I0120342

Honor
and
Defiance

Honor
and
Defiance

A History of the Las Vegas Land Grant in New Mexico

James Bailey Blackshear

SUNSTONE
PRESS

SANTA FE

© 2013 by James Bailey Blackshear
All Rights Reserved.

No part of this book may be reproduced in any form or by any electronic or mechanical means
including information storage and retrieval systems without permission in writing from the publisher,
except by a reviewer who may quote brief passages in a review.

Sunstone books may be purchased for educational, business, or sales promotional use.
For information please write: Special Markets Department, Sunstone Press,
P.O. Box 2321, Santa Fe, New Mexico 87504-2321.

Book and Cover design › Vicki Ahl
Body typeface › Basketville
Printed on acid-free paper
∞

Library of Congress Cataloging-in-Publication Data

Blackshear, James Bailey, 1954-
  Honor and defiance : a history of the Las Vegas land grant in New Mexico / by James Bailey
Blackshear.
    pages cm
  Includes bibliographical references and index.
  ISBN 978-0-86534-978-0 (softcover : alkaline paper)
  1. Mexican Americans–New Mexico–Las Vegas Region–History–19th century. 2. Mexican
Americans–Land tenure–New Mexico–Las Vegas Region–History–19th century. 3. Land grants–New
Mexico–Las Vegas Region–History–19th century. 4. Frontier and pioneer life–New Mexico–Las
Vegas Region. 5. Mountain life–New Mexico–Las Vegas Region–History–19th century. 6. Social
conflict–New Mexico–Las Vegas Region–History–19th century. 7. Las Vegas Region (N.M.)–History-
-19th century. 8. Las Vegas Region (N.M.)–Social conditions–19th century. I. Title.
  F804.L3B52 2013
  978.9'55–dc23

                                    2013038903

WWW.SUNSTONEPRESS.COM
SUNSTONE PRESS / POST OFFICE BOX 2321 / SANTA FE, NM 87504-2321 /USA
(505) 988-4418 / ORDERS ONLY (800) 243-5644 / FAX (505) 988-1025

To Barbara

Contents

Acknowledgements

My grandmother once told me how much my father liked to read when he was a boy. I did too. My brother and I used to share the morning paper with my dad over breakfast. We still do. Without such moments I doubt that *Honor and Defiance* would have come to publication. So it is to my father that I thank first. I am indebted to the Texas A&M University-Commerce, Department of History, particularly Ricky F. Dobbs, for supporting and directing my Master's thesis, the genesis of this book. While at Commerce, John H. Smith, Judy A. Ford, and Sharon Kowalsky also helped shape my sense of history. Their guidance was instrumental in the development of this work. During the research process, I spent many hours in the Rare Book Room of the Donnelly Library of New Mexico Highlands University. The staff at the Donnelly Library was always professional and helpful. A few streets away, Ken Macy, the unofficial historian and guardian of the Carnegie Library's "locked room," guided me to unpublished sources and relevant materials. Mr. Macy recently passed away. This "locked room" now bears his name. Las Vegas has lost a treasure. When searching for nineteenth century photos of Las Vegas and Las Vegans, I quickly found out that all roads lead back to the Las Vegas Citizens' Committee for Historic Preservation. With the help of Magee Polar, this institution proved to be a valuable resource that provided me with the type of period photos this history required. Although my submission to Sunstone Press occurred prior to my being accepted into the doctoral program at the University of North Texas, hopefully some of the professionalism I have experienced within its History Department has rubbed off during the editing process. I also want to thank Carl Condit and James Smith of Sunstone Press in Santa Fe for believing in this project. Of course, any and all mistakes found within *Honor and Defiance* are mine alone.

I began this acknowledgement with a nod toward family, and it is appropriate that I end there as well. Although their names are not in the text, my three sons are a part of this book. Their company and love underpin my ideas about family, a concurrent theme that runs throughout *Honor and Defiance*. If this work succeeds in conveying the sense of power such ties held in the mountain communities of New Mexico, I readily admit that my inspiration came from Mike, Joe, and Jake. Yet it is to my wife Barbara that I owe the most. Without her encouragement, this endeavor would not have happened. She graciously read early drafts, made helpful comments, understood where I wanted to go, and helped me get there.

Introduction

On the Las Vegas Land Grant in Territorial New Mexico, the dual nature of society often mimicked the challenges found in the surrounding countryside. Serenity and danger seemed intertwined, different coils of the same knot, pulled together by a variety of competing senses and priorities. One night in the late 1880s, Eugenio Romero experienced such conflicting natures firsthand. Romero was a member of one of the most powerful families in San Miguel County. He was the tax assessor, a local political boss, and a successful business man. After returning to his Victorian-style mansion one evening, the serenity that comes from settling under thick blankets soon eased him toward sleep. Yet it was not long before a crash shattered the quiet. Romero kept a pistol on his nightstand. Perhaps that was not so unusual. Immediately retrieving and firing it into the air probably was. Three invaders bolted into the night. Romero would testify that the men that were later apprehended for breaking into his home had been sent there to kill him. While law-abiding citizens in the region were always heartened to see justice served, if Romero's fate had turned tragic that night, many would have simply whispered that he had it coming. Eugenio Romero was a Republican. He usually sided with Anglo-American lawyers and land-speculators against local *nuevo-mexicanos* in ongoing disputes over land issues and workers' rights. Romero had been warned countless times to remove his fences from the grant's common land. Because he did not, he almost paid with his life.[1]

This event and others like it happened because of disagreements concerning the land grant laws of New Mexico. When the United States annexed Mexico's northern territories in 1848, the conquering government promised to protect Hispano land rights. Yet the men charged with keeping this promise came to New Mexico with different definitions and interpretations concerning property and law. The introduction of barbed-wire and locomotives into the western portions of the North American continent further muddied and influenced legal interpretations concerning land rights. This was largely due to the fact that these technological innovations created opportunities to make money. Such opportunities and incentives eroded chances for a smooth transition between Anglo-American and Hispano cultures and their governments. As the land west of the Mississippi River became more valuable, more Americans made their way into New Mexico looking to make their fortunes.

Previous to the arrival of the Americans, Spanish and Mexican authorities also awarded land to individuals or groups of settlers who wanted to better their lives. Called land grants, these pre-annexation allotments were given out on a conditional basis. Certain definable sets of criteria were inserted within Spanish and Mexican legal documents that established these grants. Specific criteria defined what Hispano pioneers had to do to hold on to their property. Most of the stipulations focused on goals meant to ensure the grant's survival. One mandated the settlers work in tandem to build a fortified plaza. Another required they divert the nearest water source through the heart of the new community by digging a main ditch that would supply all of the villagers' fields. Without implementation of such criteria, the odds of surviving on the frontier were minimal. The heart of these documents revolved around verbiage that detailed the role of unoccupied land within the community. In most cases, the mountains, rivers, and valleys located within the boundaries of the grant were to be shared with everyone who lived there. This property was called the common land, or *ejido*.[2]

In the last decades of the nineteenth century, the battle for the Las Vegas Land Grant, which pitted powerful politicians against rural farmers, cattlemen against sheep ranchers, and an old town against a new, was fought over the definition of what the *ejido* was and who owned it. From 1887 to 1893, many San Miguel County barns would burn to the ground because the majority population was angered by men who began to fence off sections and claim it as their own. Those who burned tons of hay to protest the installation of these fences claimed that they were speaking for people who had no voice. Leading citizens from both ends of the political spectrum were deeply involved in these disagreements. On one August Saturday morning during the period, newspaperman Felix Martinez stood in the street near the old Las Vegas Plaza arguing with Philip Milhiser, owner of the Las Vegas Land and Cattle Company, about such issues. During their heated conversation, Martinez, who would later help found the first college in Las Vegas, serve as a mediator during the Mexican Civil War, and become a member of the Federal Reserve Board, took out his pistol and hit the cattleman over the head with it.[3]

What would cause a successful businessman like Felix Martinez to act so violently? Why did so many *nuevo-mexicanos* living on the Las Vegas grant approve of the midnight barn burnings and fence cuttings? Was it true that most local Hispanos were lazy rabble-rousers? Was their main intent to disrupt the growing businesses of newcomers who came west with the railroad? Did a criminal element, as some contemporary newspapers claimed, incite a susceptible class of innocent locals to do the bidding of a few evil individuals, threatening the foundations of the Las Vegas economy? Was this simply the inevitable results of the American markets bringing civilization to another backwater on its westward march to the Pacific? This book seeks to answer such questions with a three-dimensional examination of the region.

Las Vegas, New Mexico, is located approximately sixty-five miles east of Santa Fe and sixty miles south of Taos on the southern edge of the Rocky Mountains, within the range called the Sangre de Cristos. *Nuevo-mexicano* settlers established the first land grant in this area along an ancient trade route that would later draw Americans west on the Santa Fe Trail. Due to its location, Las Vegas grew steadily during the middle part of the nineteenth century, accruing the benefits that resulted from becoming a trading-nexus along the American frontier. Yet such benefits remained incremental and selective until the arrival of the railroad. When the first train rolled into Las Vegas in 1879, it brought more than a great horde of easterners into the territory. New perceptions regarding land values also traveled west. These perceptions changed the economic landscape in San Miguel County, which covered the grant. For many entrepreneurs, both Hispano and Anglo-Americans, the locomotive solved long-standing problems associated with transporting cattle east. After 1879, land became a commodity, not a resource. Land speculators from the East Coast and Europe no longer ignored the region's vast grasslands and looked for ways to acquire it.

By the early 1890s, incremental land loss among *nuevo-mexicanos* bred a frustration that coalesced into fierce, last ditch efforts to protect their property. During this period, the will and determination of the Hispano people, at times secretive and violent, at others aggressively public in nature, provided them with the impetus to take advantage of early majorities in the territory. Such impetus created a dynamic which prevented the complete Anglicization of the political structure on the grant. Critical to this dynamic was religion, its function within Hispano culture, local politics, and revolt, all crucial to understanding everyday life in the mountains. Just as important was the idea of community, its organizational role in the survival of the village, and how that role was responsible in securing the remnants of the grant.

Neighbor is a nebulous term in New Mexico, yet even if an Hispana walked a few miles to reach her neighbor, distance had little to do with the relationship found there. Only after understanding the link between *nuevo-mexicanos* and their mountain valleys can a meaningful assessment of the economic and demographic changes that occurred after the railroads came through, take place. Much of economist Joseph Schumpeter's theory on "creative destruction" is illustrated in 1879 Las Vegas, where "stability and instability, good and harm," were all present. When the Atchison, Topeka, and Santa Fe Railroad laid its tracks into Las Vegas, two towns emerged out of one. The original settlement revolved around the Plaza, where many, though not all, traditional Hispanos and old-style European merchants resided. A couple of miles away, a "New Town" grew up next to the train depot. Called East Las Vegas, the majority of post railroad, incoming Anglo-Americans established mercantile businesses, saloons, and banks there, but not necessarily in that order.[4]

Within the pages of Las Vegas' history, New Mexican villagers rejected the notion that they were incapable of managing their own lives in a productive way. In fact, such men and women were quintessential pioneers; hardy, resolute, and determined. In the best interests of their families, they often made hard decisions to counteract the economic plight they found themselves in, moving away from established, but crowded settlements to start new lives on land fraught with extreme weather on landscapes that sometimes resembled the moon. The new land grants were also home to

Indians that considered Hispano settlers trespassers. Within such an environment, a contemporary *nuevo-mexicano* culture emerged, forged on an anvil of hardship and danger.[5]

Later in the century, countless Anglo-American pioneers contributed to the history of the Las Vegas grant. The bulk of these settlers were honest, fair, and heroic. This is not their story. Numerous accounts of such exemplary individuals can be found in academic and public libraries all around the country. Hispanos, Anglos, Indians, Blacks, and Asians all play a role within *Honor and Defiance, A History of the Las Vegas Land Grant in New Mexico*, yet this book focuses on the impact of American expansion among Hispanos living in San Miguel County and their reactions to it. It is important to resurrect this multi-dimensional past to get a better handle on what is going on in present day Las Vegas and the rest Southwest. At the time of annexation, the Las Vegas Land Grant encompassed almost 431,000 acres, yet by 1942, only 29,000 remained. Many Las Vegas Hispanos are still embittered by this loss in 2013. These feelings are directly related to what happened in the late nineteenth century. Today, many well-meaning Anglo-Americans in the Meadow City are puzzled over the residue of anger that remains among some of the Hispanos that live there. This monograph is an attempt to reveal why this is so.[6]

Within this history is a story of honor and defiance. Hay farmer José Padilla, union activist and political operative Juan José Herrera, and Hispano businessman Felix Martinez only reflect back the light which peasant farmers and ranchers living on the grant created in their quest to protect their property. What possessed these people to defy territorial law forty years after annexation? Their efforts gained scrutiny and concern from Washington, D.C., halted land speculation on the grant for a time, and threw a wrench into the old guard, political machine that held power in San Miguel County. Such feats deserve our attention. By the summer of 1890, they certainly had the territorial governor's. On July Fourth, Governor L. Bradford Prince sat in a chair on the Las Vegas Plaza, surrounded by a host of cheering Hispanos. He was not there to show his patriotism. At least that was not his true aim. He came to the Old Town to assess what was going on there. He sensed the defiance in the air. Many of those around him were obviously a part of one, or several movements, that seemed to be coming together in San

Miguel County. One was called *El Partido del Pueblo*, a rapidly expanding political party. This group threatened the very organization that brought Prince to power, the Republicans. And what of *Las Gorras Blancas*? How many in the crowd on that 4 July, he had to wonder, were responsible for the destruction of fences, barns, and other property on the grant? Leaving placards and notes, perpetrators justified such damage by claiming the fences had been illegally installed on communal property that everyone who lived on the Las Vegas grant owned. These night-riders, *Las Gorras Blancas*, also distributed leaflets that made the same arguments in Las Vegas. Several organizations, legal and illegal, were demanding that no fences be built on the *ejido*. What role did the secretive religious sect known as the Penitentes play in such events? How and why had so many seemingly divergent groups come together? Which of their concerns were legitimate? Governor Prince had traveled from Santa Fe to the Las Vegas Plaza to find out.[7]

The Las Vegas Plaza, July 4, 1890. From the Collection of the Las Vegas Citizens' Committee for Historic Preservation.

Going Home

The Captain and the Governor

By 4 July 1890, over three-hundred and fifty years had passed since Francisco Vásquez de Coronado first ventured into Spain's northernmost province. This day, Territorial Governor L. Bradford Prince listened to a host of speakers expounding upon a series of grievances they demanded be rectified. Bunting and flags were present on the buildings that surrounded the town square. People even hung out of the windows of the Plaza Hotel to see and hear each speaker. As far as Prince was concerned, the celebration did not appear to have much to do with the birth of the United States. The locals called it Fiesta. They cheered each time a speaker lashed out against the "land grabbers," the roar so loud it was at times hard to hear what was being said. "Land grabbers" was a catch-all phrase that referred to anyone seeking to acquire the Las Vegas Land Grant's common land for personal use. Las Vegas was an anti-Republican breeding ground, populated by men intent on ousting politicians like L. Bradford Prince.[1]

Governor Prince was an imposing figure. He resembled New York's infamous leader of political corruption, William Marcy "Boss" Tweed. Prince was both corpulent and elegant, a man who stood out in a crowd such as the one that had assembled on the Plaza that day. He was immaculately dressed in a custom made, dark suit, his full white beard perfectly trimmed around generous jowls. The governor's girth, beard, and dress epitomized what nineteenth century territorial power looked like. In March of the previous year he had accepted President Rutherford B. Hayes' appointment to become Governor of New Mexico Territory. A former senator from Tweed's New York, Prince was a loyal Republican, having accepted this position as reward for his efforts in behalf of the national party. Yet since arriving in Santa Fe, the seventeen months he'd spent in New Mexico sometimes seemed like seventeen years.[2]

Celebrating evening vespers the previous night, 1,000 horsemen rode through town illuminated by the candles they held over their heads. Such a procession represented more than religious ritual. It illustrated where real power rested within San Miguel County. The horsemen were riding to protest unfair wages and an assortment of injustices associated with companies tied to the Atchison, Topeka, and Santa Fe Railroad Company. Many of the riders were thought to belong to *Las Gorras Blancas,* or the White Caps. Plain and simple, the parade was an act of defiance, meant to intimidate people in San Miguel County who opposed both their day-time, and night-time operations.[3]

The stately Prince sat ramrod straight in the middle of the Old Town Plaza, listening and watching the festivities. Leading citizens such as Nestor Montoya, a publisher of the local Spanish language newspaper, *La Voz del Pueblo*, as well as a union leader, talked about honesty and equal wages for the common folk. Many Hispano laborers had recently struck their jobs at the railroad for more money. Stacks of lumber, extracted from nearby mountain forests slated to become railroad ties had recently been torched. One of the reasons the governor had come to the festivities was to show the townsfolk he was aware of their issues and was willing to listen. Since the arrival of the railroad in 1879, land speculators and construction companies had been finding ways to acquire grant land in a manner most Hispanos believed was against the law. Such encroachment was eating into available grazing lands and sometimes interrupting the *acequias'* ability to provide water to local croplands. These events, coupled with a growing sense within a majority of *nuevo-mexicanos* that the U.S. Court system seldom decided land disputes in their favor, contributed to the tensions that hung in the air that Fourth of July. Governor Prince wanted to get a better understanding of the actual extent of the unrest, yet at the same time, hoped to show he was a man of the people. He soon realized that belonged to someone else.[4]

All eyes turned as an older Hispano gentleman approached the podium. In his mid-to-late fifties, he moved forward with a solemn air of purpose. Many in the audience knew him personally, yet even those who did not still recognized him. Juan José Herrera's roots ran deep on the *Las*

Vegas Grandes. Manuel Herrera, his father, had been a brigadier general in the United States' frontier militia forces. Before the arrival of the Americans, the elder Herrera performed a similar service for the Mexican government. In both armies, the father patrolled the Pecos River region, in charge of protecting many of the parents of family members now listening to the son. Yet the younger Herrera was also remembered for his military service. In the Civil War, Captain Juan José Herrera of the Union army fought alongside many of the older *nuevo-mexicanos* craning forward to hear his words on the Plaza. Juan José had many friends and followers in Las Vegas, but like most leaders, had also acquired his share of enemies. Eugenio Romero and his brothers could not stand him. The *Las Vegas Optic* claimed Herrera was the mastermind behind *Las Gorras Blancas*. True or not, Juan José and brothers Nicanor and Pablo were rivals of the powerful Romeros. Benigno, Margarito, Hilario, Trinidad, and Eugenio Romero made up one of the most powerful family dynasties in all of New Mexico. Successful businessmen associated with the local establishment, they were disgusted with events in their county, laying much of the blame for what was wrong with Las Vegas at the Herreras' feet. Juan, Nicanor, and Pablo were union leaders, responsible for the growth of the local chapter of the Knights of Labor. This group fought to extract higher wages for Hispanos that worked for many of the companies the Romeros either owned or supported. Juan, along with Felix Martinez, was instrumental in the creation of *El Partido del Pueblo*, the new political party that threatened Republicans such as Prince and the Romeros.

Juan José spoke about civil liberties and property rights, the elimination of greed and graft, and fairness for all. A majority of the *nuevo-mexicanos* and a few disenchanted Anglo-Americans hung on his every word. When finished, the crowd cheered. The previous summer, when property owner José Ygnacia Lujan found his own barbed-wire fence cut to pieces, he rode out to confront Herrera. The angry Lujan had been visited by *Las Gorras Blancas* several times and blamed Juan José for his problems. The old Civil War veteran told Lujan to get down off his horse. In rough language he wire-brushed Lujan, explaining he had seen much "blood and shit . . ." in his lifetime, and was not about to stand accused of such a deed without a fight. Lujan turned and rode away. Regardless of one's personal opinion of Herrera, Las Vegans knew he meant what he said. Few *nuevo-mexicanos* were as articulate or galvanizing as Juan José Herrera. His ability to utilize the democratic system to defend Hispano rights in New Mexico was rarely matched during this period.[6]

The Romeros of Las Vegas. From the top left going right, brothers Benigno, Margarito, Hilario, Trinidad, and Eugenio. From the Collection of the Las Vegas Citizens' Committee for Historic Preservation.

Four decades earlier, Colonel Stephen Watts Kearney of the United States Army stood on a rooftop that overlooked the same Las Vegas Plaza and declared: "I have come amongst you by the orders of my government, to take possession of your country, and extend over it the laws of the United

States." Yet New Mexico Territory was far from Washington, and dramatic change did not occur until after 1879. That is the year the locomotive arrived. In the 1880s, Anglo-American notions of progress finally began to impact every *nuevo-mexicano* on the grant. Many historians claim that what happened in Las Vegas during the final two decades of the twentieth century was but a blip on the screen of history, hardly worth noting, yet for the men standing on the Plaza cheering Herrera, this was not so. In 1890, they were in the midst of, a part of, the Rising on the Las Vegas grant; a moment worth noting and re-examining. On the Fourth of July, with the governor of the territory making mental notes, Herrera's face reflected back the character and passions of the people he addressed. These traits, long embedded in the *nuevo-mexicanos* of San Miguel County, included resoluteness, communal spirit, and an honorable defiance.

Governor Prince listened respectfully to everyone who followed Herrera. Nicanor, Juan José's brother and partner, spoke on similar issues, yet it was clear that the eldest Herrera, the "captain," was the man most had come to hear. Since Herrera's return, the region had begun to resemble a powder keg. Prince made it a point of displaying a good deal of equanimity throughout the day, even as most of the speakers lambasted the very political structure that supported him. Perhaps he was stunned by the influence Juan José commanded over the crowd, perhaps not. L. Bradford Prince fancied himself to be something of a historian. If that were so, surely he knew this was not the first time *nuevo-mexicanos* had come together to fight for what they believed in. Strife was not unknown on the grant. New Mexico was a hard country. Wrapped within its beauty was an environment capable of killing both the two legged and four legged creatures that lived upon it. Ill-prepared travelers died of thirst. Unprotected lambs froze to death once the sun dropped behind the mountains. If a rancher's livestock survived the elements, there were always the Apache, Kiowa, or Comanche to deal with. Many times these Plains Indians were after more than animals. Women and children were the slave trader's most marketable commodities. Long before the arrival of Anglo-Americans, *nuevo-mexicanos* were familiar with hardship and tribulation. Since the sixteenth century, adversity had welcomed the first Hispano explorers and settlers who followed the Great River north.[7]

Following the River

Since the first Spanish conquests, the territory north of *Nueva Vizcaya* was known as *Nuevo Mexico*. Far from the center of power, this distant region personified geologic diversity, interspersing green-mountain forests with desert country that was etched with canyons and broken mesas. Its lands were surrounded by horizons that created illusions of emptiness. One ignored what one could not see in *Nuevo Mexico* at their own peril. Within heartbeats, a seemingly tranquil environment could be transformed into a nightmarishly violent landscape. The first conquistadores soon realized this on their journey north along the *Rio del Norte*. For the next three hundred years, explorers, settlers, and entrepreneurs experienced similar misgivings and expectations as they made their way into the province.[8]

Don Juan de Oñate bankrolled the first major Iberian settlement in the region. Contracted by the king, he led an expedition north to settle *Nuevo Mexico* in 1598. Colonization efforts grew in fits and starts for the next nine years, staving off Indian attacks, internal discord, extreme weather, and starvation. By 1607, Oñate's enterprise was on the brink of ruination. Most *pobladores* regretted the circumstances that found them living so far from Central Mexico. Just when it looked like Spanish authorities would disband the settlements, Viceroy Luis de Velasco ordered everyone; soldiers, pioneers, and Franciscans, to remain. Having approved the original expedition, he was not ready to abandon *Nuevo Mexico*.[9]

The viceroy's decision to continue Spain's presence on this northern frontier was not an easy one. He was aware that the odds of surviving in a harsh land among people that did not want them there were not good. In large part, the Spanish presence continued at the insistence of the Roman Catholic Church. Discussions in Mexico City about ending colonization efforts were met with Franciscan warnings that thousands of indigenous conversions would go for naught. In the end, the Church's argument was strong enough to convince the viceroy they must remain, if for no other reason, than to take care of their converted Pueblo brethren. Velasco agreed that it would be morally reprehensible to let the Indians return to heathenism. Oñate was replaced. Many of the settlers were frustrated with Velasco's decision. Although willing to stake their lives to such a harsh and dangerous place in 1598, nine years later several *pobladores* no longer believed in Spain's capacity to support them so far from the heartland. Many had no choice, and were required to stay and make the best of it.[10]

Phillip III designated don Pedro de Peralta to replace Oñate. He became the new governor of the province. Colonization efforts continued. During this transition period, officials looked for a new location for their main settlement. It was placed along the San Francisco River and would become the capital. Deemed Santa Fe, for the next seventy years friars and *pobladores* would struggle to maintain their homes in the shadows of the Sangre de Cristo Mountains. Surrounded on all sides by Puebloan communities that preferred to live without them, resentment continued to fester in the valley. Eventually, animosity and occasional violence bloomed into full-blown revolt.[11]

In 1680, Pueblo, Zuni, and Hopi Indians attacked the Hispanic settlements, killing hundreds of *pobladores* and as many priests as they could get their hands on. Once and for all, they were intent on ridding themselves of the foreigners who had taken their land, enslaved their relatives, and polluted their religion. Hispanic survivors of the Pueblo Revolt evacuated south to Mexico, bringing back nightmarish tales of revenge and reprisals. Twelve years would pass before Captain General and Governor don José de Vargas and a new contingent of settlers and Franciscans returned to the scene of the slaughter. About one-thousand hopeful *pobladores*, soldiers, and Indian auxiliaries backed de Vargas and the priests' *reconquista*. Their livestock, wagons, and horses created a slow-moving caravan that stretched for miles as they exited El Paso del Norte and moved north, up the Rio del Norte. It would take about a year before they reached the San Francisco River, their final destination.[12]

The various Puebloan peoples living in the river valley did not welcome the colonizers back with open arms. Once again, Hispanic settlers began to establish themselves around and among the natives' communities. To name only a few, Pueblo Tewa, Tano, and Tiwa speaking Indians did not consider their homes *tierra nueva*. They resented the accommodations de Vargas and his predecessors had both expected and required of them. Situated within a hostile nation, the *pobladores* survived in large part because of inner toughness and deep faith, character traits that refused to let obstacles, including the death of loved ones, turn them back. Still, it is debatable as to whether faith and courage would have been enough to hold together a successful colony among so many people who did not want them there. Coupled with these traits came superior, Old World, weapon technologies and Pueblo cohorts to minimize the numerical advantages they found along the river. Just as instrumental, if unanticipated, were tens of thousands of Pueblo, Zuni, and Hopi deaths due to the spread of European diseases. Although such decimation eventually denigrated native peoples' ability to maintain their majorities, in the beginning their numbers were substantial. Among the Puebloans, the introduction of gunpowder, horses, and European microbes led to land loss, enslavement, and depredations. In spite of these facts, successful Hispanic colonization was still never certain in the first years of resettlement. Like Oñate's experiences, the *reconquista* occasionally tottered on the brink of disintegration.

From the beginning, Captain General don José de Vargas believed he was in a better position than his predecessors to establish permanent colonies in New Mexico because he had the advantage of hindsight, and was determined not to make the mistakes of Oñate and his followers. Instead of demanding quick and absolute obedience, de Vargas treated many of the Puebloans as independent leaders of their own countries. Both civil and religious authorities were charged with interacting more humanely with their indigenous neighbors. Still, de Vargas was aware of the rival factions present among the Puebloan communities. Like Spanish leaders before him, he sought to take advantage of the situation, inducing the Tewas of Tesuque, the Pecos peoples, the Keres from San Felipe, and Zia and Santa Ana peoples to join him and his auxiliaries against the Puebloans who preferred to re-enact the Pueblo Revolt of 1680. De Vargas' colony was the minority population in the Rio Grande Valley, requiring he establish ties with river villagers that were willing to join him in a battle to overcome common enemies. Regardless of the captain general's charm or leadership style, many skirmishes and bloody engagements were fought between Spanish forces and local Indians. Mexican and Puebloan Indian auxiliaries played prominent roles in the Spaniards' ability to survive assaults from Tewa, Tano, and Jemez peoples who were intent on driving them out of the valley for good. De Vargas' colony also faced occasional attacks from the

Santo Domingo Keres and raids by the Apaches and Navajos.[13]

Many histories have been written of these events. Most focus on de Vargas' strategic decisions, his soldiers' actions, and the Franciscans' attempts to convert the native populations to the Christian faith. Little notice has been given to the core population, the *pobladores*. Common-folk held the settlements together. Carpenters, cobblers, and millers, grandmothers, aunts and uncles, regardless of their original ethnicity, were the heart of the enterprise. Despite the risks, Hispano settlers survived in *Nuevo Mexico* because they proved to be a tenacious, determined people forged by strong faith and a desire to find a better life than the one they had left behind in Central Mexico. Although some were disheartened after arriving along the *Rio del Norte*, over the years most persevered, and in doing so, became the first *nuevo-mexicanos*.[14]

One-hundred years after don José de Vargas led his caravan of Spanish and mestizos colonizers back into the fertile valleys of the *Rio del Norte*, soon to be known as the Rio Grande, settlement gradually became permanent, yet few had moved far from the river. *Pobladores* found a measured amount of safety living near or within the original colonies and were disinclined to move away. Even though de Vargas' original expedition was fraught with setbacks and did not prove to be the profitable enterprise most had expected, the colony survived, in the main, due to the influence of the Catholic Church.

From the beginning, civil and military authorities grappled with the Church for control of Spain's northern provinces. Since eight Franciscans had accompanied Coronado in 1540, every subsequent Spanish expedition experienced friction between soldiers seeking their fortune and friars seeking souls. As stated above, don Juan de Oñate's colonization effort was falling apart by 1607, and remained in New Mexico primarily because of to the Church's insistence. Yet in the ensuing decades, the priests alienated more Puebloans than they converted. Twelve years after the Pueblo Revolt, the seventeen Franciscan friars that had accompanied de Vargas back into *Nuevo Mexico* approached their mission with a pronounced delicacy, more sensitive to the natives' previous beliefs. When possible, priests preferred to look the other way. As a part of de Vargas' *reconquista*, these padres' mission was to fulfill their Order's original charge, which was to convert the Puebloan communities. They were also sent to re-establish approximately fifty churches that were abandoned in 1680. Conversion was never de Vargas', nor his soldiers' main purpose. Their original intent was to get rich by whatever means necessary. Most hoped to find gold, yet when valuable minerals proved to be lacking, some Spaniards looked to other resources, such as people, to develop their wealth. Conflicts between the clergy, civil authorities, and soldiers continued into the eighteenth century, yet for most of the true settlers of New Mexico, finding fortunes in the ground was the farthest thing from their minds. What their leaders squabbled about was of scant consequence to *pobladores* endeavoring to scratch out a living. They did search the soil, but usually for fertile spots to plant their seeds. Ditches had to be dug, water courses rerouted, shelters built, and churches constructed. Most were too busy to search for gold.[15]

For the next one hundred years, an evolving Hispanic community developed along the Rio Grande. It was true that under don Diego de Vargas, the *pobladores* did not have the option of going back to Mexico without facing arrest or death. Yet this fact did not minimize the ingrained spirit and grit required to succeed in this foreign land. The settlers who had migrated from Central Mexico made the northern frontier their home. Over many generations, the animosities between the colonists and the Puebloans subsided. Although New Mexico continued to be a dangerous place, occasional periods of peace between the settlers and the Plains Indians also contributed to the Hispanos' ability to strengthen their communities.

The *pobladores* who settled in New Mexico lived in a land of stunning geographic contrasts. Lush soils along the riverbanks wove between conifer-covered mountains. Deer, turkey, and bear roamed along the rivers and forest trails. Trout swirled below the streams' rapids, nestling and spawning in the shadows of river-rocks and fallen logs. In most valleys, the soil gave up plentiful crops and abundant forage. To the east, beyond the snow covered peaks, plateaus spotted with *piñon* trees and junipers rose and fell like a storm-roiled ocean of rust colored sand. Rock strewn creek beds laced the arroyos. Gradually, the defiles ebbed away from the mountain ranges, descending toward undulating prairies of grama grass. In the spring, these same empty gulches and gullies ran fast with snow melt and thunderstorm run-off, yet their flows were unpredictable where cholla cactus and juniper trees stippled the ochre-colored earth with a variety of green splotches.

Away from the Rio Grande, few streams or waterways maintained flows throughout the year. Those that did meandered their way out of the Sangre de Cristo Range, the southern spine of the Rocky Mountains. It was these downstream rivers and creeks, the Pecos and the Gallinas, the Sapello and the Manualitas, that enterprising *pobladores* would eventually follow away from the Rio Grande Valley to establish new colonies. A century after the confident de Vargas first journeyed north, expansion was still dangerous, yet needed. The older settlements were overcrowded. A new generation of *nuevo-mexicano* pioneers found they had to look elsewhere to pasture their sheep and plant crops. Groups of men, women, and children followed some of the same trails Coronado traveled east as they wound their way out of the mountain passes and through shadow filled valleys, intent on creating a life of their own.[16]

Mexican officials approved requests for new land grants for multiple reasons. They were aware that any future incursion by Navajos, Plains Apaches, Jicarilla Apaches, or Comanches would have to pass one of these new settlements first, thus creating a trip-wire of sorts for people living in the established villages along the Rio Grande. In the event of finding resistance, or perhaps after exacting what they wanted from the outlying areas, raiders might turn away before reaching the capital. As an example of the danger such early communities faced, in 1773, five-hundred Comanche warriors swooped into the village of El Valle, located on the Las Trampas grant north of Santa Fe, killing many of the settlers and stealing their livestock. The first community of Abiquiu was abandoned because of such raids. Another reason to create new colonies was because the villages in the Rio Grande Valley did not have enough cropland to sustain their growing populations. Access to fertile land remained static while the population continued to grow. For seeds to develop into agricultural produce, the soil had to be fertile. For soil to be fertile, water had to be available. Previous land allotments in the original colonies was equally bequeathed between a landowner's siblings, male and female, meaning that second and third generation heirs received little, if any land that touched water. Soil conducive to crop growth along the original Rio Grande settlements was already taken. Expansion away from the river was dangerous and never a certainty, yet officials knew such enterprises would eventually help staunch attacks in the heart of the province and also provide better futures for those with few prospects around Santa Fe.[17]

A new land grant fifty miles southeast of Santa Fe was representative of most that were established during the period. The majority of the *pobladores* involved in this enterprise were mixed-blood Spaniards or Native Americans who, as children, had been slaves or were adopted into Hispanic homes. One way to gain their independence after becoming adults was to join in the establishment of new colonies. On their journey to the newly granted lands along the Pecos River, they carried bows and arrows, spears, a few antiquated rifles, and old pistols for protection. The colonizers herded a few sheep and cows ahead of them, dreaming of harvests yet to come. On the back of a burrow or stacked in wooden pushcarts, they hauled everything they owned, including seed corn, oats, and beans. Once beyond sight of the old plaza, they found themselves on their own, isolated from parents, relatives, and friends by mountains, distance, and an environment that could kill them. In this manner, satellite colonies ventured away from the Rio Grande Valley.[18]

The new grant was called San Miguel del Bado (or Vado), established along the Pecos River, twenty miles south of the Pecos Pueblo. Long before the arrival of the Spanish, this ancient trading nexus had been a cultural melting pot where plains and mountain peoples met to exchange bison products, agricultural produce, animals, and slaves. Annual trade fairs were held at Pecos even when participants were at war, the violence halting long enough for barter to occur. In 1798, the culturally Hispanic *pobladores* who made their way past the pueblo were not interested in making enemies. By then, Spanish authorities had established a good relationship with the remaining people who lived in this multi-towered adobe habitat. Some *nuevomexicanos* even lived with the Pecos Indians before their homes were built at San Miguel del Bado. These colonists were more interested in raising their families and cultivating the earth than conquering their neighbors.[19]

Lorenzo Márquez of Santa Fe was the leader of the settlement, bringing fifty-two Hispanic and 13 Indian families with him to the designated location. The *bado*, or crossing, was a fertile spot, conducive to crop growth and the pasturing of sheep and cattle. Eventually, success bred the same overcrowding conditions that spurred colonization away from the Rio Grande. Prosperous ranchers with thousands of sheep sought the virgin valleys to the northeast. On the New Mexican frontier, wealth was defined by how many sheep one owned or how much pasture could be acquired to feed them. Yet it was not only the wealthy that had incentives to look elsewhere. Second generation families in San Miguel del Bado and additional settlers from other overcrowded Rio Grande communities needed land that touched water so they could fill their own ditches. Twenty years after San Miguel del Bado's founding, such locations were rarely available to new families. Thus, government authorities sought to please both the most influential citizens and the less fortunate by providing lots for homes and croplands near new water sources.[20]

The Gallinas River ran east out of the Sangre de Cristo Range through the heart of a sweeping meadow. In 1821, per an agreement with the local San Miguel del Bado *alcalde* and Mexican authorities in Santa Fe, Luis Maria Cabesa de Baca and his seventeen sons and sons-in-law, were awarded a grant to settle this area. Yet reluctance on the part of officials in San Miguel del Bado delayed its approval for several years. It is probable that the men dragging their feet were already using *Las Vegas Grandes* to pasture their own livestock and frowned upon giving it up to only one family. In 1826, Governor Narbona ordered *Alcalde* Tomás Sena to follow through with the claim. Only then did the de Baca clan move to take possession of this land. Luis Maria Cabesa de Baca and his heirs were charged with building homes, raising livestock, and channeling streams from the Gallinas into new *acequias* for their first crops. The grant was bordered on the west by the San Miguel del Bado grant. The Sapello River, twelve miles north of the Gallinas, was its northern limit. To the south, the border eventually rested alongside the Antonio Ortiz grant, while the eastern boundary became the *Aguaje del la Yegua*. With only a slight modification, this grant would eventually become known as the Las Vegas Land Grant. Its original proportions included almost 500,000 acres.[21]

Three ecological zones reside within the grant, sometimes found on top of each other. Terrain found within its borders does not always transition gradually from one topography to another. Sudden changes in altitude affect the climate, landscape, vegetation, and animals found in each zone.

The tallest mountains in the Sangre de Cristo Range top out at over 13,000 feet. Below the ridgelines and pine forests, arid plateaus, mesas, and middle elevation grassland prairies exist, interspersed with occasional fertile river valleys that cut through rocky, desert-like landscapes. The de Baca clan had acquired a land deceptively beautiful and dangerous from the Mexican government. In 1827, both abundant life and desolation could be found within moments of each other on the grant.

According to the principles of Mexican law, the original de Baca grant was never firmly established. No records indicate that Luis Maria Cabesa de Baca or his family members were able to convince enough people to irrigate, farm, or settle on the Gallinas permanently, as the decree demanded. At the time, the *Vegas Grandes* was still largely the domain of Native Americans. It is known that the Navajo, Pawnee, and Jicarilla Apaches caused problems with early attempts to settle there, raiding sheep from the fields and forcing shepherds and ranch-hands to evacuate the area more than once. The Indians interpreted incursions by Hispanic sheep herders as both trespassing and an opportunity. Horses, mules, and sheep were stolen. de Baca claimed he lost over 36,000 dollars due to such raids. South of Las Vegas, there were reports of shepherds being scalped. At one time, de Baca had 3,000 sheep grazing in the valley, but after continued Indian attacks, efforts to establish permanent residences there were abandoned. It is possible that after Luis Maria Cabesa de Baca died in Pena Blanca, around 1833, his sons were still trying to make a go of it, but by then, no substantial requirements demanded by the Mexican government were being met. In 1835, another group of *nuevo-mexicanos* moved in to claim the valley.[22]

Once again, a request was issued to the *ayuntamiento* (town council) of San Miguel del Bado. In the fourteen years since de Baca's original request, the membership of the council had changed. This time, some of its members were also petitioners for the new grant, which as Malcolm Ebright has pointed out, helped facilitate a quick approval. Once the local council accepted the request, the document was sent to Governor Sarracino for final confirmation. The petition asked that land be awarded for settlers to graze cattle and farm along the Gallinas River. It was signed and submitted to the governor by "principal settlers" and San Miguel del Bado residents José Antonio Casados, Juan de Dios Maese, Miguel Archuleta, and Manuel

Duran. The governor quickly confirmed the request. These "principal settlers" represented specific families, but the document also included anyone at San Miguel del Bado who lacked acceptable farmland. In confirming the grant, the governor reminded these men that in order to retain ownership, they must construct houses around a plaza so the exterior walls would form a perimeter barrier, similar to a fort. All awards for community grants in New Mexico included such language.[2]

Overcrowding was not the only reason why the grant petition found smoother sailing in 1835 than it did the 1821. As touched on earlier, American Indians had lived in the region for centuries and did not always take kindly to strangers building structures on their hunting grounds. Jicarilla Apaches, Comanches, and Navajo were reluctant to abdicate their ownership of the Sangre de Cristo Mountain Range. Any Hispanic settlement or hacienda was vulnerable to attack. Back at San Miguel del Bado, Manuel Herrera and a small militia was charged with protecting the local herders and traders brave enough to leave the confines of the community, but their resources were few and the territory vast. It was hoped that a new colony to the northeast would alleviate stress along the Pecos and reduce raids. Starting in 1831, for the same reasons, San Miguel parish priest José Francisco Leyba also lobbied the provincial governor to establish new colonies. By the time the community petition was submitted in 1835, several of Father Leyba's appeals had made their way to Governor Sarracino's desk. These requests asked the governor to set up communities in Ocaté, Sapello, and Las Vegas. The priest described these lands as perfect for settlement. Such pleas by the well-respected Leyba were bound to have impacted the governor's decision when the San Miguel *ayuntamiento* submitted the "principal settlers'" petition.[24]

Although the approval process appeared seamless, it was still three years before a majority of the *pobladores* took possession. The presence of Indians certainly contributed to the settlers' reluctance. As one of the petitioners explained to Governor Sarracino, many of the San Miguel residents slated for land next to the Gallinas were waiting to see if a grant closer to the San Miguel del Bado property would be awarded first. If it were, they would attempt to gain land there, which was closer to Herrera's militia. Settlers believed the closer they remained to the militia and the main colony, the better chance they had of putting down successful roots. Much of their hesitancy derived from an 1824 award of 48,000 acres along the Tecolote River to six private citizens, who for various reasons, had not followed through on government directives as to how it was to be maintained. For this reason, men and women of San Miguel del Bado waited to see if a new petition submitted to the governor to create a new Tecolote grant, which was southwest of the *Vegas Grandes* and closer to the older settlement, would be approved before deciding to move farther east. Various *alcaldes* and *ayuntamientos* were involved in this case, some demanding the Tecolote property remain in the hands of the few who originally claimed it. Others argued a revised grant should be opened to new settlers. As it happened, the new Tecolote grant overlapped portions of both the San Miguel del Bado and the Las Vegas grants. True colonization in Las Vegas only began after issues regarding the Tecolote grant were resolved.[25]

The Las Vegas grant was located about fifty miles to the northeast of San Miguel del Bado. By 1838, it was called the *Nuestra Senora de los Dolores de Las Vegas*. An additional community formed to the north of the Plaza. Both would eventually blend together, becoming the core settlement among several small villages that began to spring up in the mountain valleys within its boundaries. Just like in San Miguel del Bado, Santa de la Cañada, Las Trampas, and other successful satellite communities, besides requirements to build a plaza with protective walls, the *nuevo-mexicanos* along the Gallinas were obligated to develop the land through cultivation, which included installing ditches and planting crops.[26]

Along with these written stipulations, grant documents also decreed that all grantees must arm themselves before taking possession of their property. As a part of government protocol, on 6 April 1835, *Alcalde* José de Jesús Ulibarrí y Duran stood along the Gallinas River and read these instructions aloud to the settlers. He declared that the plaza was to be laid out above the main ditch, or *acequia madre*, from which the *pobladores* fields were to be oriented and located. He also noted that a Mexican officer would perform a weapons inspection on every eighth day. This was stipulated because, even though Mexico wanted expansion, officials in Santa Fe knew if the *pobladores* did not have the arms to protect themselves, the resulting failure could dissuade future Hispanos from considering similar ventures.[27]

Depending on which historical document is relied upon, between twenty-five and thirty-four colonists were allotted land on the Las Vegas grant. Like San Miguel del Bado, most grantees were the descendants of *genizaros* or mixed-blood Hispanics. These *pobladores* received allotments on the west side of the Gallinas River. Shortly thereafter, 113 more colonists arrived. Most of the additional allocations were made on the east side of the river. Each division was marked off by *Alcalde* Jose de Jesus Ulibarrri y Duran, in a "north to south" direction. The unit of measure was the *vara*, about thirty-three and one-half inches, the plots being between 100 and 200 *varas* wide. This meant the Las Vegas settlers were stretched about 2 ½ miles along the river, debunking the notion that everyone originally made their homes around the Plaza. Authorities forbade settlers from selling their personal plots until legal title was granted, usually after four years. The *alcalde* designated 125 *varas* for a public garden and seventy-five were made available to anyone needing a watering place. A common roadway was also allotted from this space. The location of this section is where the bridge east of the Plaza is located today. The colony, although threatened by Comanche, Apache, and Navajo, took root. Ten years later, over 6,000 acres of the grant were being worked and homesteaded by approximately 1,500 *nuevo-mexicanos*.[28]

Life on the *Las Vegas Grandes* replicated that of *pobladores* across New Mexico. Although the new grant boundaries were altered from the de Baca claim, not quite as large, the grant boundaries were essentially the same. On individual plots, settlers oriented their lives around water and each other. In early spring, while snow-covered peaks shadowed the valley, colonists cleared ditches and dug trenches, built dams and sowed seeds.

It took all the men in the village to ensure everyone had enough water to irrigate their fields. Not long after the first rough dwellings were put up, the entire community began work on the main ditch. Each property owner cut his own channel, called a *sangria*, off this ditch. To divert water into the *acequia madre*, a dam of logs, brush, and rocks was built upstream along the edge of the river to catch the flow. Once all was ready, the *compuertas* was raised, releasing part of the river into the main ditch. One moment each farmer's ditch was empty, the next it was filled with an onrush from the Gallinas. Like the blood pumping through the veins of the *nuevo-mexicano* farmers who watched it bleed across the earth, the water ran through the fields, giving life to the soil. *Sangria.* Community effort was paramount to creating a working *acequia* system. Success meant life for the village, just as redirecting the river gave life to each garden.[29]

Although the first settlers worked their plots up and down the river, most originally built their homes near the plaza. A wary eye was always kept toward the horizon, on the lookout for dust-clouds and war-horses. Some homes surrounded the plaza in such a manner that people and livestock could be ushered in and protected against raiders. Dwellings were built of adobe bricks, which were placed on foundations of mud and river-rocks. The ceilings were fashioned from young tree branches stripped and fastened in a herringbone pattern. Brush and leaves were placed on top, followed by a thick layer of mud. Soft-edged doorways and windows faced toward the plaza, mimicking the color and curvature of the surrounding earth.[30]

While 6,000 acres were parceled out to *nuevo-mexicanos* for their own personal plots in the first decade, the remainder of the grant remained unoccupied, shared by the entire community. This acreage was known as common land, or the *ejido.* Common lands were allocated for grazing, timber extraction, communal crop ventures and future settlement. Manuel Martinez, whose father lived on the Las Vegas Land Grant in the late nineteenth century, remembered that common pasturelands were ". . . all open and free for all to graze their herds . . ." Crops such as wheat were grown not on the small private plots, but on the sloping expanses between the mountains. At certain times of the year, between growing seasons, livestock roamed the valleys. The men were responsible for taking care of the sheep, cattle, goats, and horses which grazed on the common lands. During harvest time, at what the *pobladores* called ". . . *la soltura* . . ." herders were hired to keep the livestock away from wheat and corn. After the crops were harvested, "the herds could be allowed to wander into the fields again." Martinez said his father would harvest about 100 barrels of corn and 400 *fanegas* of wheat per year. One *fanega* amounted to about 125 lbs. This amount of flour would typically last until the next harvest. Much of a man's day was spent with his neighbors, taking care of the field crops grown on the commons. They also harvested timber for firewood and building materials from the mountain forests, also a part of the grant.[31]

Hispana women did much more than raise the children. They were responsible for family vegetable gardens that were grown on the private plots surrounding the home. They grew beans, corn, chickpeas, squash, and potatoes. This produce sustained the family throughout the year. The women dug holes in the earth to store root crops such as onions and garlic, covering them with straw. They cooked all the meals, made the homespun clothes worn by everyone in the family, and wove fabrics for carpets and bedding. Women did the cleaning and washing, made tallow from animal fat for candles, and created soap as well. In their spare time they could be found on their knees in the dirt, pulling weeds, cognizant of whether the garden was getting its share of water from the ditch. It was a hard life, but life along the Pecos or the Rio Grande would have been harder. At least along the Gallinas River, fertile soil and water was available for all willing to work it.[32]

Everyone contributed to the life of the village. Men collectively built the adobe homes, but it was women who crushed the rocks that were gathered and then mixed and burned to create plaster. Women lathered this mixture on the walls of their homes. This was an annual social event. All of the mothers, daughters, and grandmothers typically worked together, going from house to house, helping fill old cracks and smooth new layers into place, delegating the supervision of babies to the older children. While older daughters helped their mothers, boys contributed by shepherding the livestock and helping to take care of the field crops.[33]

Nuevo-mexicano communities which spread into the mountains in the last part of the eighteenth and the first part of the nineteenth century grew up isolated and independent from government authority. People counted on their neighbors and did not expect much from outsiders. Most endeavors were communal, even individual successes were deemed to be a part of a cohesive whole. Survival meant sharing success as well as failure. The ability to sustain each family was born out of everyone's collective efforts. This included both production and protection. They attributed their successes to an inner strength derived from their faith.

Spirituality had always played a role in defining *nuevo-mexicanos*. Faith was the strongest connection they shared with Mexico, however altered it became in northeastern New Mexico. From the beginning, Franciscans vied with conquistadors for dominion over the Puebloan peoples. After Oñate, a bitter power struggle between battle tested soldiers in charge of civil law and the friars, enveloped the region, contributing to the native's growing disdain for Spanish rule. The Franciscans considered themselves the true leaders of the colony, regarding the civil administrators as inconvenient intruders and nuisances. From the Church's perspective, government officials were not in charge of the Puebloans' souls, therefore, did not control the province.[34]

At the time, the Franciscans were the only religious order allowed by the king into New Mexico, and ruled as such. Between 1598 and 1680, not beholden to civil authorities, they created separate, isolated missions, feudal-like kingdoms, engines of economic vitality that depended on Puebloan labor to churn out textiles and grains. Franciscans raised more sheep and harvested more crops than any independent hacienda in the region. The Church sold its bounty to the government, making the missions of the northern provinces profitable enterprises. As a part of efforts to gain control of the Indians, Franciscans damned, castigated, and punished followers of the river valley religions as idolatrous, regulating them to an almost non-human status. Even though some friars occasionally tried to induce more religious participation by introducing structures similar to kivas within mission walls, most priests sought to eliminate the sanctity of underground worship centers altogether. Friars taught Pueblo children that the kachina spirit beings were spawns of the devil.[35]

After the Pueblo Revolt of 1680, as long as Puebloans outwardly cooperated and acknowledged they accepted Christianity, the Franciscans were more apt to look the other way regarding Indian culture and beliefs. When de Vargas led the *Reconquista* in 1692, the animosity between Church and State did not prove so great that neither could function effectively. Yet although the friars appeared to have learned from past mistakes, that did not mean they were less vigorous in converting natives to the Roman Catholic faith. The priests did realize that the strict implementation of the Catholicism their forerunners practiced had not worked. Failure to convert the masses coupled with the civil officials' inability to govern fairly, sowed the seeds of the bloody revolt, leading Spain's ouster from the Rio Grande Valley. When don Diego de Vargas returned, although his methods proved sometimes to be just as harsh as his predecessors', both he and the Franciscans approached the Indians differently. The friars adapted by looking for similarities in belief systems and drawing upon the visual elements of Catholic symbols to spark interest and respect among the river communities. The Franciscans were forced to acknowledge that it was a mistake to try and totally remove the Pueblo peoples' religion from their lives. This led to a gradual, more fruitful Christian conversion process in New Mexico.[36]

In the nineteenth century, Christianity survived and evolved as a belief system in remote mountain communities and river settlements because the Church, while maintaining its core values, adapted to the sway of existing cultures. There were never enough priests in New Mexico. Such a dirth meant most villages carried on as best they could, although sometimes their efforts did not ensure strict conformity to Rome's edicts. First and second generation Spaniards, as well as large contingents of *mestizos* and *genízaros*, began to express a faith born of Moorish and Judaic originations, spiced with hints of indigenous spirituality. *Nuevo-mexicanos* practiced a Catholicism in which they believed the replication of Christ's experience on the cross gave them an insight into God, molding believers in a somewhat different manner than mainstream Roman Catholic priests preferred. Death played a significant role in New Mexican Catholicism, evoking an awareness that hard times led to salvation, pain to revelation. Isolated from mainstream dogma, a medieval strain of Catholicism thrived in the mountains, one not practiced in Europe. Combining core beliefs with certain indigenous notions of the hereafter, beliefs separate from Durango mandates, faith bloomed on the northern frontier. An elemental spirituality born from the river valleys soared to life in the Sangre de Cristo Mountains. The lack of priests occasionally proved irrelevant to the *poblador*. His God was close. He found Him in the cerulean sky, the rich soil beneath his feet, and in the wind that chapped his lips. Referring to the Zunis, Francisco Vásquez de Coronado wrote: "So far as I can find out, these Indians worship water, because they say it makes their maize grow and sustains their life." It is almost as if the first conquistador of *Nuevo Mexico* was speaking of an 1840 Hispano farmer that fed his ditches with Gallinas river water. The Pueblo peoples' faith found a home within *nuevo-mexicano* Christianity, enriching the mountain culture. John Mackey wrote in *The Other Spanish Christ*: "The contemplation of His Passion produces a sort of catharsis . . . in the soul of the worshipper." Mountains could also be said to produce this catharsis within a *nuevo-mexicano's* soul. For him, the Lord was as much a part of the natural, as the spiritual world.[37]

Due to the shortage of priests, especially within the Sangre de Cristos, the faithful found different ways to hold services. Elderly village women sometimes preached and led the congregation in hymns and prayers. During the month of May, Hispanas met daily at the church to worship the Virgin Mary, who along with the baby Jesus, held a special place in their services. Prayer was tangible, an interaction with God that gave the worshiper a conduit to communicate and give thanks. Faith hummed through the settlements, the cornerstone of village culture. *Nuevo-mexicano* faith blended a circular spirituality that included earth, sky, water, and the Virgin Mary. The Christ-child and his Father would reward the diligent in the hereafter. Although women were integral to perpetuating this spiritual vitality, a unique, secret religious society of male men, the Penitentes, were just as instrumental in forging the independent mentality of frontier Hispano people.[38]

The Penitentes usually met near a local cemetery in a non-descript, one-room adobe building. The gathering place was called the *morada*. Sometimes a depiction of St. Andrew's cross was carved into its heavy wooden doors. Occasionally, entrances were painted blue, in honor of the first Franciscan friars of Northern Mexico. Inside the *morada*, symbols of the men's faith, *retalbos* and *bultos*, hung on the walls. The *retalbos* were paintings of the crucified Christ, the Virgin, St. Francis, and the saints, applied directly to wooden surfaces. The *bultos* were carved figures of Christ, made from soft cottonwood, sometimes with moveable arms and legs and real hair that was glued on the head. Along with drops of blood, locals gathered tree bark and leaves, mixed them with oil, and used clay and cactus juice, indigo and other elements of the earth, to create the vivid yellows, reds, and blues that colored their creations. From across the valley, there was no reason to give such a building a second glance, yet once inside, the *retalbos* and *bultos'* iridescent pigments shouted out the faith of their creators, the *santeros*.[39]

A community leader, sometimes the local *alcalde*, sometimes the *mayordomo*, known within the organization as the *hermano mayor*, orchestrated rites practiced within the *morada*. This leader led a secret society of *nuevomexicanos* that retained hints of mysticism and medieval devoutness. The Penitentes practiced flagellation, as did certain European sects in the Middle Ages. Rituals included whipping and simulated crucifixions, countering the argument that faith in a Catholic God was a false faith, one many Protestants declared was more a habit than a religion. In the mountains, many *nuevo-mexicano* men proved such declarations were devoid of truth. Sometimes, during indoctrination, small incisions in the shape of a cross would be cut into the back of new members. Historian Robert Darnton argues that entry into a culture's past begins, "when we run into something that seems unthinkable to us. . . ." Warren Beck wrote: "If the Penitente is a true believer, and most are, he feels radiant and transfigured after his religious observances . . . Like St. John of the Cross, he feels that God is a deathless spring, hidden by night; and therefore he goes into the darkness to drink of him." Much of the inner strength and personal character found within nineteenth century rural *nuevo-mexicanos* was forged out of such late-night ceremonies.[40]

Music was an important part of *morada* activities. The *pito,* a small wooden flute, was often played during services. Melodies the men learned as children pierced the night. Sometimes hymns were sung a cappella. A hint of the sixteenth century Gregorian chant haunted these songs, called *alabados*. Verses told stories of the crucifixion and burial. Many sang the praises of the Virgin Mary while others were related to Holy Communion. All of these ceremonies excluded the women and children, the men insisting this age-old custom of seclusion and repentance be strictly adhered to. Robert J. Rosenbaum argues that during the last half of the nineteenth century, there was no greater example of "religious solidarity" than that exhibited by the Penitentes of New Mexico. Although no one is sure exactly how the Order developed there, some believe it derived out of the Third Order of St. Francis.[41]

Regardless of where it originated, deep in the Sangre de Cristos, as Spanish power receded and priests from the mother country were driven out, the Penitentes and elder Hispana women filled the religious void left behind. When the Americans first made their presence known in large numbers, this was the dominant religious temperament they found in northeastern New Mexico. For twenty-five years, the Republic of Mexico struggled to protect its frontier borders and maintain a semblance of control over its people. While the American market economy seeped westward along the Santa Fe Trail, Mexican ecclesiastical and civil authorities sent directives northeast along the *El Camino Real.* As remote outside interests approached the villagers from opposite ends of the continent, locals looked to the Penitentes as "an organization of the common man against his masters, a brotherhood . . ." As always, Hispanos adopted to their changing environment including religious activities, with creativity and perseverance.[42]

Although the women did not participate in the rites of the Brotherhood, the church was never far from a village Hispana's thoughts. The women did make special meals at Lenten for the Penitentes and kept the *moradas* clean and in good order. Regardless of how distinct or important the Penitentes were during the period, it was the *Hispanas* that remained the lifeblood of the traditional Catholic faith in the mountain churches scattered across the Las Vegas Land Grant. During Holy Week processions, one man carried a fifteen-foot wooden cross, called the *maderous*, while the other Penitentes walked into the village behind him carrying painted wooden images of Christ. The women followed, carrying their own image of the Virgin Mary. The Stations of the Cross were sometimes recited as the progression made its way to the churchyard or other locations, where the large cross was placed. As the middle of the nineteenth century approached, small, timber-roofed Catholic churches of stone and adobe continued to materialize, scattered across the mountains and valleys, connected by a series of dirt trails. These trails of worship linked the communities of northern New Mexico into one people.[43]

Between 1821 and 1848, as children grew up and started families of their own, a new generation of farmers and ranchers spread out along the rivers and creeks, creating new villages. Again, primogeniture was not practiced. Family plots were divided equally, eventually whittling the land into strips that did not provide each family with enough land to prosper. Over the next mountain, sons and daughters broke ground with rough wooden plows; planting oats, beans, and wheat. Small plazas, called *placitas*, were constructed in the heart of the valleys that laced the Sangre de Cristos with green grasses and thin blue streams. Trees were felled and foundations begun. New churches were built. Men and women dug ditches to the river, channeling mountain water toward garden plots that called to a golden sun set high in a blue, New Mexican sky. In this way, deep in the swales of a remote land with no large population centers, the villages thrived, communal islands amid a rolling sea of conifered peaks and hard-scrabble mesas. Yet regardless of the land's beauty, the grant was not a part of a fairy-tale.

Danger was always present, as real as the cold-winds that blew off the mountains and caked the streams with ice. Indians could appear at any time. At the approach of Navajo or Apache bands, farmers would drop their hoes or abandon the wood they were collecting, search the horizon for their wives and children, and run toward the shelter of the *placita*.[44]

Isolated as they were, these communities, ten to twenty miles apart, still believed themselves to be a part of a greater whole. Spider-webbed and criss-crossed, well-worn paths connected Las Trampas with Mora, Mora with Tecolote de Rincon, Manuelitas with San Ignacio, and Sapello to Las Vegas. Sarah Deutsch calls this connectedness the beginnings of the "regional community." This community of villages evolved due to strategic and kin-based priorities that developed as a matter of course and logic. For a variety of reasons, people migrated from place to place through the mountains, visiting cousins and brothers, caring for parents, finding marriage partners, and sometimes just striking out on their own. Chokeberries, nuts, and oats from Mora were traded to *Tecolote de Rincon* farmers for leather goods and grains.[45]

While neighbors found ways to improve their lot by trading their home-grown produce and products among themselves, they also bartered with the Plain Indians. People on the grant were adept middle men that accumulated large quantities of bison furs and other hides in their parleys with the Comanches and the Kiowas. These Indians were particularly drawn to northeastern New Mexico by the wool products and breads these *nuevo-mexicanos* provided them. The villagers then traded the furs to Mexicans in Santa Fe and Euro-Americans venturing into the region through Taos. Scholars such as Brian Delay argue that the relationships that developed between Hispanos and Plains Indians made the *nuevo-mexicanos* less vulnerable to attack. Comanches preferred to raid in one direction, generally toward central Texas and Mexico, and trade in another, usually within the Sangre de Cristo Mountains.[46]

More Than a Desert

The first Anglo-Americans venturing into the Sangre de Cristos believed them devoid of civilization or useful life. Its landscapes were empty of tangible signs that man had made his mark. American notions of progress included installing a variety of buildings, fences, and other structures on top of their conquests. To the newcomer, a few adobe homes along a river did not constitute much of a community. To someone from the United States, the adobe huts, far from urbanity or the latest American inventions, might well have been located in the Sahara desert. Anglo-Americans did not understand, nor did they really contemplate, how homes nestled in a mountain valley might be connected to other isolated dwellings they occasionally passed. Yet cousins, brothers, sisters, friends, and trading partners lived along these dirt paths, all a part of a greater whole.[47]

Unlike the regional economy, Sarah Deutsch argues the life-blood of the regional community involved these interwoven relationships, unbroken by geography or marriage, with no inclination toward determining how to make a profit off their neighbor. People within the various villages were in touch with each other weekly, if not more often. In the light of day, they visited relatives, traded goods, and worshiped together in the mountain churches. By night, many of the men came together at the local *morada*. Life in the mountains of New Mexico had evolved with few connections to the central government. With little help from Mexico, men and women created an evolving culture and mode of transaction that suited both their interests and needs. The growth and success of the Santa Fe Trail and the opportunities it opened up in New Mexico was not lost on the citizens that lived on the Las Vegas Land Grant. Market influences had been at work within the mountains since the first days of Mexican independence.[48]

In 1821, the same year de Baca was awarded the first grant on the *Las Vegas Grandes*, Mexico broke away from Spain. The new federal government implemented a series of liberal trade policies to spur economic activity in their northern provinces, trying to initiate new methods of generating revenue and developing a tax base. By the time the Las Vegas community grant was awarded in 1835, the Santa Fe Trail trade, originating out of these policies, was in full bloom. As an example of its success, one caravan of seventy-five wagons carrying merchandise worth approximately $130,000 left Independence, Missouri in May 1835 for Santa Fe, certain to make a profit after the 770 mile journey.[49]

By 1835, a great deal of demographic flux and expansionist momentum had pushed large numbers of Anglo-Americans toward the banks of the Mississippi River. Missouri became the twenty-fourth state on 10 August 1821. Although migration into the western portions of the United States occurred on a much grander scale, just like in Missouri, a better future also motivated people living in San Miguel del Bado to look elsewhere for their fortunes. A little over a decade later, while many *nuevo-mexicanos* were considering whether to settle on the Gallinas River or acquire land on the Tecolote grant, Anglo-Americans were flooding into Texas in such great numbers that Mexico City banned further emigration from the United States. Yet by the time officials made this decision, it was too late. While Hispanos on the Las Vegas grant dug ditches and planted their first crops, Texians rebelled against the Republic. The defeat of General Antonio López de Santa Anna at of the Battle of San Jacinto set off a chain of reactions in both Mexico and the United States that would ultimately impact the future of these farmers' plots.[50]

Most rural *nuevo-mexicanos* remained unaware of what was happening to their south, yet were cognizant of some of the changes due to their dealings with the most powerful individuals in New Mexico. The largest landowners already utilized the local hamlets as their own personal sources of wealth, and expanded this practice once eastern markets began to influence their operations. After Mexican Independence, a few entrepreneurial Hispanos were able to capitalize on their relationships with officials within the Mexican government to acquire more land and power. They lived on large ranches that spread away from the mountain villages. Sometimes the *patron's* own labor force was large enough to create communities of their own. By the end of the 1830s, these *nuevo-mexicanos* were as powerful as the padres that dominated New Mexico in the eighteenth century. Known as *ricos*, they counted many influential government officials as friends. Because of their relationships with governors, land officers, and other persons of note, these Hispanos sometimes managed to extract the region's best lands for them-selves. Many used their holdings to influence and dominate the common folk by offering them land to live on, farming and ranching privileges, and advice and protection. Much of the time, the interaction between peasant farmer and *patron*, benefited both. The landless *nuevo-mexicano* needed a place to raise his family. The *rico* needed laborers and field hands to develop and improve land by growing crops and shepherding his large flocks of sheep. The price extracted from the laboring classes to farm a section of the *patron's* holdings was often steep. Similar to the arrangements southern sharecroppers found themselves tied to during the first part of the nineteenth century, rural farmers and ranchers in New Mexico often became indebted to the *patron* beyond their ability to pay, which secured for the landowner a steady source of cheap labor.[51]

Independent, land-holding *ricos* and enterprising Hispano business-men who partnered openly with French-Canadians and secretly with Anglo-Americans were pleased when the United States officially annexed Mexico's northern-most province in 1848, yet as stated above, many had made their fortunes long before the U. S.–Mexican War ended with half of the Republic's territory becoming a part of the United States.

As annexation approached, *ricos* within the territory worked to de-velop long-term business relationships with eastern newcomers. By 1846, the cost of merchandise hauled to Santa Fe each year approached 1,000,000 dollars. The *patrons* and other entrepreneurial *nuevo-mexicanos* played key roles in this trade. While economics and politics marched toward an intersec-tion that later produced war, many Hispanos acted as intermediaries along the Trail, developing business relationships with Americans who needed Spanish-speaking partners.[52]

In the decade before annexation, while the people on the Las Vegas grant worked at establishing their homes on the Gallinas River, Governor Manuel Armijo was busy approving the largest land grant petitions in Spanish or Mexican history. A few of these grants were awarded to Hispanos that maintained partnerships with French-Canadians, some of the first Anglos to venture permanently into New Mexico. Since the early part of the nine-teenth century, the French-Canadians had been transforming themselves from trappers and tradesmen into frontier entrepreneurs. The huge grants Armijo dispersed were similar to the *empresario* grants awarded in Texas to Stephen F. Austin. In both cases, hundreds of thousands and even millions of acres were awarded to a few individuals, with the understanding that once granted, men like Carlos Beaubien in New Mexico and Stephen F. Austin in Texas would spearhead and promote colonization efforts that had not succeeded during the Spanish period.[53]

Whether Spanish or Mexican, for decades, authorities in charge of the province were concerned about the United States' intentions toward New Mexico. The Mexican government was determined to discourage territorial infringements by populating the region with people indebted to their Republic. To do this, the new nation enacted liberal, innovative legislation that encouraged foreigners to occupy the extreme frontier. Populating New Mexico with pioneers willing to swear allegiance to the Republic became more important than the ethnicity of the participants. In the 200 year reign of the Spanish Empire in New Mexico, officials did not award more grants than Manuel Armijo's government did between 1821 and 1846. Mexican officials anxious to stem United States' expansion developed a policy of inclusion almost reckless in its approach, yet one they considered worth the gamble, considering what was at stake.[54]

The liberal Mexican policies that first opened the Santa Fe Trail gave many Hispanos the opportunity to use their ingenuity and business savvy to make money. Pre-annexation entrepreneur Miguel Romero, father of Eugenio, Margarito, Hilario, and Benigno, transformed himself from wagon-master to rancher, to mercantilist; along the way parlaying a vast sheep ranching empire into one of the largest wholesale businesses in the northern Mexico. In 1834, Mariano Chavez recruited 150 men for an expedition to the United States to sell New Mexican livestock. In 1835, with the help of his brother José, Chavez headed south to Mexico with over 20,000 sheep purchased with profits from the previous year's eastern transactions. Similarly, the Otero family did business with both Americans in the east and Mexicans in the south, growing into one of the most powerful families west of the Mississippi. Three-time governor Manuel Armijo took advantage of Mexico's innovative trade policies as well, using his office to help facilitate the growth of a major export business that made him a rich man. The economic boom also trickled down to the common folk. Hispanos found jobs on the wagon trains as drivers, herders, and carpenters. Farmers were also impacted, as were independent ranchers, both drawn into the American market economy by its clamor for produce and wool. Many *nuevo-mexicanos* continued to capitalize on the increased traffic that occurred along the Trail after the Treaty of Guadalupe-Hidalgo went into effect, yet it was the landed classes that had positioned themselves before the takeover who profited from the changes. Afterwards, some wealthy New Mexicans did move to Mexico. Many that stayed were unable to sustain what they had created under the Republic. Yet whether good or bad, life in New Mexico changed forever once it became a part of the United States.[55]

Upon entering the town of Las Vegas on 15 August 1846, Colonel Stephen W. Kearney, leader of the Army of the West, spoke to an assembly of locals from a rooftop that overlooked the Plaza. After establishing the obvious, which was that the United States now ruled the region, he informed the Las Vegans that Americans had considered New Mexico a part of the United States "for some time" and proclaimed, "we come amongst you as friends–not as enemies; as protectors–not as conquerors." Almost two years later, due to Congressional rewrites, the final version of the Treaty of Guadalupe-Hidalgo would not specifically verify the colonel's words as truth. Article 10 of the Treaty, which pointedly guaranteed *nuevo-mexicano* property rights, was deleted. Yet even after this deletion, the document, when taken in its entirety, still inferred that property agreements made under Spanish and Mexican rule would be honored by the United States. Yet with the exact verbiage that detailed these rights eliminated, talented American lawyers quickly took advantage of the omissions.[56]

Treaties and laws from distant authorities were nothing new for the locals who stared up at Colonel Kearney in 1846, yet this time the edicts were not understandable. In what must have been an awkward moment for Juan de Dios Maese, an original land grant petitioner and the current *alcalde*, Kearney ordered Maese to follow him onto the roof of a building that faced the Plaza and translate his words. The *alcalde*, trying to make the best of a bad situation, shouted down the colonel's proclamation. Most *nuevo-mexicanos* were unhappy and disgusted with the day's events, regardless of the rosy sounding phrases that echoed off the buildings. Not knowing quite what to expect from the American soldiers, some had hidden their wives and children outside of town.[57]

It was not that Hispanos were unwilling to fight the Americans. As the Army of the West set out for Santa Fe, a great number waited above Apache Pass, the main approach to the capital. They were armed and ready to fire down on the American soldiers if they entered the canyon. Yet they were gone before the Army of the West arrived. At the last moment, Governor

Manuel Armijo withdrew the *nuevo-mexicanos* gathered there, falling back to Santa Fe. It would have been extremely difficult for Colonel Kearney and his army to get through the pass if Armijo had held his ground. Yet it was not to be. Much speculation has since centered around James Magoffin, a Santa Fe trader on good terms with Armijo, and Magoffin's possible influence on the governor's decision to abandon Apache Pass. Days earlier, Magoffin had ridden ahead of Kearney's forces into Santa Fe. Although there is no record of any conversation between the trader and Armijo, the American was seen entering the governor's home. After the war, Senator Thomas Hart Benton arranged for a considerable amount of money be directed to Magoffin for "secret services rendered." Many bitter *nuevo-mexicanos* and relieved Americans believed money changed hands.[58]

Growth accelerated in Las Vegas after the Army of the West moved through New Mexico that August. In a land of 60,000 people, of which 90 percent were *nuevo-mexicanos*, approximately 1,700 U.S. soldiers, mostly from Missouri, claimed Mexico's northern-most province for the United States. The army set up its first base of operations just off the Las Vegas Plaza. Although the influx of military personnel impacted the local economy in a positive way, the majority population did not reap any immediate benefits. Locals watched as the army took over many of the buildings surrounding the square. A cadre of Anglo-American merchants and officials followed in their wake.[59]

Many *ricos* did benefit from this change. Families such as the Oteros, Romeros, de Bacas, and men like F. A. Manzanares utilized ties established through trade developed on the Trail to further enhance their businesses under the new regime. Most Anglo-Americans could not speak Spanish. Under the new regime, much of the existing Mexican law enforcement system was left in place, and continued to be run by prominent Hispanos. Many families were able to hold onto their positions of power and maintain the wealth they had created under the old system. The Romeros were certainly adept at conforming to the ways of the newcomers, and were more than willing to help manage the transition from a Mexican to a U.S. territory.[60]

Within six months after Colonel Kearney moved the bulk of his troops toward California, Charles Bent, the newly established territorial governor of New Mexico, was taken from his Taos home and killed by an angry crowd of Pueblo Indians and *nuevo-mexicanos*. The circumstances under which this occurred are not straight-forward. After annexation, many New Mexicans were frustrated with the new regime. In Taos, poverty and little access to cash, coupled with the realization that men who did not speak their language were in control of the community, bred a sense of frustration that required little prompting for violence to break out. Led by Pablo Montoya, an unhappy group of locals confronted Charles Bent about two incarcerated Pueblo Indians, demanding their release. Bent refused to comply, which instigated a rampage through town. The peoples' frustration escalated into violence. The governor was taken from his barricaded house, shot full of arrows, and scalped. He was not the only target. Prefect Cornelio Vigil, a prominent Hispano who was cooperating with the new government, Sheriff Stephen Luis Lee, Narcisco Beaubien, and other Anglo-Americans were murdered on the streets of Taos on 19 January 1847. The deaths ignited a series of similar attacks across the mountains, exploding into a full scale revolt that ran from Arroyo Hondo to Mora. While violence did not erupt in Las Vegas, unrest simmered there as well. An outbreak of paranoia swept the Anglo section of town, creating minor panic and a pervading sense of fear that affected everyone. In July 1847, *Acalde* Juan de Dios Maese was implicated in revolutionary activities that led to his arrest. Found innocent of charges, Maese soon realized the damage to his reputation had destroyed his ability to do business in Las Vegas. The Revolt was not isolated to the northern villages of New Mexico. Its impact was felt throughout the northeast, a wide-ranging event that negatively impacted most *nuevo-mexicanos* that lived there.[61]

Charles Bent and his brother, William, made their names and fortunes as traders on the Santa Fe Trail. Along the Arkansas River, on the edge of the United States border, Charles operated Bent's Fort with partner Ceran St. Vrain. This was the most successful trading post west of the Mississippi. Taos priest Antonío José Martinez had long held the opinion that the Bent brothers were neither trustworthy nor loyal to Mexico, and was not shy about communicating his beliefs to Mexico City.[62]

Many Americans later argued that Padre Martinez was one of the masterminds behind the Taos Revolt. Father Martinez believed Bent and his cohorts had corrupted the region with guns, alcohol, and other illegal contraband. He believed the owner of Bent's Fort, Charles Bent, the future governor of the territory, was the key player in any U.S. attempt to take over the country. After Governor Manuel Armijo approved the Beaubien-Miranda grant in 1841, one of the largest grants in Hispanic American history, Martinez cried foul, claiming Charles Bent was a silent partner in the transaction. The padre declared those involved did not have the best interests of the Republic at heart. Father Martinez felt so strongly about the matter that he traveled to Durango to argue the award should be nullified. After hearing the persuasive priest's argument, which also included the assertion that the Jicarilla Apaches would be displaced, and that it was unfair to the Pueblo Indians of Taos, the Mexican government agreed with Martinez, canceling the award. Yet the cancellation of the Beaubien-Miranda grant only stood for a few months. Governor Armijo explained to government officials that much of the underhandedness the padre accused him of was untrue. Ultimately, authorities in Durango declared the grant a legal transaction. Father Martinez was not alone in his frustration. When this grant was approved, many *nuevo-mexicanos*, Jicarillas, and Taos Indians felt cheated of property they believed they owned. Annexation fueled those sentiments.[63]

A series of letters between Bent, Carlos (Charles) Beaubien and the Mexican consul to the United States reveals they maintained a long-standing, high-level of animosity and disrespect toward the Taos priest, feelings that would not change after annexation. In an 1842 letter to consul Manuel Alvarez, Charles Bent expressed his disdain for Father Martinez, noting the padre was taking credit for Beaubien's appointment as a local Justice of the Peace. Bent wrote:". . . doubt very much if he [Martinez] had been consulted." A short year had passed since the priest fought to have Beaubien's grant denied. Charles Bent sarcastically related to Alvarez that he did not believe Martinez had vouched for Beaubien in the past, nor would he in the future. In 1843, Prefect Cornelio Vigil, the acting Justice of the Peace, killed on the same day as Bent, declared the grant was legal, even walking a portion of it, as custom dictated. After Padre Martinez ventured to Mexico and convinced authorities not to honor the award, Vigil wrote Guadalupe Miranda in 1844, making fun of the padre's efforts, apparently not much concerned with the decision. In 1846, soon to be Territorial Governor Bent, also in a mocking tone, wrote Manuel Alvarez that Father Martinez believed he was so afraid of the padre that he buried gunpowder around his own home, and planned to blow up the priest if he paid a visit. Martinez, Vigil continued, only discounted this rumor after sending some people over to dig around the governor's house. A clear tone of ridicule pervades any reference to Martinez between Vigil, Alvarez, and Bent. It seems to have been a common practice of the padre's adversaries to make fun of him.[64]

The most disturbing letter was written by Charles Bent on 8 April 1846. The Army of the West's march into Las Vegas was still six months away when he wrote Alvarez: "The priest will spair [sp] no means to injure me, but if he will attack me fairly publicly and above board, I am certain he will not accomplish his end, but under handily as he no [now?] doing, wishing to make [indecipherable], of Superior authoritys, to due his dirty work, if he can suxxead [succeed] in this thare is no telling what he may accomplish. . . .The priest will make use of every means to injure up, and his strong hold is falsehood this he will use to its extent, as he is in the habit of doing." No evidence ever came to light that linked Father Antonio José Martinez to Charles Bent's death. Testimony in fact details how he helped save many of the Americans once violence erupted in Taos, yet it appears the territorial governor would not have been surprised if the padre was involved. Oddly enough, after Donaciano Vigil uncovered a plot to kill Bent in December, the territorial governor still chose to return home to Taos without bodyguards.[65]

U.S. troops from Las Vegas and a group of Taos trappers and traders led by Ceran St. Vrain joined the effort to put down the insurrection that originated with Bent's death. St. Vrain had known Charles Bent and his family for over twenty years, serving as his primary business partner at Bent's Fort. The revolt revealed many in New Mexico were not as thrilled with Colonel Kearney's proclamation as he claimed they should be. Some Americans who failed to acknowledge or take seriously the seething resentment of so many *nuevo-mexicanos* and Pueblo Indians paid the ultimate price. The previous fall, U.S. newspapers were hailing Colonel Kearney's bloodless campaign as proof that most citizens of New Mexico approved of United States annexation of New Mexico. What happened on 19 January 1847 changed that.[66]

Although the "conquest" came quickly, for many in New Mexico, the continued occupation by the foreigners was never a certainty. In the days that followed, the Taos Revolt spread across the mountains, drawing more Hispanos to Pablo Montoya's call. A large contingent of rebels made their way toward Santa Fe, only to be turned back by Ceran St. Vrain, his cadre of trappers, and a contingent U. S. soldiers. A running gun battle ensued, the Americans chasing the rebels back through the mountain villages of the Rio Arriba highlands. After two major clashes, the remaining insurgents returned to Taos, taking refuge within the Pueblo and a Catholic Church located there. The U.S. Army followed. Using bombs and cannon balls, the Americans breached the church's walls and captured or killed the remaining rebels.[67]

On 20 January 1847, the day after Bent was pulled from his home, scalped, and killed, five Missouri traders on their way to Taos were stopped in the village of Mora by a group of local *nuevo-mexicanos*. Manuel Cortez has just arrived from Taos when American traders attempted to pass through town. They were on the final leg of their return to Missouri. Cortez and several hundred Hispanos would not let them pass. Merchants Lawrence W. Waldo, Romulus Culver, a Mr. Noyes, Benjamin Prewitt, and Lewis Cabanne, all from Missouri, did not get out of the village alive, robbed and murdered in Mora. Colonel Kearney's Las Vegas proclamation and Governor Armijo's retreat from Apache Pass still angered Cortéz and many of the men that joined him in mountain community. Resentful of Americans as a whole, these *nuevo-mexicanos* took their anger out on the Missouri traders.[68]

U. S. Army Captain R. I. Hendley, in charge of a grazing detail near Las Vegas, was ordered to find and arrest the Mora insurgents. Captain Hendley led eighty troops into Mora, where they were met by small-arms-fire that seemed to come from every house. As the soldiers proceeded through town, they were caught in a vicious street battle. For the next three hours they fought house to house, killing twenty-five of the insurgents. During the firefight, Captain Hendley was shot in the groin. He died shortly thereafter from an artery rupture in his leg. Some of the rebels found protection in an old adobe fort a few miles west of town. Others took cover within the courthouse on the Square. At the end of the day, the soldiers decided they were in no position to dislodge the armed and fortified *nuevo-mexicanos* from their positions and decided to return to Las Vegas and reassess their situation. A week later, 1 February 1847, the army, led by Captain Morin, returned to the

Mora Valley with cannon. The battery brigade set up their heavy artillery across from the courthouse and obliterated the town square. Before the day was done, the cannon was moved and also destroyed the old fort. Manuel Cortez and several of his followers escaped into the surrounding mountains. Although these men would continue to spar with the U.S. military for the next few months, by and large, the violence ended with the destruction of Mora. The Taos Revolt was put down.[69]

A trial quickly followed in Taos. The only eyewitness account ever published was written by seventeen-year-old Hector Lewis Garrard (known as Lewis H. Garrard to his reading public). He noted the trial took place just a few weeks after the uprising. One of the sitting judges was Carlos Beaubien, whose son Narciso was drug from under an outhouse and killed. The court interpreter for the trial was Ceran St. Vrain, Bent's old partner. Throughout *Wah-to-yah: And The Taos Trail*, Garrard's recollections of his adventures in New Mexico amply illustrate the racial prejudice most Anglo-Americans brought into the territory, but occasionally this young man's common sense shines through. One of the charges the Taos insurgents faced was treason. Garrard found this a bit odd: "It certainly did appear to be a great assumption on the part of the Americans to conquer a country and then arraign the revolting inhabitants for treason." Later, describing the rebels sitting in the courtroom after their death verdicts were read, he noted: "The poor wretches sat with immovable features; but I fancied that under the assumed looks of apathetic indifference could be read the deepest anguish. . . . I left the room, sick at heart. Justice! Out upon the word, when its distorted meaning is the warrant for murdering those who defend to the last their country and their homes." On the day several of the rebels were brought out to be hanged, Garrard commented: "The one sentenced to *treason* showed a spirit of martyrdom worthy of the cause for which he died–the liberty of his country; and, instead of the cringing, contemptible recantation of the others, his speech was firm asseverations of his own innocence, the unjustness of his trial, and the arbitrary conduct of his murderers." With the executions in Taos and the leveling of Mora, resistance weakened. It would be several decades before another organized force rose up against perceived injustices.[70]

Soon afterwards, leaders in Washington ordered plans for a military base be drawn up for the area. It was decided to build a fort east of Mora and north of Las Vegas to deter further revolts, act as a distribution point for bases further west, and protect travelers on the Santa Fe Trail from Indian attack. Fort Union was completed in 1852. It was built on rolling, red dirt hills near the intersection of the Cimarron and mountain branches of the Santa Fe Trail. After the construction of the post, the Anglo-American presence grew stronger in New Mexico.[71]

As the smoke settled over the ruins of what was once the town of Mora, a new reality gripped the local populace. Many more chose to leave for Mexico. Businesses and homes around the Las Vegas Plaza were vacated by Hispanos and quickly filled by Anglo-Americans and European immigrants. Records are not available regarding the purchase price these evacuees settled upon, but based on sales documents of a later era, it is doubtful the victors were willing to pay much to those who left.[72]

In 1850, W. W. H. Davis, the first U.S. Attorney for the territory noted, "a few Americans living here . . . seem to control the trade of the place." With the exception of five properties near or around the Plaza, by 1853, all businesses were dominated by men from the east, whether Anglo-American or European. Although *nuevo-mexicano* businessmen would rally in about a decade, Miguel Romero was one of the few who never left. In the face of Anglo-American expansion, he was able to sustain and grow his businesses, which, as stated earlier, he began along the Trail as a wagon master and mover of freight. Even as Anglos continued to file into Las Vegas, Miguel Romero's businesses prospered. As the first generation of *nuevo-mexicanos* grew up under United States' rule, Miguel added a creamery and a mercantile store. José Albino de Baca also remained in Las Vegas. By the mid 1850s, he had become one of the wealthiest men in New Mexico. North of the Plaza, de Baca built an extravagant, three-story home in the village his family had begun back when the grant originated, called Upper Town. Romero and Baca were examples of men that took advantage of the changing market economy while continuing to utilize old world patronage as a means to control local citizens. Local farmers knew them as *patrones*, men they leased land from, sold their crops to, and persons that could be depended upon in hard times to help them out. Yet the common-folk were also cognizant of the fact that these men's benevolence generally came with a price. Such *patrons* demanded loyalty, often-times manifested in how they expected the common folk to vote. Such reciprocity kept these *ricos* in positions of power long after the Americans came.[73]

The town of Las Vegas, designated the San Miguel County seat in 1852, remained one of the primary engines of capitalist growth within Territorial New Mexico throughout the 1850s, 60s, and 70s. The few Hispano business-men who remained during this period used their contacts and experience to facilitate successful operations. At the same time, they were able to maintain their vast properties outside of town, which allowed them to create wealth out of the ground. Much of their prosperity derived from the grazing fields that surrounded Las Vegas. Landless *nuevo-mexicanos* lived on the *ricos'* ranches, often managing their sheep operations for that privilege. As these *patrons* accumulated more wealth, they gained additional political power. They used their influence as cultural intermediaries to grow their businesses and develop their political power bases as *jéfe politicos*.[74]

By the 1870s, more *nuevo-mexicanos* were back on the Plaza, reassert-ing their position among the majority population. The Romeros, de Bacas, and the Lopez family continued their influence as town leaders to create a vibrant, cohesive political network, using communication channels that already existed to facilitate trade and ballot-box influence in the surround-ing mountain villages. Although select Anglo-Americans were sent to New Mexico to run the territory, much of the on-the-ground management re-mained in the hands of local Hispanos. Several decades passed before the United States government was able to send lower level officials with enough ability to counter-act the dominance of regional political networks in New Mexico. One person who did have an early impact was Surveyor General William Pelham. Pelham was charged with assessing the validity of all land titles in the territory.

Only after annexation did American officials, sifting through stacks of government documents, begin to realize the magnitude of the Spanish and Mexican land grant system. Over decades and centuries, both community and private grants had been dispersed over the best parts of the country. The "best parts" always meant where water flowed. Once in New Mexico, territorial officials slowly realized what a grand task they had before them. First, they had to investigate the different types of landholdings and attempt to understand why they were created as they were. As touched on earlier, owners of large private grants were still obligated to improve the land and encourage settlement. Men and women who homesteaded on these individual grants made agreements with the owner to work land they had never owned. They prospered or failed in large part according to the efforts and fairness of the local *patron*. New settlers on such private grants were also obligated to ensure crops and grains were produced and livestock was taken care of, albeit under a system where a portion of what they grew or raised was given to the owner as payment for being able to live there. When attempting to understand the various types of grants in New Mexico, the most important questions concern what common lands were meant for, and what would the United States government do about them.[75]

Community grants were different animals than private grants, and ferreting out the specifics of each is still confusing and controversial. On a community grant, each settler was issued his own personal plot for a home and garden. Unlike a private grant, this allotment became the settler's personal property. On the other hand, the grant's common lands were to be shared by everyone. According to both Spanish and Mexican law, no portion of pasture or timberlands could be rationed out percentage-wise as a part of a *pobladores'* private property. The issue of how Americans understood Spanish and Mexican law regarding the sharing of common lands is the most relevant point concerning the future loss of *nuevo-mexicano* land rights. Hispanic notions and rules on common usage originated with the Castilian idea that a person could not own naturally reoccurring resources such as water, wood, or grass. American surveyor generals who were in charge of assessing the validity of grants could not read or speak Spanish, and had no background in ancient Castilian land-laws. Claiming property as a shared venture was as foreign to the American concept of ownership as the Castilian tongue, which many *nuevo-mexicanos* still spoke.[76]

When New Mexico became a territory, there were sixty community grants in place. This book's focus is on the Las Vegas Land Grant, yet it is important for the reader to understand the basis of the land grant system in general before an investigative assessment of the Las Vegas grant can take place. The Las Vegas grant was a community grant. Each person who lived on such a grant, as stated above, received an allotment for a home, called a *solar*, one for cultivation, known as the *suertes*, and use of pasturelands or *debesa*. The surrounding forests were also considered common, used for firewood and building materials. At the center of most was a plaza or *placita*, which usually ran near a water source managed by everyone on the grant, sharing equally.[77]

When Colonel Kearney rode into the middle of the Las Vegas Land Grant in August of 1846, many in his army wrote that they had entered a small town of "mud huts," interpreting their surroundings according to their own pre-conceived notions of what was normal. The soldiers believed they had crossed hundreds of miles of empty territory and occupied a village in the middle of nowhere. Yet for Hispanos on the Plaza who stood listening to the *alcalde* interpret Colonel Kearny's words, Las Vegas was neither empty nor irrelevant. *Las Vegas Grandes* was the center of their universe.[78]

Besides the sixty community grants that existed when the Army of the West bivouacked on a slight rise east of the Plaza (where New Mexico Highlands University now stands), there were over 6,000 private grants in New Mexico. Articles 8 and 9 remained within the Treaty of Guadalupe-Hidalgo, but lacking the clarity found in deleted Article 10, gave only "general guarantees" to property owners. As stated above, clear statements upholding *nuevo-mexicano* land rights were omitted. Fogginess and deleted portions of the documents left many openings for legal counsel representing newcomers that followed the army west.[79]

In a land of little water, *nuevo-mexicanos* held title to most of the property along the rivers. One hundred and thirteen total grants were submitted by Hispanos to the United States government when asked for proof of ownership. At about the same time officials started the process of interpreting the petitions, a new dynamic began to influence decisions about property in New Mexico. Capitalism and the draw of eastern markets were no longer a novelty. As more Anglo-Americans ventured into the region, ideas about growth, land, money, and community began to change on the Las Vegas Land Grant.[80]

2

The Barter Economy, Capitalism, and the
Arrival of Civilization

Southwestern Capitalism

Nuevo-mexicanos were cognizant of the new regime's power, but paid little attention to United States officials unless directly confronted by them. Hispanos living on the Las Vegas grant focused on providing for their families, a task that required more hours than there were in a day. The Taos Revolt was common knowledge on the grant and everyone was keenly aware of what happened in Mora, yet winter would not wait on an uprising to play out. Settlers could ill-afford to be unprepared for three-foot snowfalls. Even if they approved of the actions their neighbors were taking, maintaining sufficient stocks of wood for warmth and cooking, scavenging enough water from ice-choked streams, and taking care of the livestock prevented most from participating in the revolt. Stored grains and fresh meat reaped from the common lands were all that stood between most families and starvation. Hard winters sometimes lasted until early May. Enough food had to be put up to sustain people on the grant for seven months. Other than the occasional visit by a Catholic bishop, prior to annexation men of power seldom visited their rural constituencies. Most farmers and ranchers on the grant preferred it that way. There was wood to stack and animals to look after. It was no different in the winter of 1847.[1]

In the first decades after annexation, entrepreneurs from the East Coast and Europe made their way west in quest of a new start. Europeans traveled into an alien world, far removed from the trade centers of France and Germany. For some, the cities and towns along the Atlantic Coast were just their starting point. After experiencing a cultural cataclysm in the bustling port-towns of Boston, New York, and Baltimore, many moved on, transported by ox-drawn wagons, horse-drawn coaches, and mules toward the Mississippi River and beyond, joining a host of Americans that were escaping the congested seashore towns.[2]

Contrary to most federally appointed officials, foreign-born merchants who came to Las Vegas were already bi or tri-lingual, having become conversant, to a certain extent, in both English and French before traveling to New Mexico. Already familiar with the struggle to communicate with Americans in New York, or French Canadians in St. Louis, men such as Charles Ilfeld of Germany found it easier to adapt in a town like Las Vegas. They understood success required conforming to the existing social and economic playing field without re-writing the rules. Anyone serious about developing a business on the grant knew the first priority was to learn Spanish. Charles Ilfeld was serious. At nineteen, he left Homburg, Germany, for America. Already knowing some French, on the trip over he focused on learning English. The Spanish language seemed like a natural progression for motivated Europeans like Ilfeld. When he first entered New Mexico Territory, he worked for merchant Adolph Letcher in Taos. It was not long before both men realized that Las Vegas, perched as it was along the main path of the Santa Fe Trail, was a more promising site for a mercantilist. When Letcher moved his enterprise there, Ilfeld followed. After partnering for a while with Letcher, the young German started his own business on the Plaza. Soon, he successfully established himself as one of the most prominent merchants in town.[3]

Ilfeld needed local resources to stock his stores and fill the big orders he began to receive from Fort Union. He and other Las Vegas merchants created partnerships with local farmers and ranchers. To meet the military's growing demands, he purchased buffalo meat, beans, oats, and hay from Las Vegans and the mountain villagers that lived on the grant. When more soldiers filed into New Mexico, they brought hundreds of horses. Forage became a popular energy resource. Hay was grown in the mountain valleys and on the upland prairies east of town. The army became more established in the region just as the bison began to disappear. This was no coincidence, for part of General William T. Sherman's strategy to control Indians included eliminating this animal from the plains. Beef and wheat crops were soon introduced as replacement staples. Rural farmers plotted out fields for hay and wheat while ranchers accelerated sheep and cattle operations.[4]

Merchants such as Charles Ilfeld were only able to expand because of their growing business relationships with the grant's *nuevo-mexicano* farmers. Although freighting goods to the East Coast added 30 percent to the cost of doing business, men such as Joseph Rosenwald and Frenchman Jean Pendaries were still able to double their profits by bartering for goods received from local communities and then selling them to the federal government and large wholesale operations in Kansas City. In return for the wheat, beans, hay, and livestock, the villagers were offered refined sugar, wood matches, metal farming utensils, and iron bed frames. The seemingly timeless subsistence lifestyle that had been in place since the late eighteenth century was altered by this Anglo-American demand for *nuevo-mexicano* goods. Not to say trade with varying cultures was not unknown in San Miguel County, exchange of goods had always been a part of village life, yet with the introduction of American manufactured products, a gradual transformation within the rural economy began to affect the material world of Hispano communities on the grant. This economy was also impacted by the newcomers interpretations of old-world property laws.[5]

Historian Richard White argues that the majority of officials sent west to administrate the new territory were honest men that took their roles seriously, yet good intentions were often not enough. For most, this was their first visit to New Mexico and they did not speak the language. To make things worse, the government did not provide them with adequate resources to carry out their responsibilities. One of their most important tasks was to confirm whether or not Mexican notions of land ownership were legitimate.[6]

In years past, up to and through the 1830s, much of colonized New Mexico operated similar to a feudal society. Similarly, like the land barons of Europe, the *ricos* depended on peasant farmers living on their property (private property) to furnish them a portion of their harvest and livestock each year. Farmers and ranchers paid these *patrones* with produce, wool, wheat, and lambs. Any excess left after such payments was what most *nuevo-mexicanos* lived on. After 1848, if any goods remained after setting aside provisions for the family, they traded with merchants like the Rosenwald Brothers, Romero, and Ilfeld. In most cases, businessmen dealt with the *patrones*. Such *ricos* and owners of private land grants had more to trade, having acquired produce and goods as rent from tenants living on their lands. With the continued emergence of sedentary merchants in the American Southwest, old mountain cultures and economies were forced to accept the new realities of annexation. Cash quickly became the dominant means of transaction, yet the majority population had little access to it. After the coming of the railroad, life on the grant would change even more drastically, yet that transition remained twenty to thirty years in the future.[7]

One of the first photos of Old Las Vegas. Note the Catholic Church, the large white wooden structure, is the most prominent building in town. From the Collection of the Las Vegas Citizens' Committee for Historic Preservation.

By 1850, a passenger stage was running between Las Vegas and Independence, Missouri; a distance of 770 miles. Passenger fare was $250 per person, which included a forty pound baggage limit. Anything over the limit cost a traveler an additional fifty cents per pound. Many of the first to use these stages were the immigrants from Europe, but United States citizens also migrated into the new territories. Would-be bankers, land speculators, and cattlemen cast their eyes across the rolling plains east of the mountains, marveling at the sea of grasses. Intrepid businessmen calculated the possible profits from the endless stream of freight wagons that moved across the Santa Fe Trail. Others cast their eyes toward the mountains, attempting to deduce where veins of gold might rest within the deep crevices and peaks of the Sangre de Cristos. In an effort to draw more Anglo-Americans into New Mexico, newspapers hailed the bountiful wonders of the region, ensuring readers in Missouri and Illinois were aware that the hardest part about making a living in Las Vegas or Santa Fe was getting there.[8]

The military's presence in and around Las Vegas was comforting for those traveling on the Trail, but it was impossible for soldiers to police such a large area with more than just a perception of success. The focus at Fort Union remained on protecting settlers, freighters, and corralling wayward Indians, yet an additional, unanticipated mission was soon taking up their time. Territorial officials and military officers soon became familiar with New Mexico's own long-standing, wide-ranging market economy. The co-manchero trade funneled horses and cattle stolen in Central Mexico into an exchange system that included Hispano hard-breads, wool, bison-hides, American gunpowder, and cash. This robust economy incorporated Pueblo Indians, Kiowas, Utes, Navajo, Comanche, *nuevo-mexicanos*, and Missouri bankers into an inter-ethnic trade-zone that started in Saltillo and ended along the Mississippi River. After annexation, this southwestern, shadow-economy continued, remaining for the most part just out of the reach of the U.S. Army.[9]

This indigenous form of raw capitalism had existed in the mountains for over 100 years. In the seventeenth and eighteenth centuries, trade fairs drew various tribes and villagers to Taos, Pecos, and Santa Fe each year. These events eventually included Anglo-American and French-Canadian mountain men. Like the comancheros to the southeast, this trade was not restricted to produce or man-made products such as pottery, robes, or blankets. After the Utes acquired horses, they took advantage of the Paiute tribe's lack of mounts, swooping into their villages to steal women and children. These captives became valued commodities who were traded for wools, horses, and other valuables at the fairs. A ready market for victims of tribal warfare had existed in New Mexico for centuries. Although the Comanche were perhaps the most successful native capitalists, in 1853, Captain Henry Dodge, Indian agent of the Navajo, observed 6 percent of that tribe held forty percent of the wealth, while 12 percent lived in a virtual starvation state. Some of the richest of the Navajo owned forty to fifty slaves each. One hundred of the wealthiest, Dodge claimed, owned 100,000 of the sheep and 15,000 horses.[10]

The Comanche, like other native tribes, found their lives and business activities disrupted by the steady expansion of Anglo-Americans into their domain. Coupled with drought, these Indians harvesting of bison for their own needs and as marketable commodities had reduced the herds to a point that only required Anglo sharpshooters a couple of decades to practically eliminate them from the plains. By the time of annexation, Comanches were already adapting to this reality. As the bison herds shrank, Plains Indians ventured deeper into Texas and Mexico, returning with horses and cattle to the Texas Panhandle or the breaks beyond the *Llano Estacado*. There, they bartered with the comanchero for axes, bridles, sugar, maize, and hard breads. The comancheros then herded these animals into New Mexico Territory where they found plenty of buyers.[11]

Patricia Limerick argues that Indian depredations along the Santa Fe Trail and the illegal trade between the Comanche and *nuevo-mexicanos* was a stimulus to the region's economy. If the comanchero had no place to sell stolen horses and cattle, this illegal trade would not have thrived along the Sangre de Cristo Range. If it had not thrived, Texans would not have demanded the military stop the Comanche's from stealing their horses and cattle. If there had been no demand, more troops would have not entered New Mexico, which would have meant local farmers would not have benefited from the goods they sold to the frontier outposts. Charles Goodnight declared that Comanches stole over 300,000 cattle and 100,000 horses in the 1860s, proving the New Mexicans' talent for trade, not to mention their brazen attitude toward U. S. occupation. As stated above, Fort Union became the main distribution point for goods that supplied other bases. One such base that focused on the illegal trade was Fort Bascom, positioned in the Canadian River Valley about 90 miles east of Las Vegas. This fort was located in the heart of one of the main comanchero trade routes, the Canadian River. The construction of Fort Bascom, like Fort Union to the north, and Fort Sumner to the south, created an increased demand for *nuevo-mexicano* agricultural products. As a sidebar, the very officers sent to disrupt the contraband sometimes became entangled in the illicit trade, strong-arming those involved for a part of the profits before allowing them to pass through the valley they were sent to police.[12]

The military's increased demand for food and forage afforded an opportunity for those with the means to convert untilled land into agricultural profits. Ceran St. Vrain, the ex-mountain man and old partner of Charles Bent, built a grist mill in the Mora Valley about twenty miles west of Fort Union, prepared to take advantage of the increased military demand for wheat. Bent's avenger accumulated much of the Mora grant for this enterprise. It is rather ironic that St. Vrain would one day settle in a place known for its hostility toward Americans. Although he was not involved in the army's annihilation of Mora, he had participated in putting down the revolt in Taos. Not long after the mill was put into operation, a traveler passing through the Mora Valley commented that he had never seen such wheat harvests. Using only animals and their own backs, *nuevo-mexicanos* annually furnished St. Vrain's Mill with 60,000 bushels of wheat to grind. Less than twenty miles to the south, Frenchman Jean Pendaries built another mill in the Tecolote de Rincon Valley. With the spread of corn and wheat crops, other mills sprang up on the grant, including one just west of the town of Las Vegas.[13]

Ilfeld, St. Vrain, Miguel A. Otero Sr., and others signed government contracts to provide the army with a variety of produce. Sam Watrous started a cattle enterprise near the junction of the Sapello and Mora Rivers to supply beef to Fort Union. By 1869, John Rosenwald was furnishing 300 pounds of corn to Fort Bascom and filling orders for hay and beans. None of these merchants broke the ground, planted the seeds, nor hauled the harvests to the grist mills. Peasant Hispano farmers turned the earth, managed the *acequias*, tended the crops, and in most cases, herded the cattle that fed the soldiers stationed throughout the territory. These farmers and ranchers were integral to the development of the agricultural and livestock industries of New Mexico.[14]

About this time, Eugenio Romero and his brothers were beginning to step out of their father's shadow. As they branched out on their own, Miguel's sons developed their own followings in Las Vegas. On most political issues, they aligned themselves with the San Miguel County Republicans, yet each proved to be independent thinkers and talented individuals. Eugenio married in 1856. In doing so, he gained both a wife and a partnership. Ascension Lopez came from one of the most influential Hispanic families in the region. They would have ten children together. Eugenio was a brilliant businessman. As Las Vegas grew, so did his assets, expanding his lumber business into Santa Fe, Duran, and Estancia. His younger siblings proved just as adept. Trinidad founded the Romero Mercantile Company and became a future delegate to the territorial congress. Although he was his own man, he followed in Eugenio's footsteps, marrying Ascension Lopez's sister, Valeria. Benigno became president of the Plaza Hotel and Improvement Company. Margarito owned a Las Vegas lumber mill and was a prominent local politician. Much later, Margarito built *El Porvenir*, a resort hotel on the outskirts of town. In the years to come, Hilario Romero would make his name in law enforcement, serving as both a county sheriff and U.S. marshal for the territory. Toward the end and into the next century, both Eugenio and his sons, like their uncle Hilario, would serve the county as law officers. What is clear is that in the first decades of American rule, the Romero clan grew stronger, and were prominent players in the future of the Las Vegas Land Grant.[15]

The Pull of the American Market

To meet government contracts, Charles Ilfeld maintained business relationships in several mountain villages with groups of small farmers. He also did business with large land owners like Eugenio Romero. From Mora and Sapello, Ilfeld acquired lumber, oats, wheat, and corn. Jean Pendaries, Telesfor Jaramillo, Milnor Rudolph and S. A. Clements sold wool, hay, corn, and timber to Ilfeld and other Las Vegas merchants. These men also sold their goods directly to government agents.[16]

The same mountain villages that produced crops and forage for Rosenwald and Pendaries had existed as subsistent societies with few outside needs for over one hundred years. It was still rare for a local farmer to enjoy a sliver of the profits his land produced, as most had entered into agreements that kept them in or near debt. An inequitable balance existed between the agriculturist and the entrepreneur. Both St. Vrain and Pendaries owned the mills that processed the local farmers' grains. These mill owners set the rates per pound just like the town merchant determined how much was required for specific manufactured products. Although merchants received cash for the produce they delivered to the army, in most cases, the rural Hispano received merchandise or a reduction of their debt for previous purchased seed or tools. Although such arrangements generally favored the merchant and the mill owner, wagonloads of wheat did help pay for glass windows and other home and lifestyle improvements. Bushels of corn were traded for bolts of calico cloth. Metal shovels and hoes were introduced. Such marvelous products entered both the urban and rural Hispano exchange system that also included the military's demand for agricultural and meat products.[17] The U.S. government instigated the increased trade between town merchants and *nuevo-mexicano* farmers. As Limerick argued, Washington directives to protect travelers along the Trail and expand their control in the new territory also ignited production on the grant. Acquiring locally produced foodstuffs for the military proved to be both cost productive and fresher than what could be delivered from St. Louis and points east.[18]

This dynamic continued to evolve in the 1860s. Farmers and ranchers grew the crops and raised the livestock. Town merchants funneled Hispano agricultural products and butchered meat to the army for cash. With funds accumulated from these sales, merchants purchased steel ranges and iron bed-frames to use in barter with farmers to acquire more of their produce. Each season, this cycle played out, with the *nuevo-mexicano* accumulating household goods and farm implements, yet little cash, for their efforts.[19]

Although technologically advanced house-wares and agricultural tools affected life on the grant, Hispano cultural values did not change. A decade earlier, manufactured metal items were non-existent, yet in the 1860s steel kitchen ranges and iron plows were available. Although Hispana women controlled what came into the house, whether the family was considering acquiring plows or kitchen utensils, all goods were viewed from the perspective of what item best benefited the family. On the whole, villagers did not equate their value as people by what they owned. In most of Las Vegas and the surrounding communities, individual ownership remained a foreign concept. People perceived themselves as a part of a greater whole. Indeed their survival as a community sometimes required the subjugation of personal wants. These concepts of ownership and ideas about land differed from most Americans. In the United States, documents and receipts were considered cornerstones to a free economy. Proof of ownership, as declared by the printed word, was everything. This was not so among the descendants of the original *pobladores*.[20]

Hispano Farmers on the Las Vegas grant. From the Collection of the Las Vegas Citizens' Committee for Historic Preservation.

Proof of ownership was obvious to the *nuevo-mexicano*. Wheat growing in the valley was proof. Sheep dotting the hillside was proof, as was smoke curling up from the chimney of a flat-roofed adobe home. A father could point to children chasing chickens and grandmothers weaving blankets and ask, what further proof was needed? Farmers believed a good crop of oats growing along the river was more credible than an odd scrap of paper. The grant, as Hispanos knew it, was something God had given them. Its boundaries were cold-water streams and snow-capped mountains. Ownership was both spirit-filled and tactile.

Two years after Fort Union was built, Texan William Pelham, the first surveyor general of the territory, arrived in New Mexico. His task was to assess Mexican and Spanish land grant claims and make a recommendation to Congress as to whether they were valid. Mr. Pelham was faced with a daunting, if not impossible task. Like most American officials, he did not read, write, or speak Spanish. Still, he was charged with investigating the particulars of each case. He had to interview the claimants, visit the sites, and determine if submitted claims were valid and whether their boundaries were correct. Many Hispanos had lived on property handed down to them for generations. Few had what would be considered proper documents. Some *nuevo-mexicanos* petitioned Pelham for land they claimed Mexican or Spanish officials had tricked them out of. They wanted it back. William Pelham and subsequent surveyor generals were sent to New Mexico with little power or money to adequately assess the situation. All annexed lands, not just titled property, were their responsibility to sort out. Surveying included charting landscapes a mountain goat would have trouble traversing. In 1854, the call for landowners to bring their titles and arguments before Pelham was distributed across the territory.[21]

In 1855, two separate parties petitioned Pelham for title to the Las Vegas Land Grant. One of the petitions was put forth by the heirs of the 1835 grant. This was the enterprise that established the successful settlement of Las Vegas. Another petition came from John S. Watts, an attorney representing the original 1821 Luis Maria de Baca heirs. After reviewing each, Pelham was convinced that both were valid. In his report to Congress, he noted that the de Baca clan had protested to Mexican authorities when a community grant was approved for the same location in 1835. In his mind, this corroborated their argument that they had never renounced their claim. He explained to authorities in Washington that his job had been to ascertain if land grant claims put before him were valid. He believed both petitions were, regardless of what that meant to his superiors or the courts. He argued that it was not his place, nor was it within his job description, to decide ownership. He was sent to New Mexico to establish legitimate title. It was not his problem that there were two legitimate claims to the Las Vegas Land Grant. Instead of letting a judge rule on the issue, Congress instead chose to award the de Baca heirs territory equal to the Las Vegas property, eliminating a court fight. Four separate parcels of land, totaling almost five-hundred-thousand acres, were given to the de Bacas as compensation. Some of these awards later became a part of Arizona and Colorado. The second group of petitioners, heirs of the 1835 community grant, were awarded the "the town of Las Vegas" grant in June 1860. Issues regarding what this term actually meant would fester and blister into the next century.[22]

From an Anglo-American perspective, the next decade was one of steady growth. Traffic and trade along the Santa Fe Trail and the federal government's need to supply the military with competitively priced, local food sources fueled this growth. Although Las Vegas was gradually maturing into an established territorial town with a more American appearance, many newcomers still yearned for the benefits that might accrue once a railroad made its way to the Plaza.[23]

Not that everyone on the grant pined for the locomotive. Some were happy with the status quo and looked askance at those who dreamed of train depots and cattle cars. Many locals had no idea what a locomotive was, nor had ever contemplated seeing one. These Las Vegans, rural farmers and ranchers and a few of the merchants with whom they did business, were comfortable with a barter system which complemented the old world subsistence economy so many on the grant were used to. Hispanos had few choices within this system, but it closely replicated the manner of trade they had been practicing all their lives.

Life on the Las Vegas grant was free of technological excess, dependent on nature, the weather, hard work, and communal cooperation. The Industrial Age and its money-making apparatuses were foreign concepts to the Hispano farmer. Although men in the East had been working toward bringing the coal-powered engine and its powerful hauling capabilities west, San Miguel County gained a reprieve from such ingenuity in 1860. Abraham Lincoln was elected president and the Civil War began.

Distance did not equate to irrelevance during the war. *Nuevo-mexicanos* played a significant role in foiling Brigadier General Henry H. Sibley's advance into New Mexico and Territorial Colorado. Sibley's ultimate goal was to march to the West Coast and claim California. There was also a secondary consideration to the Confederate thrust north, one that contemplated bankrolling future campaigns with an infusion of Colorado gold. The march toward the territorial minefields began in Texas, and would not be stopped until passing through Socorro, Albuquerque, and the capture of Santa Fe. After winning a hollow victory at the Rio Grande crossing of Valverde, Confederate forces, made up mainly of Texans, took Albuquerque and the capital without a fight. At that point, Sibley was intent on moving his forces past Las Vegas and then marching north another forty miles to Fort Union, the federal army's main western command post. Here, the Confederate leader hoped to find caches of food and arms. In a previous life as a Union officer, Sibley spent time as the commander of this frontier outpost. After capturing his old base, he planned to strike out for the Denver gold mines. Northern officers knew that holding Fort Union was crucial to stopping Sibley's advance, yet they did not have enough troops in the area to do so. The Colorado First Regiment of Volunteers, under the command of Colonel John Chivington, moved south, covering over forty miles per day, intent on reaching Fort Union before General Sibley and his Confederate army.[24]

Ceran St. Vrain, the ex-trader, one-time partner and avenger of Charles Bent, as well as being a veteran of the Indian Wars, was again called to duty. He was instrumental in creating volunteer regiments of *nuevo-mexicanos* from the region to serve with Union forces in the conflict. After having done so, at the age of fifty-nine, he deemed himself too old to lead the troops into battle. The Mora grain merchant deferred his command to General Christopher "Kit" Carson, who decades earlier employed St. Vrain as a hunter on John Charles Frémont's first trek west.[25]

Captain John M. Chivington pushed his Colorado troops hard to reach Fort Union ahead of Sibley's rebels. Shortly after arriving, Chivington continued west, attempting to steal a march on the Confederates he knew to be heading in his direction. The two forces met in the same mountain pass where General Armijo once assembled an army of civilians to block Colonel Kearney's Army of the West. In the Battle of Glorieta Pass, Union and Confederate soldiers brought the bloody realities of the Civil War to the mountains and pine-forests of New Mexico. Although the battle did not prove disastrous to either, when Union troops swung into the Confederates' rear and attacked their baggage trains, destroying their supplies, the Southern assault of New Mexico came to an end. In a hostile environment without provisions, the Confederates were forced to retreat to Texas. Northern New Mexico remained within Union control throughout the rest of the war and the gold fields of Colorado were kept out of rebel hands.[26]

Much has been written of Union officers criticizing *nuevo-mexicano* actions in this campaign. Although there is an occasional aside that relates to isolated incidents where New Mexican Volunteers stood fast and fought bravely, the most publicized histories characterize the majority of these volunteers as undependable. Some were noted in various battles to have deserted in the face of enemy fire. Yet if Hispanos were so undependable, how did so many get killed or wounded during these campaigns? Although Company B of the 5th New Mexico Volunteers suffered a 53 percent casualty rate defending Captain Alexander McRae's battery at the Battle of Valverde, this fact seldom came out in the weeks that followed the battle. Instead, Union officers used the *nuevo-mexicano* soldiers as scapegoats to excuse their own failings during this fight in New Mexico. Most Hispano soldiers were local farmers who joined up because they knew the majority of the invaders came from Texas. The promise of payment for service rendered also induced many to join, yet in the heady days before the Colorado Volunteers arrived, Hispanos were the eyes and ears of the existing Union forces, both to the south, at the battle of Valverde, and in the north, watching the approaches to Las Vegas. Hispano soldiers were required to do much of the backbreaking work involved in preparing for the anticipated assault on Fort Union, reworking its walls and digging trenches. Since the first battle of the first war ever recorded, men have lost their nerve and fled. White northerners ran at Manassas, deserted at Fredericksburg, and dropped their weapons and ran at Antietam, just as southerners did at Shiloh and other battles too numerous to mention. The fear of death is not racist, yet perhaps some of those who survived the Battle of Valverde were selectively prejudice in their recollections of who was brave and who was not.[27]

When war broke out in New Mexico, Hispano farmers and ranchers answered the call. Between 1861 and February of 1862, the Fourth Regiment, including Captain Juan José Herrera, made up of six companies, mostly locals living on the Las Vegas and Mora grants, joined up at Fort Union. They enlisted for three years of service. Additionally, independent of St. Vrain's volunteers, Jose I. Martinez raised more men, creating the Mora County Militia. An additional forty-three Hispanos traveled fifty-seven miles to join the fight, arriving at Fort Union on 25 September 1861. After the war, many surviving *nuevo-mexicano* veterans came back to their villages on these grants, returning to their families, their fields and their *moradas*. Captain Herrera was one of these men. Yet he did not stay long. He left, it was rumored, under a cloud. Captain Herrera would not return until the late 1880s.[28]

The Civil War stymied the Industrial Revolution's advance into New Mexico, yet once the conflict ended, the federal government, not enterprising businessmen, jump started its westward advancement. The move toward New Mexico was led by capitalists, not captains. Land was the key. Government enticements encouraged entrepreneurs to invest in the territory. Both before and after the war, Congress used its ability to distribute public lands as incentive to promote the country's various interests. Prior to the conflict, land was used to entice young men to join the army. Afterward, it was used to reward veterans. The Homestead Act of 1862 encouraged migration westward by granting 160 acres to any man willing to settle and cultivate unimproved acreage in outlying areas. In retrospect, this act was perhaps too successful, as many families ventured into unchartered territory and claimed the best property as their own before it could be properly plotted out. The Homestead Act was later altered to accommodate intrepid squatters who settled choice land before it was surveyed. Few veterans became pioneers, yet were able to make a quick profit by selling the land awarded to them by the government for service to their country. Speculators were more than willing to pay cash for this, "land script." Land agents who bought these parcels would then turn around and sell them in bulk to corporations looking to graze livestock herds on western grassland prairies. America, Richard White wrote, was "a capital-short and land rich-country." Land was also given away in various forms to help propel the locomotive across the continent. One way the federal government did this was by encouraging vast, Armijo-like grants across the paths the railroads were sure to follow.[29]

A settled community was already in place in Las Vegas long before the rail-lines came through, making it unique. Towns such as Leadville, Colorado and Otero, New Mexico were established only as a result of the creation of the railroad. Generally, the few women found in boomtowns were prostitutes. Normally, churches followed saloons, as did the local government needed to function within any civil society. That was not the case in Las Vegas. When the Atchison, Topeka, and Santa Fe Railroad arrived in the summer of 1879, a town council was already in place. Several non-alcohol related mercantile establishments were long-established in the old Mexican town. A strong Roman Catholic presence dominated civilian life, although Protestants were also making their presence known. John Annin had founded the Presbyterian Church a decade earlier. Methodist preacher Thomas Harwood gave his first sermon inside the Hamilton House Inn five months before the first train rolled into the depot at the corner of Railroad Avenue and Jackson Street. No doubt most of the ministers in Las Vegas knew what was coming, and preached accordingly.[30]

The Onset of Civilization

By United States standards, Las Vegas was considered a sleepy trading post waiting for the arrival of the future. Some elite Hispanos begged to differ. As mentioned above, a few miles to the north of the Plaza, Don José Albino de Baca had established a second community among the remnants of his ancestor's first settlement. He built an opulent three-story home there in the mid 1850s, yet even so, the heart of the town remained centered around the Plaza. In 1852, the multi-story Exchange Hotel, a fine example of territorial style architecture opened, along with its barroom, Buffalo Hall. Across from National Street, freight wagons fresh from Missouri off-loaded goods on the mud trampled road that rounded the circular yard. It might not have been New York City, but it was more than a stage stop.[31]

Adobe homes surrounded most of the Plaza beyond the Gallinas River. Dirt roads leading out of town wound around ditches and hills. Topography guided how these original village paths were formed. Consideration was always given to ease of travel with little regard for the shortest trail between two points. Just to the west, what became South Pacific Avenue led to Santa Fe. Homes and businesses lined this path, their inner courtyards facing away from the clouds of dust that hung in the air after freight wagons passed.[32]

The Las Vegas Plaza, looking west. The Exchange Hotel is on the left in front of the building with the scaffolding. The Plaza Hotel is the three-story brick building on the right. Charles Ilfeld's first store is the center, single-story, white building to the right of the Plaza Hotel. The far right, single-story building is the one Colonel Stephen Watts Kearney stood on top of on 15 August 1846 to address the citizens of Las Vegas. From the Collection of the Las Vegas Citizens' Committee for Historic Preservation.

In 1857, the charter for the Atchison, Topeka, and Santa Fe Railroad was created by the Kansas Legislature. Cyrus K. Holliday gained control of the enterprise in 1859. In 1864, Congress gave the go-ahead to begin construction. The legislature agreed to award twenty sections of land for each mile of track laid. In March of 1879, as the company's contractors angled their way into the mountains of New Mexico's northern border, a local Las Vegas newspaper warned its citizens that it was time to put their paperwork in order. Once the railroad came, rising land values would put their titles in jeopardy.[33]

South Pacific, leading out of town. From the Collection of the Las Vegas Citizens' Committee for Historic Preservation.

Town leaders were soon schooled in the realities of the outside world when they met with railroad representatives to discuss the location of the station. Businessman José Albino de Baca and other city leaders were surprised when the A. T. & S. F. Railroad representatives declared the tracks and depot would be located one mile east of the Plaza. In anticipation of the train's arrival, de Baca had recently built a new hotel just off the square. It would now be positioned far from the depot. To even consider coming as close to the old Plaza as they planned, the railroad people demanded right of way through the Las Vegas Land Grant in writing, as well as a $10,000 bonus. The document, which they required Las Vegas town leaders to sign, noted: "The said Committee shall be and is hereby authorized to donate and concede to the constructors of the Railways, such unoccupied lands of the aforementioned Grant as shall be necessary for the tract; provided that the Railroad should pass through lower town Las Vegas or in its proximity and that the depot shall be erected in close vicinity of the town." The "constructors" also demanded twenty acres for the depot and rail yards. The "town" referred to in the document was not old Las Vegas. Instead, the Atchison, Topeka, and Santa Fe Railroad demanded an additional 400 acres for a completely new "town."[34]

Communities such as Las Vegas had little choice in the matter. At the time, the *Las Vegas Gazette* argued all the demands should be agreed to, with the exception of an additional town-site. The paper claimed such a gift would kill Las Vegas. The sentiments of most citizens proved to be irrelevant. All the railroad men's demands were met. Plans began on a "new town," located one mile east of the Square. Designs were largely put together by Anglo-Americans recently drawn west in anticipation of the locomotive's arrival. The site was christened East Las Vegas. A new era was about to begin on the Las Vegas Land Grant.[35]

Almost immediately, buildings began to go up where the train station would be located. Some of these structures were temporary, created for short-run profits. In El Moro, Colorado and Otero, New Mexico, transient railroad enterprises packed and followed the tracks south. Proprietors unfastened the nails and bolts that held pre-fabricated buildings together, took the walls and roofs apart, stacked the various sections on wagons and followed the railroad workers toward San Miguel County. The first approaching dust-trails of these vagabond communities foretold that Las Vegas would never be the same.[36]

Territorial chief justice and future governor L. Bradford Smith wrote that the coming of the locomotive was the courier of "American civilization being brought forth to this former Spanish colony." *Nuevo-mexicanos* soon found out that the American promise of "civilization" included some queer notions about advanced society. When describing establishments similar to El Moro, John Hoyt Williams wrote that businesses thrown up along the path of the Union Pacific Railway were meant to provide vice-filled diversions to railroad workers after a hard day's work. Williams described these businesses as nothing less than, "mobile Gomorrahs." The temporary buildings were erected near the designated depot area well in advance of the railroad workers' arrival. Such establishments were prepared to provide whiskey, a place to gamble, and other activities known for their "general mayhem and depravity." As stated above, these raucous shanty towns normally came out of the ground along an isolated rail junction in the middle of nowhere. Such creations became the playgrounds for youthful indiscretions. Installing tracks required strong backs, not strong principles. Young men with money filled the saloons and dance halls that cropped up along Railroad Avenue.[37]

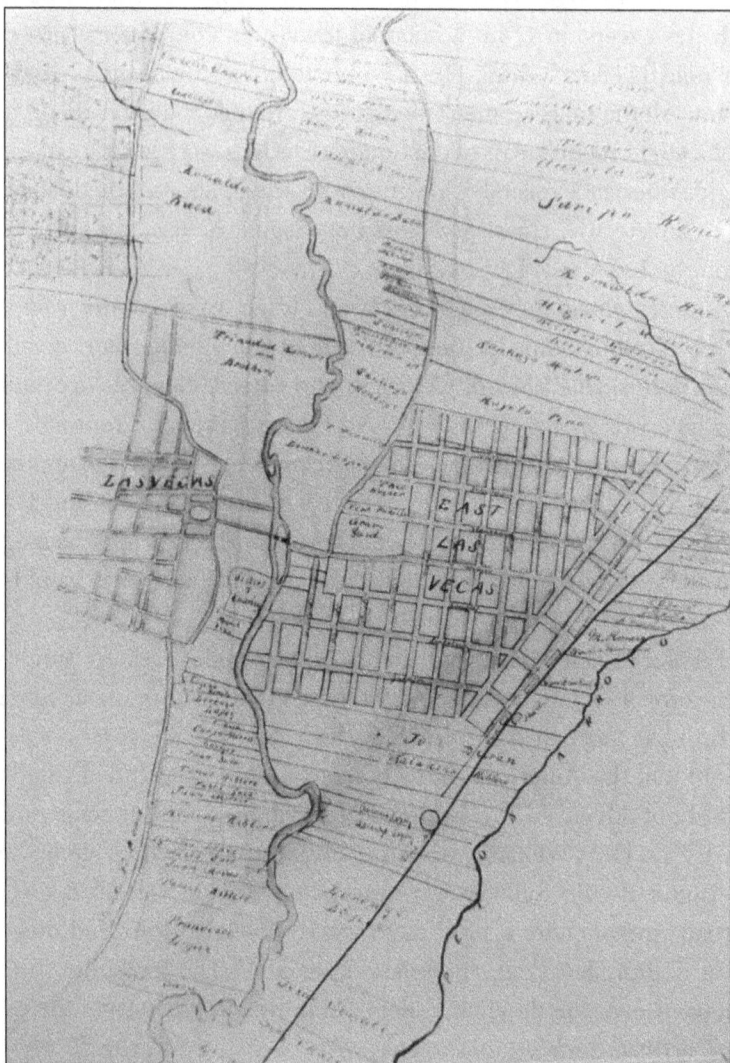

Surveyor general's layout of Las Vegas Land Grant plots in and around Las Vegas. From the Collection of the Las Vegas Citizens' Committee for Historic Preservation.

In Las Vegas, far from the watchful eyes of parents and peers, "mayhem and depravity" indeed arrived with the locomotive. For fifty cents, a man could get two dances and a drink in East Las Vegas. The notorious "hell on wheels" ramshackle businesses were usually the first sequence in the evolution of establishing an orderly frontier community, yet the bells of the Presbyterian Mission on Chavez Street in Las Vegas could already be heard from Close and Patterson's dance hall, one of a string of saloons and gambling dens that took root near the depot. For locals who ventured out of the *Nuestra Senora de los Dolores*, the Catholic church west of the Plaza and traveled east over Bridge Street and the mile to the depot, they would see the tents, temporary buildings, and eastern laborers who congregated in and about these businesses at all hours of the day and night. Proprietors entreated one and all to venture in; Chinamen, Irishmen, Germans, and Black Americans. In 1881, one visitor counted at least twenty-four saloons. These were the first impressions many *nuevo-mexicanos* gained of Prince's new "civilization."[38]

According Miguel Otero Jr.(who would later become territorial governor), money was fluid in Las Vegas after the creation of the New Town, as some called it. Railroad traffic proved his point, garnering at least two and one-half million dollars in freight receipts between 1886 and 1891. Passenger trains raised another one-half million in cash. From the beginning, railroad workers from Raton and Lamy lived and played in Las Vegas. Hard-earned wages boosted the local economy. Indeed cash was available, if you knew how to acquire it.[39]

The Revolutionary Instrument

In the summer of 1879, as the train's first stop into town grew near, the clatter of hammers and saws swelled around the depot. Miguel Otero Jr. recalled: "Everywhere buildings were going up, while tents and hastily built shacks of all kinds were being used as restaurants, saloons, and living quarters." East Las Vegas rose out of the dirt alongside the temporary buildings. Fresh concrete cured while mortar was mixed in wheelbarrows among stacks of freshly-fired bricks. A variety of curses and shouts in numerous languages echoed between construction sites. With the exception of a few territorial homes being built along new dirt roads, all that could be seen between the depot and the Plaza were rows of corn, wheat, sheep, cows, and *nuevo-mexicano* adobe homes. Chickens scratched and pigs oinked within a rock's throw of the new saloons and hotels.[40]

On 4 July 1879 at 11 a.m., a crowd gathered to celebrate the train's arrival. They were disappointed. Due to mechanical problems, only a few cars were able to roll in, less the locomotive. Two days passed before the steam powered engine was able to puff into the depot. Wanting to be the first to ride into Las Vegas, Miguel Otero Jr. and other dignitaries traveled up to Trinidad, Colorado and got on the train there. When it finally arrived in Las Vegas, the locomotive was decorated with bunting, evergreens, and ribbons. A great crowd came to celebrate its belated arrival. Many were East Las Vegas businessmen. For years they had anticipated the opportunities this event would create for them. Others, mostly the rural Hispanos, not at the forefront of the activities, stood back in guarded awe, wondering what would happen next. That night, parties for territorial dignitaries and railroad representatives were held at Close and Patterson's near the station and the Exchange Hotel, celebrating the arrival of Las Vegas' future.[41]

Donald Meinig argues that modern capitalism was the "persistent basis" of the West's "identity" in the latter part of the nineteenth century. He contends that the railroad was the "revolutionary instrument" that stoked the flames of that identity. Las Vegas in the 1880s was a good of example of what he was talking about. Within two years of the Atchison, Topeka, and Santa Fe's arrival, gas lines were installed to light the town's streets and businesses, a new water-works system was created, and telephones became operational. East of the Mississippi, the Industrial Revolution had advanced incrementally, allowing Americans the time to adjust to each technological advancement gradually. On the Las Vegas grant, the wooden match was still a novelty in 1879. The town's citizens were faced with trying to assimilate several decades of accumulated advancements almost overnight. Few had puzzled out the mystery of the electric telegraph when telephone poles began to be installed. Gas-fueled flames from cutting-edge street lamps illuminated the Plaza every night. Horses and mules pulled sparkling new trolleys between East Las Vegas and the Square, ferrying Anglo-American strangers in wool suits to business meetings and bars. In 1881, six churches held services in Las Vegas. Machine shops, lumber mills, and a wheel house for the train station offered employment opportunities to newcomers. By then, one-thousand homes dotted the growing community.[42]

Las Vegas' location was the key to the boom. Since the first settlers had measured off the Plaza's footprint, locals had taken advantage of the town's placement. Spaniards, *genizaros*, and Anglo-Americans all utilized the pre-existing footpaths and horse trails that wound around the southern tip of the Rocky Mountains, as had the Kiowas, Utes, Puebloans, Navajo, and Apaches that came before them. Until other railroad tracks in Albuquerque and Texas drew trade away from the region, Las Vegas was the central shipping hub for an area which stretched for hundreds of miles in all directions. Cattle, hides, wool, and grains were shipped east along the Atchison, Topeka, and Santa Fe, accentuating what the people of the Pecos Pueblo knew for centuries. The mountains running north made it impractical to carry a reasonable load of trade goods over steep inclines. The Sangre de Cristo Range, a purple wall of jagged, snow capped peaks, funneled traders around its spine along one tried and true path; the same path Missouri freighters and railroad engineers followed all the way to Santa Fe. After 1879, two towns thrived on the grant. Both claimed to be the real Las Vegas.[43]

The past and future were in some ways foretold by the layout of Las Vegas' streets. A current map of the town reads like the index of its own history book. West and south of the Plaza, the streets hold names like Delgado, Valencia, and Santa Fe. By the late 1870s, the grid-like road pattern familiar to Americans in Topeka and Boston was replicated east of the Gallinas River. Closer to the train station, straight lines were the consideration, not topography. As the 70s ended, territorial-style homes rose where farmlands used to fall toward the eastern prairies. Street signs identified the straight-lined lanes with names such as Washington, Garfield, Lincoln, and Jackson. In 1879, after 60 days of construction, an ornate steel bridge rose over the river, connecting old Las Vegas with National Street. National originated at the depot, crossed Railroad Avenue, then ran through new neighborhoods and farmers' fields until it reached the bridge connecting the new world to the old.[44]

The arrival of the locomotive changed many eastern capitalists' notions about Las Vegas. Commerce accelerated. The technological revolution that was occurring in the United States at that time was similar to that instigated by the Internet a century later. For decades, the town had profited from its location along the Santa Fe Trail, yet with the arrival of the railroad, the Industrial Revolution landed in the heart of the grant.

As a result of the locomotive's arrival, the physical face of Las Vegas changed as much as its infrastructure. Architecture reflected the variety of cultures that met on the edge of the Sangre de Cristo Range. Two-story Greek Revivalist structures complemented with both stone and adobe, brick facades with cast-iron columns, stepped parapets, elongated territorial style porches, and arched windows sporting decorative cornices modeled after Italian commercial buildings sprang up. Wave after wave of changes refaced the Old Town while the New Town grew along the tracks. Facing the depot, three-story buildings rose out of the ground as fast as the bricks could be stacked.

With the arrival of the railroad, new inventions seemed to be unloaded on the docks every day. The telegraph's technology was outdated shortly after its first messages were transmitted east. Miguel Antonio Otero, Sr. already owned a bank on the Square and a vast wholesale operation before starting the Las Vegas Telephone Company in 1880. Horse-powered trolley cars soon moved up and down its dirt streets, ferrying businessmen and tourists along National to the Plaza. Six miles to the northwest, the Hot Springs Hotel was built. Established next to a bubbling hot springs in the shadow of the mountains, the resort was located on a site once sacred to the Pueblo Indians that used to travel there. As many locals soon found out, what used to be, was irrelevant, to what would be.[45]

With the financial backing of eastern business partners, F. C. Martsolf made a fortune building hotels along many different railroads' tracks. He moved to Las Vegas to search out a suitable area to build another lavish resort. He knew the hot springs was a perfect location. Within a year of completion, representatives of the Atchison, Topeka, and Santa Fe purchased the sandstone fortress-like structure and renamed it the Montezuma Hotel. It was three stories tall, included 207 rooms, a world-class restaurant, and exclusive bath houses for its guests. The railroad company built a narrow gauge track from the depot to the Montezuma's front door.[46]

Employees of the Santa Fe Railroad became Industrial Age folk heroes in Las Vegas. Just as Steven Jobs and Bill Gates became idolized leaders for their innovations and grasp of new technologies, locomotive engineers and conductors were put on pedestals of esteem out west. Some were able to convert their lofty status into business opportunities. When the first steam-powered locomotive came into the train station, Charlie Brooks was the conductor. Soon after he arrived, Brooks quit his job and opened a saloon with Fred Locke. Unfortunately, after a short illness, Brooks died. Previous to the construction of the Montezuma Hotel, one-time freight conductor W. Scott Moore operated the "Old Adobe House," in the same location. Charles W. Wiley worked for the Atchison, Topeka, and Santa Fe as a grading contractor. He became the first mayor of an incorporated East Las Vegas. In 1881, Wiley built a grand, two-story Victorian mansion in the popular Italianate style north of the Carnegie Library. Both the library and the house still stand.[47]

It was the much larger class of general laborers who made it possible for Wiley and Brooks to garner so much attention. Conductors and engineers were celebrated because they knew what few men did, how the steam engine worked. Yet it was general laborers seeking escape from the stifling conditions found in East Coast slums and sweat shops that propelled the locomotive west. Hundreds of transient young men of all ethnicities pounded down the railroad ties, linked the iron tracks across the mountains, and shuffled the wood and coal into the smoke-belching belly of the blazing engines. While many of these workers followed the trains into Arizona and California, some stayed and opened laundries, hired out as farm labor, and worked in the hotels and restaurants of Las Vegas. Chinese, Filipinos, and Mexicans filled most of these positions. Free Blacks also worked on the railroad. Some stayed in Las Vegas, finding work in the same occupations as other men of color. By the end of the 80s, there was a Black Methodist church in town. Although Anglos did not accept Blacks on equal terms, they were not socially segregated. More the exception than the rule, it is still significant that Montgomery Bell, an ex-slave from Missouri, became a successful entrepreneur in Las Vegas. He operated a general store and made money investing in real estate and livestock on the grant.[48]

Generally, the labor system in place was structured to make such advancement a rare occurrence. Work practices were set up on a two-tiered platform. Anglo Americans usually filled the foremen and skilled labor positions. Skilled carpenters, freight wagon teamsters, brick layers, iron-work craftsman, printers, and store managers were typically Anglos. They could make up to $3.50 per day. The men who got down in the mud, dug the ditches for the sewer lines, hauled the timber to construction sites, and tended the beasts of burden that hauled wagons and trolleys through town were minorities and transient, poorly-educated whites. Their average rate for a day's work was approximately $1.50. A workday usually meant at least twelve hours of labor.[49]

It was these young men whom the traveling hell towns preyed upon, although visiting eastern capitalists were also lured to such places. Writing about the rootlessness inherent in forward frontier enterprises, future Surveyor General Julian Rolf wrote: "Men without restraint of law . . . unburdened by families, drink whenever they feel like it, whenever they have money to pay for it, and whenever there is nothing else to do." By 1880, violent death was so common on the streets of Las Vegas that a local newspaper commented on March 10, "Well, who was killed last night?" The *Las Vegas Optic* pleaded for laws restricting firearms be enforced, but such a requests fell on deaf ears for many years.[50]

Although Anglos were the minority, they perpetrated the majority of violent crimes that were reported in the newspapers. For a short time, during the height of the boom, Doc Holliday ran a saloon out of East Las Vegas. He first attempted to establish a dentist office in town, but this venture failed. Wyatt Earp was said to have helped out at Holliday's establishment for a while. Only in town for about a year, the famous dentist/gunslinger was still there long enough to kill Fifth Calvary veteran Mike Gordon in a shootout. Several saloons and dance halls around the depot tended to lure certain kinds of activity and people. One visitor to Las Vegas in 1879 said: "Gray and baldheaded reprobates, who have wives, sons and daughters in the east, can be found nightly in this place, with some demimonde on their knees."[51]

The Las Vegas establishment resented such activities. Middle class merchants such as Charles Ilfeld believed he was just as much a part of Victorian society as any family man back in Philadelphia. In fact, Ilfeld was known to take buying trips to that city as well as New York because he enjoyed the culture and lifestyle that could be enjoyed there. Such men were appalled by what was going on in the twenty-four hour gambling dens and barrooms. Several merchants organized efforts through Protestant churches to reform those who had come west to get rich but ended up penniless in an alley behind Close and Patterson's or the Harvey House Hotel. Merchants were determined to re-establish the societal norms they had enjoyed before the New Town became a reality. There were similar reactions within the *nuevo-mexicano* community. Local Spanish newspapers derided the arrival of so many Anglos and the rampant spread of the saloons that followed in their wake.[52]

Charles Ilfeld was not enamored with the pull of East Las Vegas. He remained on the Plaza for several years. In 1883, he built a large three-story department store there which he called the Great Emporium. William Parish, his biographer, argues that Ilfeld was reluctant to endorse the New Town because he was wary of the railroad people's power and influence. Ilfeld felt that Otero and Sellars, a mercantile establishment that set up next to the depot, was in cahoots with railroad interests, in effect receiving favor and orders from the Atchison, Topeka, and Santa Fe Board. Ilfeld believed Plaza interests were being ignored because of such influence. This put a bad taste in his mouth concerning East Las Vegas businesses and the financial institutions that sprang up to support them. Banker and cattleman Jefferson Raynolds had no such qualms. He moved to Las Vegas to make money. Raynolds offered Ilfeld the director's chair of his bank. At first the merchant accepted, but a week later, had second thoughts and declined the post. Early on, the growing influence of railroad interests and banks in Las Vegas made the old German immigrant uneasy. He did not like being associated with them.[53]

Everyone on the grant was economically affected by the coming of the railroad. Town merchants continued to barter with *nuevo-mexicano* farmers, but not as in previous years. Although prior agreements between merchants and farmers had seldom been equitable, Hispanos were still able to realize some benefits through this trade. Yet their barter-based buying power decreased after 4 July 1879. Wage-based job growth in Las Vegas put more money in the pockets of upper rung, managerial types and skilled craftsmen. When these workers began to trade with cash, mercantilists no longer depended on the old barter system, the only economic transaction method most *nuevo-mexicanos* were capable of. As a result, businesses no longer found it necessary to maintain personal relationships with rural farmers to be successful, which made it much easier to play economic hard-ball on the Las Vegas grant.[54]

As noted above, Jefferson Raynolds was a prominent banker in Las Vegas, coming to town with his brothers, Frederick and Joshua, in 1876. Jefferson, the third son, was twenty-eight years old when he began in the banking business in Pueblo, Colorado in 1871. After working at the Thatcher Brothers' Bank for five years, he moved to Las Vegas. The Raynolds Brothers' Bank operated in Las Vegas for three years, then on 22 September 1879 Jefferson opened the First National Bank of Las Vegas on the Plaza. It was less than a year later that Miguel Otero Sr. opened the San Miguel National Bank on the west side of the Square. Raynolds later moved his bank to East Las Vegas.[55]

Like hotel builder F. C. Martsolf, the Raynolds brothers had also followed the railroad's path west, insinuating themselves into the towns the Santa Fe, Atchison, and Topeka ran through; anticipating the growth that was sure to follow. Ilfeld's uneasiness was due, in part, because banks in the territory were not regulated and could charge whatever interest rate the market would bear. At first, bankers did not gain much business from the local farmers or general laborers, but such individuals had never been Jefferson Raynolds' main focus. What Raynolds anticipated was the arrival of the cattle companies. He had personal aspirations of profiting from such enterprises, and at one time was treasurer of the National Beef Producers' and Butchers' Association. Train hauling capabilities expanded both corporations' and cattlemen's ability to seek prime grazing lands far from eastern markets. Cattle companies required occasional loans to stay afloat, perched as they were on the edge of the prairies. Raynolds' and Otero's Las Vegas banks facilitated the growth of this industry in San Miguel County.[56]

As American financial institutions grew stronger in the West, *nuevomexicanos* ability to barter for manufactured goods weakened. Cash became king. Jefferson Raynolds was a key contributor to Las Vegas economic transformation. His goal was to lure eastern funds into his bank. He used the railroad as a powerful instrument to meet that end. By extending prospective cattlemen credit, he was able to draw the industry into his debt. Many easterners were enticed by the potential New Mexico's natural resources contained, yet they were not interested in trading plows for wool or corn. They wanted the land. They believed once they had it, it could be converted into cash. This was the age of Andrew Carnegie, Jay Gould, and William Vanderbilt. Miguel Otero Jr.'s comment that there was plenty of money in boomtown Las Vegas might have been true, but he was not talking about the general *nuevo-mexicano* population when he said it. It was well-positioned and wealthy Hispanos and Anglo Americans, skilled craftsman and upper management personel, cattle corporations and cattlemen, that he was referring to when he spoke about the triumph of capitalism in San Miguel County. If you knew the right contacts, there was money to be made on the grant.

Yet this was not the case for the majority of people who lived there. Most *nuevo-mexicanos* derived satisfaction and pride from their ability to sustain their way of life just as their grandfathers and grandmothers had. A good crop, a warm fire, plenty of food, a strong family and sense of community; these were the markers that guided their lives. What happened beyond the village had never been of much consequence. Within Anglo-American hearts pumped the blood of nationalism. Growth and expansion meant success. What had been achieved in Vermont, Tennessee, and Missouri were great sources of pride for all Americans. They believed success was self-replicating as long as one worked hard and kept faith with a Protestant God.

Most *nuevo-mexicanos* were locked out of the celebration. Their inability to acquire dollars, as well as their cultural recalcitrance, made it hard for them to embrace the region's changes, and eventually led to a loss of control over much of the Las Vegas Land Grant. In the next chapter, I will investigate culture clash, both religious and economic, the effect of Anglo-American exceptionalism, and the incremental frustrations rural Las Vegans experienced once land became a valued commodity. To place what happened on the grant within its historical context, it is appropriate to review neighboring land grant issues of the same period. Many of the same land usurpation practices that played out on the Las Trampas grant to the west and the Maxwell Land Grant to the north were also used in San Miguel County. Anglo-American speculators and their Hispano counterparts took similar approaches in their attempts to accrue land throughout New Mexico. People on the Las Vegas grant did not live in a vacuum. They were certainly aware of the precarious position they found themselves in. Although three decades had passed since the Taos Revolt, resentment never left the mountains. Nor had defiance. Or faith. Juan José Herrera would soon return from the north and remind everyone how embedded such traits were in the mountain people who lived on the Las Vegas Land Grant.

A Tangled Web

God in the Mountains

The railroad brought more than Anglo-American ideas of growth and capitalism to Las Vegas. In lock-step with the arrival of the Industrial Revolution came an influx of Protestant missionaries intent on eradicating what they deemed the backward notions of the Catholic Church. Back east, Protestant denominations raised tens of millions of dollars for the "proper" conversion of Hispanos and Indians. In the early 1880s, Presbyterians opened eighteen schools in New Mexico. Some Hispanos eventually converted. Of those who did, many became ministers or teachers in missionary schools. When Alice Alta Blake arrived in the village of Rociada to establish a Presbyterian school, she was surprised that many locals were resentful of her attempts. Priests were especially defiant regarding the intrusion of idealistic newcomers. Conversely, many missionaries were dumbfounded that Hispanos did not thirst for Protestant salvation.[1]

Alice Blake and Harriet Shaw personified the contradictions inherent in most Anglo-American Christians who came west to convert the masses. Blake was a teacher in Las Vegas but decided to found a mission school in Rociada. Knowing just a few words of Spanish, she was determined to convert a "priest-ridden people" of a religion, she believed, that was lost to the dark ages. While on the one hand, her journal entries characterized *nuevo-mexicanos* as "dirty and ignorant . . . " she was just as certain they "were not a primitive race." She was confident the Protestant religion would eventually take root, and was convinced her meshing of education and Christianity would have a good effect on the surrounding communities. Although some of Blake's ideas concerning Catholicism and the people that practiced it do not stand the test of time, her earnest attempt to do good eventually overshadowed her early misconceptions. She later developed a loyal following in Trementina, about twenty miles east of Las Vegas along the Canadian Escarpment. Hispano parents were known to accompany or send their children up to fifty miles to acquire her instruction and guidance. Alice Alta Blake came to be loved by many in the region. Missionary Harriet Shaw initiated a school for girls in Albuquerque. She found the locals to be just as faithful to their God as she was to her own. The only way to ensure student enrollment at her school was to promise Hispano parents the Protestant faith would not be a taught there. Over time missionaries realized they would have to adjust their zeal to gain entry into the Hispano world of New Mexico.[2]

While incoming Protestants may have been naïve about *nuevo-mexicano* faith, they remained confident about what it took to save young Anglo men lured into the saloons and gambling dens of Las Vegas. Local merchants, regardless of their church affiliation, supported all denominations' efforts to stem drunkenness and halt violence. Men such as Charles Ilfeld, Jean Pendaries, and the Romero clan preferred that local wage-earners spend more of their money on store merchandise and less on liquor and prostitutes. Jean Pendaries, no prohibitionist, once operated a billiard hall on the Plaza, yet he also ran a grocer and was part owner of a hotel. Pendaries was on personal terms with French Bishop Lamy and like most practicing Catholics, knew rampant vice was not good for Las Vegas' health. Pendaries and his fellow business associates stood to benefit from recapturing some of the balance that had prevailed in "old" Las Vegas before the arrival of the locomotive.[3]

Most newly-arrived easterners held no concept of the multi-layered array of beliefs that flourished under the umbrella of Catholicism in New Mexico. Anglo-Protestants that came to Las Vegas saw this faith as a single entity, one most believed to be more a medieval cult than a true religion. Missionaries saw their efforts to convert Hispanos as a struggle between good and evil. Few Protestants were aware of the turmoil that already existed within the Catholic Church in New Mexico. Father Antonio José Martinez of Taos had fought many battles against the Mexican theological and civil authorities in Durango before tangling with Charles Bent and other Americans. The famous padre was skeptical of outsiders, regardless of their title. He continued to defy his superiors when French Bishop Lamy became the region's first archbishop. Such recalcitrance ultimately led to Martinez downfall in Taos. In general, there were never enough priests of any ethnicity to cover all of the mountain villages with any kind of regularity. Regardless of who was in charge of the Church, the secret Penitentes continued to worship as they had during Spanish rule. Father Lamy was cognizant of the Church's problems in New Mexico. He hoped to solve some of them by sending an influx of Italian Jesuits into the region. This new Order imparted a great deal of influence in Las Vegas and other territorial towns. Protestant missionaries stumbled into a multifarious brew of faiths which converged under the Roman Catholic umbrella in New Mexico, generally unaware that the religion practiced by the old Spaniard padres was different from that of the Jesuits or rural *nuevo-mexicanos* Penitentes.[4]

One of the most prominent of the new Jesuit priests was Father Donato M. Gasparri. In 1875, he founded the Spanish language newspaper, *Revista Católica*, in Las Vegas. While much of the French clergy reviled Hispano religious customs, the Neapolitan fathers saw something familiar in New Mexican rituals, coming as they had, from a more traditional, Mediterranean culture. The Italians were also aware of the Penitentes and did not feel threatened by their activities. Similar societies were present off the coast of the Mediterranean Sea. Father Gasparri was virulent in his condemnation of Protestant missionaries' attempts to convert the locals to another faith. In 1878, he urged the territorial legislature to approve a bill chartering his Jesuit order into a tax-free corporation. Although Governor S. B. Axtell vetoed the proposal, the legislature over-rode his veto, illustrating the Jesuit's political influence. His newspaper promoted *nuevo-mexicano* Catholic faith and condemned Anglo attempts to disparage their piety. His editorials denounced secular schools which did not use Jesuit textbooks. Others saw a conflict of interest in the lobbying of Congress for tax-free status. His press printed most of the textbooks used in Catholic schools throughout the territory. Under Father Gasparri's direction, the *Revista Católica* urged *nuevo-mexicanos* to hold strong to their faith and stand up for their rights. To do otherwise, Gasparri editorialized, meant loss; loss of their identity as a people, loss of their culture, and loss of their land.[5]

Technological and architectural transformations in the 1880s gave Las

Vegas an exterior facade similar to eastern towns, yet this physical transformation was not a true economic barometer of general conditions that existed only a few miles from the train depot. The majority of the population was not experiencing income growth. A few minutes from Bridge Street, the main road into the Plaza area, the key indicators of successful westward expansion were not apparent to the naked eye. The surrounding mountain valleys and rolling prairies appeared untouched by humanity, unmoved by clocks or some Americans' notion of progress. Nor was the impact of the cash economy on the majority of the region's people easy to discern. Religion and the dollar, two visually elusive dynamics, were the true agents of change on the Las Vegas grant, not buildings. Mission-work, Anglo-American exceptionalism, the growing power of the dollar, and the fear of losing their property, all created a climate of growing concerns and resentments among most of the people living on the Las Vegas grant. To the casual observer, life in the mountains appeared much as it always had. Each spring, Hispanos and Hispanas cleaned their *acequias*, plowed their fields, and tended their animals. They repeated the seasonal rites; whitewashing walls, sowing seeds, and praying to their God. When the snow began to melt, just as their fathers before them, Hispano men led their sheep into the high country to forage on lush mountain meadows. Yet a creeping sense of foreboding shadowed the men and women that lived on the *Las Vegas grandes*. It was no longer their father's country.

Land and Money

The Las Vegas Land Grant originally consisted of 431,653,000 acres. The greatest portion contained the commons, or *ejido*; pastures, farmland, mountain timber, rivers, and mesa-lands. Whoever controlled these resources controlled the grant. As already noted, railroads allowed cattle to graze far from market. New Mexico was flush with millions of acres of prime grasslands, most of which were located along the rivers, within the *ejido*.[6]

It was over these lands that the battle for the grant was fought. The majority of newcomers were willing to use any means available to acquire title to the common land. Cattle companies intent on grazing large herds needed a ready, free-flowing supply of water. Construction contractors required timber for railroad ties. Both stepped up the pressure on federal authorities to force local landowners to acquiesce to their demands for a share of these resources. Through intermediaries such as lawyers and *ricos*, *nuevo-mexicanos* were led to believe that the procedure to register their land with the new government was fraught with difficulty and risk. Such men explained to rural farmers and ranchers that they needed legal representation so their interests could be protected. In an effort to do the right thing, many did hire lawyers. Hispanos soon realized bartering livestock for these types of services was unacceptable. Lawyers, mostly strangers who spoke a foreign tongue, handed them papers in a foreign script, and then required cash for services rendered. If cash was not available, and it seldom was, then the only acceptable substitute for payment was land.[7]

The cattle industry boomed in the latter part of the 1870s, in part, because British demand for beef increased fifteen times what it had been in the 60s. In the Southwest, a calf could be purchased for five dollars during the 1880s. When this animal grew into an adult, it fetched between 45 and 60 dollars at market. Capitalists on the East Coast and in Europe did the math. Due to their need for meat, the British alone invested over 45 million dollars in the American cattle industry. With boxcars now available to haul beeves, Easterners and Westerners alike began to establish cattle herds in New Mexico. Typically in the West, grass, the fuel needed to raise a calf into a cow, was free. A cattleman could graze his herd on the public domain for what it cost to watch over them. Even so, in New Mexico, entrepreneurs who did not have access to grant land, none of which fell within the public domain, were unlikely to find free access to water. The land surrounding most rivers and streams had long ago been awarded to *nuevo-mexicanos* and their ancestors. Enterprising Americans looked for ways to rectify this problem.[8]

One such American was Thomas Benton Catron. After serving in the Confederacy as a highly decorated second lieutenant, he came to New Mexico hauling two wagonloads of flour. He sold the flour and the wagons for approximately 10,000 dollars, then began a career as a territorial lawyer. By 1893, he owned over 237,000 acres on eight different grants. Later, Catron was district attorney in Mesilla for two years, was originator of the Republican Party in New Mexico, became attorney general, served as territorial governor, and was one of the state's first senators. Thomas Benton Catron is still vilified in New Mexico as the poster boy of Anglo-American expansionism. He was a talented lawyer and powerful politician. He used both Anglo and Hispano Republican party ties to create business opportunities, using patronage, strong-arm tactics, and money to get what he wanted. Many were entranced by his ability to create networks of power across racial and political lines. This network, a loose confederation of lawyers, businessmen, and politicians, was collectively known as the Santa Fe Ring. Although many of their plots were hatched in Santa Fe, their influence impacted all of New Mexico. Cohorts of Catron worked to gain control of the government by dominating the territorial political system. Once in office, they established centers of official control that allowed them to acquire vast amounts of land and its derivative, money.[9]

An example of Catron's ability to acquire property through the Ring's manipulative abilities was his use of Surveyor General Henry M. Atkinson to gain preferential treatment in the pursuit of land on the public domain. According to U.S. law, a land claim could not be filed by a settler on the public domain until after it was surveyed. Surveyor Atkinson would wait to plot out certain sections until after Catron's men found a property which contained a viable water source. After being notified of the location, Atkinson would plot out the ground and file a freshly minted survey at the closest courthouse. Someone who worked for Catron would then immediately file a homestead claim before anyone else knew of its existence. Afterward, the men Catron had hired to purchase the lots would sell them back to him. In this way, after accumulating the parcels that touched the only streams in the area, he gained control of the surrounding property as well, denying access to others unless a profitable compromise could be reached.[10]

In an ironic twist, lawyers such as Thomas B. Catron and one-time partner Stephen B. Elkins accumulated large swaths of grant land in New Mexico by representing *nuevo-mexicanos* in land disputes. Elkins acquired the deed to his portion of the Town of Mora grant by defending a citizen in a criminal case. Elkins eventually owned sixteen of the original seventy-six shares of the Mora Grant by accepting acreage in lieu of cash for his services. Although his attempt to gain control of the entire grant failed, the fact that Elkins acquired so much illustrates how vulnerable people were who faced a foreign legal system. Still, an even more ingenuous method of wresting away grant lands was devised by other creative legal minds. It was called the partition.[11]

The partition was a device the United States legislature created to give Anglo-Americans more opportunities to legally acquire communal property. According to both Spanish and Mexican law, common land was available to everyone who lived on the grant, yet no one specifically possessed it as they did their home and garden plots. The idea that the greatest portion of each grant was shared equally was repugnant to most Americans. Easterners associated Mexican land laws with legalities that conformed more to old-style European societies that had failed. From the American perspective, only barons, feudal lords, and contemporary Hispano *patrónes* profited from such allocations.[12]

Yet at the conclusion of the Mexican - American War, Mexican authorities were promised that such property rights would be respected. When Mexican officials signed the Treaty of Guadalupe Hidalgo, they believed their concepts of land ownership, which included the viability of the *ejido*, was protected. Based on both Spanish and Mexican law, *nuevo-mexicanos* did not believe an individual could purchase exclusive rights to land everyone owned. Such Spanish/Mexican usufruct rights were re-evaluated by the U.S. Courts. Anglo-Americans argued that common sense dictated if someone purchased a Hispano home plot that turned out to be 4 percent of the total home plots located on the grant, the buyer was also due a corresponding 4 percent allotment of the commons. As an example, excluding the plots for a home and garden, 4 per cent of 450,000 acres would mean the purchaser was due an additional 18,000 acres. How the U.S courts came to interpret ownership of common lands proved devastating to the people of New Mexico.[13]

In many court proceedings, U.S. judges concurred that a personal plot on a land grant included a corresponding percentage of the *ejido*. To initiate a partition suit, which was based on the above interpretation of grant ownership, only one of five-hundred landowners was needed to file a claim to individualize the commons. Such a suit usually began when a person on the grant wanted to sell his or her plot to someone else. He or she then filed their suit in court. The next step involved a judge selecting a panel to determine the feasibility of carving out the single, designated allotment.

This meant all the valleys, ravines, canyons, and mountains on the grant had to be professionally surveyed, with the ratio of personal acreage to common lands gridded out. If such work was impractical, the grant's entire commons could then be sold out from under those living there. If dividing up the commons seemed unfeasible, the panel then considered if such an action, selling only one parcel, decreased the value of the whole. If it was determined the entirety was diminished, all of the *ejido* could then be thrown open to purchase by outsiders. Such an action required that all landowners on the grant be notified. In sleight-of-hand legal maneuvering worthy of a magician, the court required such notification to be by means of the closest local newspaper. It did not matter if the paper was located thirty miles from the interested parties' home, as long as it was the closest. Nor was it much of an issue that the specifics of the case were printed in the King's English. Typically, rural *nuevo-mexicanos* did not travel to town nor rarely did they read the English versions of the local gazette. This meant they were not made aware that someone on the grant had filed a partition suit and that the adjoining meadows were about to be sold on the court-house steps in the near future. Only after the transaction occurred did most folks find out they no longer had unrestricted access to the commons. A local Hispanic hired for the occasion went door to door explaining what had happened. Only after the farmer heard the words in Spanish did the full gravity of events settle on him like a dark cloud.[14]

Profit, not land acquisition, was generally the outcome sought by such partitions. Sometimes those involved were rewarded for their efforts. Needing money, Jose Chavez sold his 5/36 share in the Tierra Amarilla grant to Elias Brevoort for $8,500. The next day Brevoort turned around and sold the same parcel for $15,277. About sixty days later, the buyer, William Pinkerton, sold the same property to Thomas B. Catron for $25,000. Land flips could happen in a hurry. Profits were derived as much from heated speculation as any true improvement in land valuation. Lawyers and entrepreneurs gambled land costs would rise even more after New Mexico became a state. Eventually, Brevoort would work for the Land Office in Santa Fe.[15]

An illustration of a partition suit occurred on the Las Trampas grant, located west of Las Vegas on the western side of the Sangre de Cristo Range.

David Martinez, an heir of an original colonizer, was about to default on a $1,000 loan he owed to the National Bank of Santa Fe. To cover this debt, he decided to sell his share of the grant. In the year 1900, after attorneys confirmed Las Trampas' boundaries, Martinez, along with four other grant descendants, brought a partition suit before the local courts. The judge appointed a commission to have the property physically inspected to see if a partition was feasible. One of the surveyors hired for this job, Ireneo Chavez, was brother to an assistant of Alonzo McMillen, David Martinez's lawyer.[16]

The commissioners found the Las Trampas grant could not be physically partitioned. After court appointed referee Ernest A. Johnson set aside a ridiculously sparse 650 acres for all the homes and garden plots located there, the entirety of the commons was auctioned off on the court house steps in Santa Fe. The only bidder was H. F. Raynolds. As payment for representing Raynolds, his lawyer received ¼ interest in all the common land on the grant. Not one of the defendants to Martinez suit were represented in court. Raynold's purchase was eventually annulled, due to a complaint filed in court that stated both the purchaser and his lawyer had bribed referee Johnson to cooperate in their land scheme. Incredibly, the court's decision to partition the *ejido* stood. Eventually, the land was resold to rancher and land baron Frank Bond. Although Elias Brevoort and other speculators had flipped their share of Jose Chavez's Tierra Amarilla property for nice profits, Bond was not so lucky. There were no quick dollars to be made off the Las Trampas *ejido*. The only men who profited from this partition were the lawyers. High in the Rio Arriba highlands, Hispano farmers and ranchers whose fathers and grandfathers had owned the surrounding countryside found out it was no longer theirs. Most of this land was eventually sold to a logging company.[17]

Governor Armijo had attempted to populate the Mexican frontier with new settlements to prevent exactly what happened at Las Trampas. In a gamble that appears foggy when seen through the lens of history, the plan to counteract encroaching American expansion with buffer colonies failed. Yet similar land awards took place in Texas. Both Spanish and Mexican officials struggled to find a successful way to colonize their barren provinces. They knew if they did not, eventually someone else would, whether it be the French, the Americans, or as it was the case for most of the nineteenth century, Texas Indians. That Armijo profited from such attempts does not entirely dilute his intentions.[18]

In 1841, north of the Las Vegas grant, Armijo awarded what became known as the Beaubien-Miranda tract to two of his friends. This is the award that sent an angry Padre Martinez to Durango in protest. Forty years later men were still fighting over this grant. The battle was always over its boundaries. The Beaubien-Miranda grant eventually became the Maxwell Land Grant. Lucien Maxwell, Beaubien's son-in-law, acquired the property from Beaubien, his wife, María de la Luz, and their daughters. Thirty-one years later, in 1879, after the grant had passed through several owners and a bankruptcy, Land Commissioner James A. Williamson ruled the property included over 1.75 million acres. In doing so, he disregarded the decision of previous commissioners who claimed the land was privately held. Under Mexican law, a private grant only contained 97,000 acres. Although portions of the larger allotment eventually went to the lawyers and politicians who were instrumental in influencing the Land Commissioner's decision, much occurred between the time Maxwell decided to sell and Williamson made his decision. Once the smoke cleared, Williamson owned a large ranch in New Mexico.[19]

By 1848, men like Lucien B. Maxwell, as well as *pobladores* and local *ricos* had all vied for this property, located within the Jicarilla Apache's ancient domain. Guadalupe Miranda, wanting no part of the American experience after annexation, sold his share to Maxwell and moved back to Mexico. After working the grant as its *patron* for several years, making profits with sales from trade along the Santa Fe Trail, his circumstances changed. Fort Union soldiers found gold on the grant in 1866. Although Maxwell reaped profits from both the minerals and the supplies he furnished to an influx of prospectors, by 1869, he felt it was time to get out, and looked for a buyer.[20]

The surveyor general at the time, T. Rush Spencer, hired private land surveyor W. W. Griffin to map out the property. With Lucien Maxwell's help, Griffin inspected the land and exaggerated its boundaries. He reported to Spencer that the Maxwell Land Grant encompassed close to two million acres. Elizabethtown boomed near the site of the gold find. While Colorado Senator Jerome B. Chafee helped look for a buyer on the East Coast, *nuevo-mexicano* farmers warily eyed Anglo miners rooting around the mountains.

The grant, all 1.7 million legally declared acres, was sold to English and Dutch investors for 1.35 million dollars. Cattleman Wilson Waddingham, who helped broker the deal, W. A. Bell, Hispano mercantilist Miguel A. Otero and Stephen B. Elkins bought shares in the enterprise. At approximately the same time, Senator Chafee was instrumental in killing House Bill 740, which would have restricted Mexican grants approved by the United States to 97,000 acres. The Secretary of the Interior, Jacob D. Cox, was incensed with Chafee. He believed the amount of land Maxwell claimed as his own was obscene. By executive order, Cox declared Governor Armijo had awarded a personal grant to Beaubien and Miranda, not a community grant. As stated above, community grants had no land limit. Cox intent was to open the extra land to public domain so private plots derived from the excess land could be filled with Anglo-American farmers and ranchers.[21]

Although some of the early surveyor generals earnestly attempted fair appraisal of titles, many that did not were entangled within the Santa Fe Ring's web. Three weeks after James K. Proudfit replaced T. Rush Spencer as surveyor general, he became partners with Thomas B. Catron and Steven B. Elkins in the Consolidated Land, Cattle Raising, and Wool Growing Company. Catron also partnered with Surveyor General Henry Atkinson in 1876 in the Boston and New Mexico Cattle Company. Over the next nine years Catron continued to involve the men responsible for determining both the validity and size of land grants in business ventures such as the New Mexico Land and Livestock Company, the American Valley Company, and the New Mexico and Kentucky Land and Stock Company.[22]

Meanwhile, the Dutch learned the federal government had an issue with the land they had purchased from Maxwell, but the foreign investors chose to ignore it. The buyers refused to believe that their 1.35 million dollar purchase of 1.75 million acres was anything less than what it had been represented to be. The Dutch reasoning concerning its boundaries were based on the verification of such by the surveyor general. That a fee simple, absolute conception of ownership was overlaid on top of Jicarilla and *nuevo-mexicano* ideas of land ownership seemed an irrelevant consequence to the parties of the sale.[23]

As the nineteenth century entered its last quarter, a cauldron of legal maneuverings and property manipulations began to boil across New

Mexico. The statute that implemented the partition suit went into effect in 1876. Shortly after Secretary of the Interior Jacob D. Cox ruled the Maxwell Grant was only 97,000 acres, the General Land Office informed homesteaders that the remaining lands connected to this property were now a part of the public domain and available for settlement. At the same time, English and Dutch backed owners of the newly named Maxwell Land Grant and Railway Company began to practice the partition suit and subsequent sale of divided common lands.[24]

The *nuevo-mexicano* farmer found himself trapped between federal government edicts and European interests. Regardless of the claims, counter claims, and distant power struggles, the fields needed attention and children had to be fed. The next rain was far more important than the shouted declarations of some self-important territorial politician. Small-time Anglo-American farmers and ranchers living on the grant often found themselves in the same position. Trouble brewed in what became Colfax County.

The new Maxwell Land Grant and Railway Company did not fare well. After assessing their purchase for the first time, the Dutch and English owners were shocked to find so many Hispanos and Anglos living on their property. Early attempts to eject them led to sporadic violence. The English opted out of the partnership. The Colfax County War, which involved officials attempting to eliminate the "squatters," is beyond the scope of this work. Suffice to say that as early as 1873, *nuevo-mexicanos* and Anglos resisted having to pay company agents for the land they had already acquired and were reluctant to leave. Numerous monographs have covered grant issues and the Colfax County Wars in depth. Maria E. Montoya and William H. Keleher both shed valuable light on these crucial events.[25]

Due to troubles gaining control of the land, coupled with an inability to pay taxes on 1.7 million acres, the railway company filed for bankruptcy in 1875. By late 1876, the territorial government stepped in and sold the grant to M. W. Mills. Mills was acting as a front man for Thomas B. Catron. Afterward, the bankrupt Maxwell Land Grant and Railway Company was allowed to buy back its shares from Catron, although he continued to retain an interest in the enterprise. Acting on behalf of the company, Catron's old partner, Stephen B. Elkins requested the General Land Office issue a new survey. Once and for all, questions regarding the grant's boundaries would finally be put to rest. Noted earlier, in 1879, J. A. Williamson, the new commissioner of the General Land Office, agreed to Elkin's request, with one stipulation. Any new survey would be carried out by an uninterested third party. Apparently, the fact that Elkin's brother was hired to verify the boundaries "once and for all," carried little import with Williamson. Low and behold the new survey verified the grant was closer to two million than 97,000 acres, just as alumni of the Santa Fe Ring had always claimed.[26]

Surveyor General Henry M. Atkinson approved John T. Elkin's work and submitted the re-platted survey. Interior Secretary Carl Schurz approved the grant's new patent. It turned out Mr. Atkinson owned shares in the grant. That fact was probably unknown to Schurz, but it was the federal government's responsibility to ensure a fair appraisal of the submission. They failed miserably in this endeavor. This was due, in part, because of the smokescreen of corruption that ran rampant within the territorial government at the time. The lure of market capitalism played a powerful role as well.[27]

The fight for Hispano land rights on the Maxwell Grant would move to the courtroom where it remained for another century. After 1888, there was little violence or anti-grant activity. The company began to have more success ejecting both *nuevo-mexicanos* and so-called Anglo squatters from the property. After 1894, U.S. judges refused to hear any more arguments about its boundaries. Large land owning companies with financial backing from both Europe and New York eventually won out over New Mexico's own citizens.[28]

Even if they would not admit it, as they struggled to understand what was going on with their land, rural Hispanos found the draw of the market economy still too strong to resist. A gravity based economy filled with American made manufactured goods pulled them away from Old Mexico. Who would not want a plow made of iron instead of wood, or matches instead of flint? Yet, at what cost were they acquiring such innovations?

What of the Americans? For them, land was as viable a market as anything traded on Wall Street. T. Rush Spencer, James K. Proudfit, and Henry M. Atkinson were all surveyor generals who speculated on the same lands they were charged to assess. Along with judges and lawyers, they looked to acquire as much acreage as possible and quickly flip it on the open market for cash. To achieve this end, they took advantage of their positions within the legal community to denigrate the integrity of *nuevo-mexicano's* grant titles. Under the crushing weight of this dynamic, farmers and ranchers faced an unrecognizable future. Whether through the partition suit or by reinterpreting ownership of the common land, the Anglo-American quest for land and water in New Mexico continued.[29]

Small landowners who were able to avoid lawyers, suits, and cash enticements still faced property taxes. Such fees could not be bartered with wheat. Some *nuevo-mexicanos* resorted to working for the railroad while others, in an ironic twist, found employment with the very surveyors assessing their pastures and timberlands. Those who could not find work or decided it was impossible to raise crops and animals while laboring elsewhere, were forced to sell off a portion of their property to pay the taxes. Hispanic and Anglo entrepreneurs and speculators were always available to purchase lots as they became available. Like a virus, the cash economy filtered its way out of town and into the Las Vegas grant's surrounding mountain communities.

In the last decade of the nineteenth century, resistance to encroachment was beginning to wane in Colfax County, but that was not the case sixty miles to the south. On the Las Vegas Land Grant, when some of the same legal actors put similar plans into action, *nuevo-mexicanos* did not consider acquiescing to Anglo-American intent so early. As the results of decades of legal maneuverings crept like an obscure stain toward the rural villages of San Miguel County, a common passion burned within the people. Guided only by an iridescent moon, *nuevo-mexicanos* began to gather in greater numbers within the small adobe dwellings scattered along the feet of the Sangre de Cristo Range. In silence they rode across well-worn trails to their *moradas*. Carrying axes, rifles, and unlit torches, they came together inside their chapter houses. Union organizers were there, as well as wheat farmers, sheep ranchers, and *mayordomos*. Just as resistance was waning to the north, defiance was building on the Las Vegas grant.[30]

4

Incremental Ambitions

With the arrival of the Southwestern cattle boom in the 1870s, the fence became a powerful symbol of American expansionism. As far as most *nuevo-mexicanos* were concerned, such devices seemed more hindrance than help, were insulting, and when strung across the commons, became symbols of theft. Pine-branch fence posts stood like sentinels of past victory and future peril. Entrepreneurs such as Amsterdam cattleman Wilson Waddingham, lawyers John S. Watts and Thomas B. Catron, and businessmen Eugenio and Trinidad Romero used fences as protection against squatters and recalcitrant New Mexicans. Most never believed locals had proper title, or simply chose to ignore the truth. Many newcomers to the grant believed the land was theirs to fence as they pleased, discounting prior titles as foggy, foreign documents rendered meaningless by annexation. Most sought the meadowland for their cattle. Anglo-Americans and some wealthy Hispanos argued that the rural farmers and sheepherders had squandered the land's potential and were determined to rectify that problem.[1]

The railroad made it economically feasible to raise cattle in a land of four million sheep. Sheep dominated the region because they were easily managed and did not require containment or much water. José Leandro Perea managed over 2,500 flocks across New Mexico. When the Colonel Kearney made his proclamation in 1846, Perea's empire included 200,000 sheep. Each spring, miles of wagons full of wool lined the roads to Las Vegas, waiting to broker agreements with the dealers. In the first thirty years after the Mexican cession, livestock demographics in New Mexico experienced a dramatic change. Cattle-herds escalated from 33,000 head in 1850 to 350,000 in 1880. Cattleman did not think much of sheep or sheep owners. Contrary to local sheep men, recently arrived Anglo-American cattlemen, along with the land-rich Hispano elite, tended to vote Republican.[2]

Wool wagons in Las Vegas. From the Collection of the Las Vegas Citizens' Committee for Historic Preservation.

Prior to and after annexation politics in New Mexico was a full-contact sport. If on the wrong side of the political equation, the press vilified participants not only as poor representatives, but poor humans, thieves, and sometimes murderers. Most involved in politics considered such treatment par-for-the-course. If being slandered in the *Las Vegas Optic* was all that happened to a politician, he considered himself charmed. For the most outspoken, physical harm was a real possibility. Doña Ana politician Albert J. Fountain came up missing one day and was never found. Santa Fe Ring antagonist, José Francisco Chavez was assassinated in broad daylight on the streets of the capital. Some politicians were mugged, others knifed. Democrats accused Republicans of skullduggery and vice versa.[3]

Politically and geographically, Territorial New Mexico was a hard country. It was run by Anglo and Hispano men with sharply-honed political skills, not above taking violent action if it suited their needs. As a body, they were frustrated about their inability to enact legislation without the approval of federal officials, yet their differing opinions on how to approach statehood fueled a rift that was legislatively counter-productive.

Local politicians' failure to correct chronic structural problems and get legislative reforms passed could not be traced to any want of vision or plans. New Mexico did not become a state until the second decade of the twentieth century. As long as it remained a territory, the federal government retained final say on major issues. In the decades following the Civil War, key appointments were ladled out from Washington D.C., usually to loyal Republicans. With a distant, and usually uninterested, or distracted national government in charge of New Mexico, little regulation, jurisdictional oversight, or civil reform took place. In Washington, committees created to enact legislation had a hard time getting things done because it took time for elected officials to get situated in their jobs. By the time many had settled in and were ready to get down to business, their terms were about over. The political process was also infected by a coercive patronage system. Usually, politicians in the States were more interested in getting re-elected than focusing on a territory irrelevant to their own personal constituencies. Many U.S. Congressmen were earnest in their desire to carry out their duties as the nation's representatives, but found the federal system terribly inefficient and practically incapable of affecting the welfare of distant communities in a meaningful way.[4]

The New Mexico Territorial Congress requested statehood fifty different times between annexation and 1912. Reasons for delays were numerous and complicated. From a national perspective, prior to 1865 the slavery issue impacted any territory's future consideration, New Mexico included. It is also important to note that inner-territorial conflicts delayed statehood. Men like Stephen B. Elkins, Thomas B. Catron, and Wilson Waddingham preferred not to operate under the confines of state officials that might prove to be more diligent in their duties protecting the rights of *nuevo-mexicano* farmers than distracted Washington bureaucrats.[5]

On the other hand, New Mexicans had never been shy about crossing party-lines when they believed the other side held the proper position. Because of this flexibility, in New Mexico, political outcomes were driven more by the personality of the person running for office or platform priorities, than party-dogma. Many Republicans pushed for statehood because they believed it would usher in another wave of prosperity. Some party members opposed this movement because they feared the Hispanic majority in the region would create a Democratic stronghold. There was also a large block of Democrats who opposed statehood because they feared the tax burden would fall on the poor. Conversely, while many Anglo-American Republican businessmen anticipated statehood windfalls, a contingent of railroad men and merchants disagreed, fearing, like many Hispano Democrats, the common man, and that included middle-class whites, would bear the burden of funding state taxes, and therefore opposed it. For many years, the Catholic Church also opposed statehood, but not for economic reasons. Priests throughout the area believed state-supported, non-secular schools would incrementally destroy their flocks' faith by removing students from their care and tutelage. While people in the largest towns consistently voted for statehood, those in the rural areas, which was most of New Mexico, did not.[6]

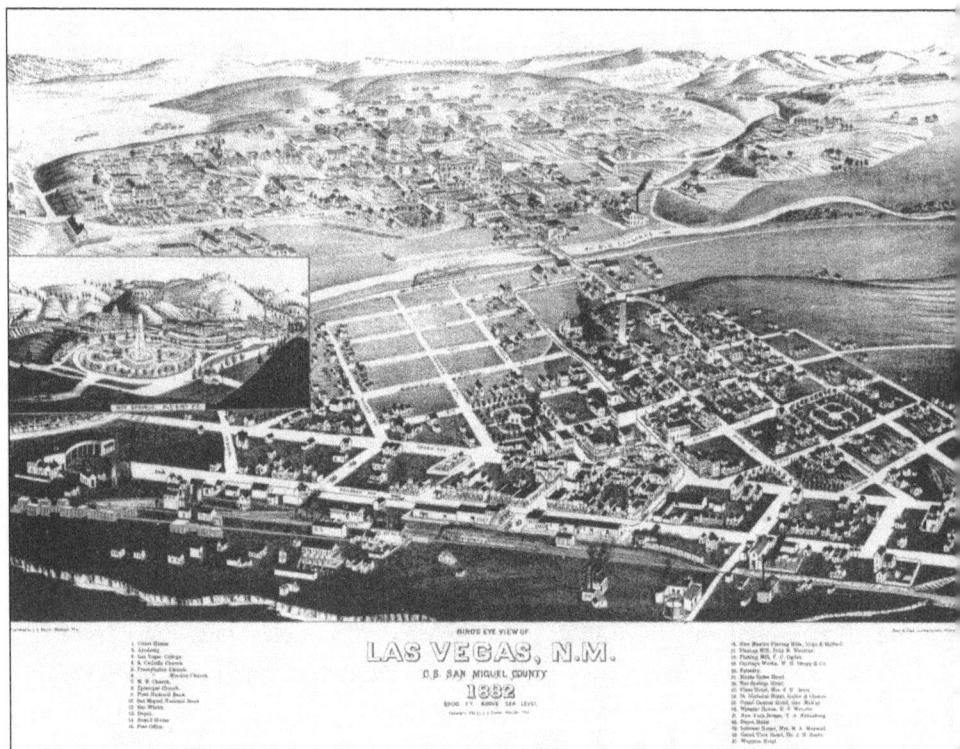

Las Vegas, New Mexico, 1882. From the Collection of the Las Vegas Citizens' Committee for Historic Preservation.

Catron had grown rich in Territorial New Mexico, and at different times saw the advantages expressed by both camps. The staunchest Republican in the region, his support generally depended on the political climate of the time. As an example, one year, while many of his cohorts feared higher taxes were sure to follow, Catron professed the actual tax rate would go down and championed statehood. He reasoned tax-rates would remain low but with an influx of immigrants, the volume of income gathered from an increased base and business growth would go up considerably. Later, he opposed a plan combining Arizona and New Mexico into one state. Hispanos were seldom involved in politics in Arizona. In New Mexico, their vote was critical to any election. Within the territory, they served on juries and many had become politicians in their own right. In Las Vegas and Santa Fe, both political parties worked diligently to garner *nuevo-mexicano* support in numerous ways. Over the years, Catron utilized patronage in large doses to cultivate a powerful constituency for his party and did not want this influence disrupted by a new prejudicial class of Arizona politicians over whom he had no control.[7]

Some within the United States Congress were wary of New Mexican statehood. In 1889, a territorial delegation arrived from Santa Fe to push their case. Upon meeting these lobbyists, Senator George F. Edmond snidely commented, "Since having seen the delegation from New Mexico, I am more than ever convinced of the necessity of public schools in that territory." The chairman of the Committee on Territories, Indiana Senator Albert Beveridge, continually threw a wrench in attempts for statehood. He believed the people of New Mexico to be backward and did not deserve acceptance until more white people populated it.[8]

For over sixty years, New Mexico remained a territory. It languished in a pseudo-transitional state because the U.S. Congress never afforded it the same priority as it did California, where large deposits of gold were found. Application also failed due to constant political in-fighting. In the meantime, a system of federal patronage provided easterners with key positions in a land they did not know.[9]

While New Mexico remained within a legal system which resembled a judicial purgatory, land speculators, under the cover of United States ambivalence, took advantage of its people, which depended on a distant central government to look after their rights. Such conditions proved a fertile ground for fraud and malfeasance. The same congressmen who voted against statehood used the fruit of their inactions as reasons to maintain the status quo. Writing about such paradoxes, Richard White commented, "Locals resented the federal government for its failure to use power to improve conditions while at the same time, resented that power." Meanwhile, legal proceedings that facilitated and required the sale of land grant parcels continued. *Nuevo-mexicano* farmers were forced to sell lots to pay county taxes. More fences began to show up as boundary-lines on the commons. Such ambivalence impacted common-folk that lived on the Las Vegas grant.[10]

When talking about Jean Pendaries and other newcomers' entrance into the Tecolote de Rincon Valley, Manuel Martinez said, ". . . this ambition came from the Americans. The people were not ambitious. The gringos come here grabbing all the land and throwing out the natives." Although Martinez's remembrances of his father-in-law's time in the valley drip with bitterness, such oral history is important. The tone reveals and becomes a part of the evolving history of the area. "Ambition" is a pejorative term here. Neither Frenchman Pendaries nor most Anglo-Americans understood the *nuevo-mexicano* concept of the word.[11]

Hispanos who worked their portion of the grant as farmers and ranchers did not consider themselves ambitious. Within the village community, their moral compass forbade them from making a profit at the expense of others. This innate quality, *vergüenza,* was rooted in the belief that one could not advance while leaving others behind. One's value as a human came not from money or materials. A sense of satisfaction was derived from the land on which they lived, the bounty of the harvest, and the strength of the community.[12]

The *pobladores* who established the first settlements already displayed these traits when they ventured onto the *Las Vegas Grandes*. While Anglo-American culture forged a spirit within individuals that allowed them to succeed on their own, sometimes at others' expense, this was contrary to *nuevo-mexicano* notions of honor. Many looked at the new professions cropping up in town as unacceptable. To become a profitable banker or a merchant sometimes required impersonal treatment of prospective clients. Although a select Hispano elite did succeed in the Anglo-American world, they did so without ever having to live as the majority of the population in Las Vegas did.

The *patrón* was better prepared to adapt to the American concept of profit and success than the men and women who worked for him. The Romeros had more in common with Charles Ilfeld than the subsistence farmers who scratched out a living along the Gallinas River. Those who worked the *acequias* and raised crops and livestock for a living found such business enterprises repulsive to their nature as honorable men. For this lack of ambition, newly immigrated Anglo-Americans believed most *nuevo-mexicanos* were incapable of learning, or flat-out lazy.

Many of the *ricos* were able to parlay their value as intermediaries into positions of political power. Both Eugenio Romero and his brother-in-law, Lorenzo Lopez, retained a strong influence over the common-folk on the grant. Many Hispano farmers were obligated in several ways to such men, living on their land under some type of indebtedness. Some depended on their *patron* to act as buffers between their culture and the society of American strangers that seemed to be taking over large parts of Las Vegas. Such *patrónes* were long-standing leaders in *nuevo-mexicano* culture and were often looked upon as a positive force in their lives. They provided funds during hard-times, made sure relatives were looked after when sick, organized balls, paid for weddings, insured continuity of culture, and the old way of life. Lorenzo Lopez was known as *"el amo des los pobres,"* the poor people's overseer. These men converted this power and influence into political capital in the land of democracy. Lopez, Inspector General of the Second Militia during the Civil War, held many political positions in San Miguel County in the latter part of the nineteenth century, including county sheriff.[13]

Hispano land-loss continued in a number of ways in the 1880s. Through the partitioning, the selling of parcels to pay county taxes, and payments to lawyers for a number of questionable and legitimate services, acreage was extracted. An Hispano loss often meant an Anglo gain on the grant. As more Americans edged into the valleys, an incremental, seething, sense of shame crept into the *nuevo-mexicano* psyche. To be shamed by ambitious men inflicted a humiliating ache in the hearts of everyone who believed the Las Vegas Land Grant to be sacred and untouchable. *Vergüenza* hung like a shadow over mountain communities, a stain on their ancestry. Soon, this shame would manifest itself into anger. The land was at stake. And honor.

Lorenzo Lopez. San Miguel County Sheriff in 1888. Head of the wealthy Lopez family on the Las Vegas Grant. From Ralph Emerson Twitchell, *The Leading Facts of New Mexican History*, vol. 2.

It is unknown if the Frenchman Jean Pendaries was familiar with the term *vergüenza*, but he was obviously an enterprising pioneer who adapted well in his new country. He had arrived in America with his wife and two daughters in 1857. It would have been impossible for him not to be aware of growing resentments on the grant. Little is known of Pendaries, but he is an important figure because his name and influence still impact the valley in which he eventually settled. That Manuel Martinez spoke with such bitterness about him and the issues relevant to this book requires a closer look.[14]

Pendaries first surfaced in New Mexico with the purchase of the Las Vegas Hotel on the Plaza in 1864. As related earlier, he owned property on this square with his wife, Mathilde, later known as Mathilda. At different times, they ran a grocery, a billiards hall, and a hotel. Americans called him John. That is how he was designated in the 1870 San Miguel Census. Some Hispanos knew him as Juan. He and his family immigrated from Villebrumier, France, near Gascony. Unlike many early settlers, he was already married when he entered the region. Few Anglos brought their wives west. The 1870 Census reveals that twenty-two Anglo-Americans were married to Hispano women during the period, with only four Anglo women represented as being married to Anglo men.[15]

Jean Pendaries' Ranch in the Rociada Valley. The mill, the large building on the far left, has been preserved and still stands. From the Collection of the Las Vegas Citizens' Committee for Historic Preservation.

By the time Pendaries established himself in Las Vegas, he was a family man with two daughters. In 1869 or 1870, a son was born, but Henry Pendaries would die in early childhood. As Manuel Martinez so acidly recounted, Jean Pendaries turned his attention toward the Tecolote de Rincon Valley sometime in the late 1860s. Juan Nepomuseno sold him land there in 1868. Soon after, he built a ranch-style home, as well as a gristmill that supplied Ilfeld and the military with grains. From the same mill he ran a local post office and general store. Such was Pendaries' growing influence that in 1884 he renamed the valley community Rociada. He named it such; so the legend has it, because of the layers of dew or *rocio* that coated the valley floor each morning. He also christened the valley that ran west up the eastern slope of the mountain range. He named this village Gascon, after Gascony, France. Tecolote de Rincon would never be printed on territorial maps. Rociada would remain the name of the mountain hamlet that skirted the edge of the Las Vegas Land Grant.[16]

Like many other nineteenth century patriarchs, Pendaries (pronounced

Pondaray) mixed family with business. His granddaughter, Consuelo Baca, recalled that Bishop Lamy liked to visit the ranch when he was in the area, giving him a chance to savor food from his homeland and speak in his native tongue. Pendaries used the bishop's influence to counter Protestant missionary's attempts to convert the locals.[17]

If he did not choose his children's spouses, the record certainly indicates Pendaries had a major influence on decisions about whom they would marry. Emilie, later called Emilia, the oldest, would wed Charles Rudolph, the son of Milnor Rudolph, the Territorial Congress' Speaker of the House. A first cousin to President Garfield's wife, the elder Rudolph had also purchased land in the valley. He sold it to Jean Pendaries in 1878. At the time, Charles ran the Plaza Hotel on the Square. Another Pendaries daughter, Marie, later called Mary, married Richard Dunn, a businessman who came from Nova Scotia via Maine, where he had owned a lumber operation before moving west. Among other enterprises, he would set up a similar lumber business in Gascon, close to his wife's family.[18]

Dunn became steeped in Las Vegas business and politics, running a store on the Plaza, being employed as a manager for Charles Ilfeld, and partnering with his father-in-law in Pendaries and Dunn. He built an elegant home in Gascon just a mile or so from the Pendaries Ranch. Dunn was, at one time, President of the Board of County Commissioners and Chairman of the Democratic Executive Committee for San Miguel County. With Charles Rudolph's father being one of the most influential Republicans of the era, family gatherings at the Pendaries Ranch must have provided an interesting spot for after-dinner conversations. One has to wonder if the subject of politics was left at the front door.[19]

Yet the most high-profile Pendaries betrothal was yet to come. His youngest daughter, Marguerite, married prominent Hispano, José Albino Baca Jr. This union garnered much attention in the county and future history books. A wealthy Las Vegas merchant and entrepreneur, Baca had followed in his father's footsteps, taking advantage of trade opportunities presented by the proximity of the Santa Fe Trail. He later became Lt. Governor of New Mexico. Baca's life was cut short in 1924 when he died of a heart attack while running for governor. One of José and Marguerite's children, Consuelo, married Oliver Lafarge, a future Pulitzer Prize winning author.

Lafarge recounted Consuelo's Rociada childhood in the book, *Behind the Mountains*. It recalled Consuelo's life in the valley, an idyllic childhood tale about the family who inherited the Pendaries Ranch. Rociada, a little more than a day's ride from Las Vegas, was thirteen miles west as the crow flies, but twenty-two along a series winding, dirt roads. Through several vignettes, via Lafarge's powerful pen, Consuelo told several warm-hearted tales of growing up on a large sheep ranch that was nestled at the feet of the Sangre de Cristos. The ranch house is no longer there, having burned to the ground in 1964.[20]

Today, not far from Santo Nino Church, located next to the old Tecolote de Rincon *placita*, a resort community sprinkled with cabins, modern mountain homes, and a golf course hugs the eastern rim of the mountains. It is called Pendaries Village. Other than his name, little remains of Jean Pendaries' legacy. His gristmill still stands, refurbished now, a reminder that the American market economy reached deep into the heart of the Las Vegas grant. The Frenchman is known as a pioneer who "settled" the valley and gave it its name. As with the rest of the grant, the history of this mountain community runs deeper than Pendaries' legacy or American concepts of place. Jicarrilla Apaches once roamed there. *Nuevo-mexicanos* settled along its streams a generation before annexation. Although Jean Pendaries' intentions were perhaps honorable, that is of little consequence to those who wove their own patterns on the land's history. Whether voluntarily or through coercion, after selling off their lots, many Hispanos born in Tecolote de Rincon became hired hands in Rociada, working first for Pendaries and then the Bacas. *Behind the Mountains* reveals little of what *nuevo-mexicanos* thought as their circumstances changed during the last part of the nineteenth century.

Voices in the Night

Ten years after the railroad's arrival, Las Vegas had experienced more than the obvious changes. Each of its architectural marvels hailed the coming of the Americans with a steady sprouting of three-story brick wonders. Buildings were decorated with artistic cornices and graceful ironwork. Although the volume of elaborate Victorian homes which rose off their elevated foundations revealed the vibrancy of the local economy, changes were afoot that could not be admired or touched. It was no secret that Anglo-Americans had used the United States' legal system to great advantage, applying their familiarity with its procedures to acquire land. A steady flow of eastern entrepreneurs had infiltrated the area. Emotions were simmering among the rural Hispanos who lived on the grant. Ambitious men were about.

Looking west down Bridge Street toward the Plaza. From the Collection of the Las Vegas Citizens' Committee for Historic Preservation.

Soon, Juan José Herrera would return from Colorado to San Miguel County, stepping into the emotional breach that rippled just under the surface of the mountain villages that dotted the grant. Coincidently, or so it seemed, about the time Herrera returned, an event in Las Vegas set the stage for him to draw alienated Hispanos, disenchanted with Anglo-American notions of fairness, into a counter-acting, recognizable force. A lawsuit brought by a cattle corporation against a *nuevo-mexicano* family initiated the most successful resistance in New Mexico since the Taos Revolt. Herrera would lead that fight. Oddly enough, it began with the installation of a fence, one that an Anglo-American demanded a *nuevo-mexicano* tear down.[21]

Looking east down Bridge Street toward the Gallinas River bridge. From the Collection of the Las Vegas Citizen's Committee for Historic Preservation.

After purchasing of property within the grant's boundaries, Philip Milhiser, a partner in the Las Vegas Land and Cattle Company, brought a suit against José L. Padilla and his brothers, claiming they had fenced off a portion of land his cattle company had acquired. Milhiser and partners Gustavos Milhiser, Emanuel Milhiser, and Sampson Hirsch meant to have the Padillas' barbed-wire removed and the families vacate the area. The Milhisers, like other easterners, had bought their New Mexico property from someone who owned a chain of title that could be traced back to one of Las Vegas' first colonizers. Louis Sulzbacher and his wife, Paulina, were the sellers. They had acquired their share of the Las Vegas grant by buying out

William H. Meyer and Henry L. Waldo, who had earlier partnered with them in the acquisition of land from original *pobladores* Pablo Ulibarri and Elugio Segura. Sulzbacher was a local lawyer who employed Waldo early in his career. Waldo would one day become Chief Justice of the New Mexico Supreme Court. Sulzbacher also did business with Thomas B. Catron, as well as representing a host of Las Vegas businessmen such as the Rosenwald brothers of Las Vegas in land transactions. Sulzbacher also occasionally engaged in real estate deals of his own.[22]

The last link in this chain of transactions occurred between Louis Sulzbacher, his wife Paulina, and the Las Vegas Land and Cattle Company, twelve days after the lawyer finalized his purchase of Henry L. Waldo and wife Lucy's property. Philip Milhiser believed this 27 June 1887 purchase gave him Sulzbacher's private plots and a representative portion of the *ejido*, in this case about 25, 860 acres. He did not waste much time making these beliefs public, filing a suit against José and brothers Francisco, Pablo, Faustino, and Clemente Padilla. The cattleman argued that these men were squatters and had illegally built fences and houses on a portion of the common land he now owned.[23]

The defendants in the case countered that the land in question was theirs, and had been for years. In court, they backed this up by furnishing homestead deeds and testimony that proved Milhiser's chain of title was not linked to theirs. At the time, each brother worked an adjoining 160 acre tract. One month after the Las Vegas Land and Cattle Company's 27 June purchase, Philip Milhiser filed his suit in the county court house. It would not come to trial for another year.[24]

Milhiser claimed this acquisition entitled his company to "an undivided one-sixth part of said granted lands." As noted above, this included private lots and roughly 26,000 acres of the Las Vegas Land Grant. He testified that his purpose in filing the suit was to, "secure a decree of the court denying the defendants any right in the tract of land . . ." being contested.[25]

The land in question was called "*La Monilla.*" In *Milhiser v. Padilla*, José testified this property was, "one mile south of the road leading from the town of Las Vegas to the Olguin Hill, and about thirteen miles east of the town. . . ." Although the southern edge of the Rocky Mountains loomed on horizon, the Padillas' property was no pine-forested, mountain paradise. *La Monilla* was a separate geologic entity from what existed in the nearby mountain valleys. Its undulating topography rolled eastward toward the ominous Llano Estacado and south toward the Bosque Redondo. Its golden prairie grasses were interspersed with deep ravines, high mesas, and red-sand washouts. The immensity of this land's barren qualities included a stark harshness that was both beautiful and dangerous. Although only a day's ride from the thick pine-forests and fertile meadows of the Sangre de Cristo Range, the Padilla homestead was an arid grassland punctuated with rocky outcrops and isolated junipers.[26]

José Padilla and his brothers testified that they had lived on the site since at least 1877, farming, ranching, and growing hay. In court interviews, José claimed he had built two houses there, stacked stones for a corral to contain his horses, and maintained a few cattle. José further stated that about a year after he arrived in 1877, he began to string barbed-wire across the property. José Padilla testified he spent over 10,000 dollars building homes, installing fences, and growing hay. When awarding acreage, both the Mexican land grant system and the U.S. Homestead Act stipulated settlers must maintain and improve their properties or risk losing them. José was trying to establish that he met the Homestead Act's requirements.[27]

Santiago Garcia, testifying for Milhiser, claimed José Padilla could not have lived at *La Monilla* before 1879, because if he had, Santiago would have seen him. Garcia said he was living in a nearby cave at the time, occasionally herding livestock for others. Garcia did admit he had seen Padilla building a house on the property in 1879, but had not seen any fences or building structures before that time. When cross-examined, the cave-dweller could not say for sure when he had lived near the Padilla home-site.[28]

José Padilla stated he had "known" of *La Monilla* for thirty-four or thirty-five years and had lived there for over a decade. The court records backed up his testimony. One item noted Padilla filed a property claim for 160 acres on 10 February 1879. In 1885, two documents in the San Miguel County records corroborate the earlier claim. Additionally, together, the Padilla brothers purchased an "undisclosed interest" in the Las Vegas Land Grant from Felix Martinez and his wife, Virginia, in September of 1887.[29]

It is reasonable to assume that the Padillas knew that eventually, installation of barbed wire, even on their own land, might cause a confrontation, regardless of how secure they felt about their title. John Taylor testified that José Padilla told him he put the fence up in 1881 or 1882. Taylor said the fence was about two miles long and a mile and a half wide. Taylor also verified that there were certainly homes and corrals on the property by then. Even though the Padillas installed their fence long before Milhiser's arrival, it is possible this was one *nuevo-mexicano* family's attempt to establish land sovereignty in the face of Anglo-American, westward migration. It is somewhat ironic that a cattleman seeking property in New Mexico went to court to have a fence removed. This proved to be a perplexing case for the judicial system. If the judge found for Milhiser, that meant the Padillas would have to remove barbed-wire from grant land, something most Hispanos had been demanding of eastern cattlemen for years. What would the ramifications be for other cattle companies stringing wire throughout New Mexico if such a decision was reached? On 21 August 1888, Chief Justice of the Territorial Supreme Court, Elisha V. Long, presiding, in this case as a District Judge, brought the suit up before the San Miguel County Court.[30]

Philip Milhiser lived in East Las Vegas, but the Las Vegas Land and Cattle Company's ranch was out of town, about six miles from the Padilla homestead. Milhiser admitted the defendants had lived at *La Monilla* for some time, but argued they were illegal squatters encroaching on his company's property. He stated the land in question was between six and seven hundred acres. Milhiser had lived in town about a year, the time that had elapsed since he had bought his last parcel of land from Sulzbacher. County records show he had previously purchased two separate deeds from lawyer Sulzbacher and his wife, one for $3,100 on 2 December of 1886, and one for $600 on 30 December 1886. Milhiser found it completely irrelevant that the Padillas had been living at *La Monilla* for several years before his arrival. The Las Vegas Land and Cattle Company ran about 600 head of cattle and twenty horses on the grant. The Padilla's fence, he claimed, was preventing him from full utilization of his property.[31]

It is interesting to note the involvement of Felix Martinez in this court case. Martinez was a very influential newspaperman in Las Vegas. That he sold an interest in the land grant to José Padilla for 300 dollars in September of 1887, about six months after Milhiser's final purchase from Sulzbacher, indicates that from its inception, this suit was of critical interest to contemporary leaders in Las Vegas. Many such leaders were both interested and involved in the proceedings. Felix Martinez testified in the court case in Padillas' behalf, claiming the *La Monilla* property could be traced back to original *poblador*, Tomas Baca. This, Martinez argued, proved that the Milhiser claim, originating as it did from Pablo Ulibarri and Elugio Segura, was a separate allotment from José Padilla's, therefore could not be considered part of the Las Vegas Land and Cattle Company's spread. Martinez was a force in the Democratic Party of San Miguel County and would become one of two key leaders of a grassroots political movement that was just beginning to build momentum in the county. This movement was intent on protecting Hispano land rights. That the other leader of this party, Juan José Herrera, also testified in Padilla's behalf is just as eye-opening. Herrera also verified that José's chain of title was separate from Milhiser's. That these two well-known advocates of *nuevo-mexicano* rights stood up for José Padilla in this landmark case has never come light. As the crow-flies, the Herrera homestead was about twenty miles west of *La Monilla*. Such distance practically made the Padillas and the Herreras neighbors. It is obvious that restricting Milhiser's purchase to that of the original private plot would have had the full support of most local Hispanos anyway, yet the fact that Martinez and Herrera testified in this case is important. It signifies this case had more than the moral approval of local *nuevo-mexicanos*. The growing movement to protect Hispano rights on the Las Vegas Land Grant helped to shape the outcome of *Milhiser* v. *Padilla*.[32]

Several citizens testified in Philip Milhiser's behalf. One, Hilario Romero, Eugenio's brother, a member of the Republican Party and future U.S. marshal, swore he had never seen a house at *La Monilla*. Max Nordhaus, at the time a bookkeeper for Charles Ilfeld, later to become a ranch foreman for one of the merchant's livestock enterprises, also testified to the veracity of Milhiser's claim, as did José Maria Montoya.[33]

Early on, Judge Long, a pictorial cross between Moses and John Brown, hired Colonel R. M. Johnson as referee to sort out the case and take testimonies of persons pertinent to the suit. A man by the name of Johnson was also hired to perform a similar task for the judge presiding over the Las Trampas grant court case. His first name was Ernest. This examination could not verify that the two grant referees were related, but it seems likely that they were. The Trampas suit revolved around the feasibility of partitioning the commons, similar to what Milhiser was claiming. Part of his argument included the idea that if a person bought a private lot on a land grant, he was also entitled to a representative share of its *ejido*. Milhiser also belonged to the group that believed the grant was private property, owned by heirs of the original settlers, or the persons who had purchased their titles. Judge Long did not get Colonel R. M. Johnson's report until 3 July 1888, almost a year after the suit was filed. On 21 August 1888, the case was finally heard. Before making a decision, Long took an additional year to review the referee's findings and do his own research. The judge reviewed Spanish and Mexican law to clarify what the Republic of Mexico intended. What would Mexican officials have done? The question before Long involved the core argument of all land grant battles. Expansionists and speculators claimed that, like Milhiser, the *ejido* was a part of their purchases, a closed system that could not be diluted by future settlers. They claimed no one had the right to purchase or settle unused portions of the grant. Milhiser believed the Padillas were squatters. He discounted any witness who vouched for how long the Padilla's had lived there and certainly would have been suspicious of Felix Martinez selling José Padilla land, and then coming to his defense regarding the property's chain of ownership. The involvement of Felix Martinez and Juan José Herrera did not sway Philip Milhiser from his belief that he had clear title to the land in question. Milhiser also supported the theory that fewer owners meant a larger piece of the common land pie, and was not about to be swayed otherwise.[34]

After careful study, Judge Long concluded that since its origination, settlers had always been welcome on the grant. This would include Padilla. As an example, the judge used the fact that not long after the original *pobladores* came to the *Las Vegas Grandes*, another hundred followed. This led him to conclude that the Las Vegas Land Grant originated as a colonization grant, and later settlers could not be excluded. The judge interpreted Mexican law to mean that unoccupied lands not specifically designated to particular persons should be open to settlement and farming purposes, as community and colonization grants were. Such settlers had common rights to the remaining entirety of the *ejido*. Therefore, Long believed owning a private lot did not give the holder, i.e. Milhiser, a legal share of the commons, and even if it did, this would not have prevented Padilla from staking his claim in 1877. Common land, the judge ruled, was meant to remain common land, its resources available to existing property owners and future colonizers.[35]

Judge Elisha V. Long. Twitchell, *The Leading Facts of New Mexican History,* vol. 2.

Elisha V. Long's interpretation of Mexican law flew in the face of most Anglo-American definitions concerning New Mexico's common lands. Although the General Land Office and Surveyor General George Washington Julian agreed with Thomas B. Catron and Jefferson Raynolds that the judge had come to the wrong conclusion, they differed as to why. Since 1887, Julian had been pushing the Land Office to resurvey the grant.

He wanted land officers to focus on existing personal allotments. Once private home plots were identified, the remaining land, which Julian's believed to be untitled public domain owned by the government, could be carved into homestead plots for incoming Anglo-Americans. Catron and Raynolds disagreed with Surveyor General Julian. Like Milhiser, they argued the grant was private property and outsiders had no rights there. In their estimate, if the commons became public domain, the 400,000 acres that they desired would be frittered away to squatters. Upon coming to his decision, Judge Long determined the commons was the property of "the town of Las Vegas." It is important to note, when Surveyor General William Pelham submitted his findings on the original petitions to Washington, D. C., he also classified the grant as "the town of Las Vegas." Almost thirty years later, like Pelham, Judge Long did not clarify what "the town of Las Vegas" included, but his decision did run counter to the notion that the common lands were closed to the select few who owned title there.[36]

Milhiser's original suit required Judge Long to investigate whether he and other landholders held exclusive property rights. The judge did not think so. "The Mexican government . . ." he wrote, "had never intended that they [the original grant owners] . . . have exclusive right to appropriate to themselves the whole of the said land to the exclusion of actual settlers coming later. . . ." The case was two years old before Long reached this decision.[37]

Life on the grant was not suspended while the judge reviewed the documents, nor did tempers cool. The General Land Office's approval of Surveyor General Julian's argument that common land was public domain only confused the issue. In an effort to separate the commons from personal plots, Julian hired Will Tipton and Russell B. Rice to survey private lots on the Las Vegas grant, yet angry residents often prevented them from completing their jobs. For the next six years, these men, Rice in particular, attempted to plot out the various land titles in San Miguel County. In the end, Julian's attempt to fasten the government's hold on the *ejido* failed because he ran out of funds. Even so, dragging survey chains across personal property surely added to emotional upheaval on the grant.

Based on Julian's and the government's actions, speculation increased and more fences were installed on the commons. Along with Max Frost, the head of the land office in Santa Fe (as well as a prominent newspaper publisher), local merchant Charles Ilfeld was enticed into participating in some of the land schemes which were hatched. He was later indicted for involvement in a plan to sale fraudulent homestead claims on the grant. Surely the general belief that all of the commons would soon become public domain encouraged such activities.[38]

Louis Sulzbacher represented many of the speculators. He also was personally involved in the process, purchasing land from grant heirs and then representing to potential buyers that he owned the deed from the heir plus an equal amount of the commons. This is what happened to Milhiser. Sulzbacher's name comes up several times in the documents related to the purchases of such property. Sheriff Lorenzo Lopez also participated in land flips, purchasing as many as 250 acres from a land grant holder and then turning around and selling smaller parcels to other individuals. Sulzbacher left Las Vegas in 1890 for Kansas City, becoming a legal representative for the Atchison, Topeka, and Santa Fe Railroad Company. He moved to Puerto Rico at the turn of the century, serving as Justice of the Supreme Court for the island.[39]

Before he became available to testify for José Padilla, Juan José Herrera was in Colorado. While there, he watched how the coming of the railroad spurred speculators and landed elites to go after the prime pasturelands found on most *ejidos*. Like Sulzbacher, Colorado cattlemen and outside interests used the court system to argue that common lands were a part of privately held deeds. While up north, Herrera worked in the mines alongside angry Anglo laborers who felt absentee East Coast owners were cheating them out of honest wages. It was in Colorado that the Knights of Labor first found success dealing with labor problems, anti-monopolism, and other issues the railroad companies carried west. *Nuevo-mexicano* discontent may not have been apparent to Anglo-Americans, but Herrera would immediately have recognized it when he returned to San Miguel County. He had seen what could happen if that discontent was not channeled properly. As Robert Larson pointed out, it was out of the Knights of Labor's ability to organize and form a united front that the Populist Movement was born in the Mountain West. Juan José Herrera helped bring that movement to New Mexico.[40]

When Herrera returned to Las Vegas, he was already a well known figure. His father was a trusted soldier and officer in both the Mexican and U.S. militias. Grant documents pertaining to the Salitre grant, awarded in 1841, illustrate the respect the Republic of Mexico held for Manuel Herrera. When Santíago Ulibarrí made this award, he declared that since there was little water on the property, only Herrera would be allowed to irrigate there. The elder Herrera commanded troops that protected the settlers from roving bands of Indians. Manuel would later become a Brigadier General for the Unites States' Territorial Militia. He led several companies in battles against the Apache and Navajo.[41]

Juan José Herrera had been gone for approximately twenty years, yet was still well connected in the area. After moving in with his mother and brother on the family property in *Ojitos Frios*, he reacquainted himself with old friends. The Herrera homestead was about fifteen miles south of Romeroville, and a few more from Las Vegas. A familial interconnectedness woven together by a generational web of cousins tied one mountain village to the next, grafting stories of grandfathers and grandmothers, uncles, aunts, and cousins, onto the same regional tree. This familiarity bred a variety of traits among the people of the Las Vegas grant. Being related by distant blood or through marriage bred bonds of loyalty and trust that were hard to break. In the rare case where such a trust was violated, the consequences could prove harsh and long standing, creating feuds that never seemed to end. The Herreras were related to the Romeros on their mother's side, who was a Baca. José was also a friend of Lorenzo Lopez, brother-in-law to both Eugenio and Trinidad. He also knew future Territorial Governor Miguel Antonio Otero Jr., who claimed him as a friend in the early 80s when he passed through the region in search of gold. Juan was an honored guest when Lorenzo's daughter married. As stated above, *Ojitos Frios*, as the crow flies, was not that far from *La Monilla*, where the Padilla clan resided. Family and neighbor were important concepts tied to traditional core values, yet such bonds could also prove troublesome, especially when everyone did not share the same values or beliefs.[42]

In the latter part of the 1880s, the Knights of Labor began to offer legal assistance to Hispano farmers concerned with protecting their pastures on the Las Vegas grant. They did this through an organization called the

"Las Vegas Land Grant Association." Union chapters also started making contact with wageworkers. Efforts to organize bubbled along while Judge Long struggled to come to a decision on *Milhiser* v. *Padilla*.[43]

Like his father, Juan José was a man of influence. He too had served the United States military. He could speak both French and English. It is also possible he knew some native dialects, since while up north he had worked as an Indian agent in several territories. At some point, he married Luisa Pinard, a young French woman, possibly the daughter of pioneers from La Cueva, a settlement near Mora. Sometime before 1866, he apparently left her, because in 1867, the *Santa Fe Weekly* wrote about it. It is rather telling that a newspaper in the capital would write about a man leaving his wife in the Las Vegas area. What was written is not the point. That it was written about at all is. Juan José was a marked man by those who opposed him long before he began to assemble union chapters on the grant. Oddly enough, twenty-five years later, newspapers were still writing about Herrera's past marital problems. In 1891, an unflattering poem about Juan José Herrera was published, one stanza declaring, "he is the same nobody who abandoned the French lady . . ."[44]

That Herrera's separation from his wife was still a newsworthy event a quarter-of-a-century after it happened reveals something of the times and the man. He obviously maintained an aura about him that some felt inclined to denigrate. In Territorial New Mexico, men not afraid to express their beliefs occasionally found themselves within an editorialist's cross-hairs. This was the case with Juan José Herrera.

When Juan José returned from Colorado and settled with relatives southwest of Las Vegas, he found himself situated next to the Black Tree Trunk Ranch. It was not long before his disgruntled neighbor accused him of cutting up his fence. In reply to this accusation Herrera stuffed him in a rain barrel. When José Ygnacia Lujan expressed a similar opinion a couple of years later, only by turning his horse and riding away did he escape a similar fate. In 1887, union activity began to spike in San Miguel County. Local chapters of the Knights of Labor started cropping up all over the region. Herrera proved to be a proficient organizer and a natural leader. During the Civil War, he was promoted to captain of the Fourth Infantry, Company D, New Mexico Volunteers. He served the Union cause alongside many of the Hispano farmers and ranchers with whom he was now becoming reacquainted. By 1888, with the help of brothers Nicanor and Pablo, twenty new chapters of the Knights of Labor were created. These new groups were scattered from Santa Fe to Mora, spreading the union's message through the mountains. At the same time, under the cover of darkness, much of the barbed-wire that had lately been strung across the commons was destroyed. The victims of these acts, usually Anglo-American cattlemen, suspected the growth of unionism was contributing to the destruction of private property on the grant.[45]

The year Milhiser filed his suit, such incidents had almost become commonplace. Fence cutting was attributed to a group of riders that roamed the countryside after the sun went down. They hid their identity by covering their faces with parts of white sheets or scarves, and were known to wear white hats. *Nuevo-mexicanos* called these men *Las Gorras Blancas*. The *Las Vegas Optic* preferred the English version of this name, White Caps. *Las Gorras Blancas* were presumably an organized group of several hundred *nuevo-mexicanos* who visited landowners they believed were trying to take over the *ejido*. Both Anglo-American and Hispano landowners felt the wrath of these men. Of sixty-nine recorded acts of destruction attributed to *Las Gorras Blancas*, at least eighteen were perpetrated upon Hispanos who, like the Anglo-Americans, were trying to claim a portion of the *ejido* as their own.[46]

Such gatherings and acts of destruction were not unique to San Miguel County. Throughout the history of the United States, small groups of rural citizens had taken matters into their own hands when they believed their government was not concerned with, or capable of, protecting their property rights. After the Civil War, ex-Confederates in Missouri could not stand to see men who had sympathized with the North appointed sheriff. Deep-seated fears based on both real and imagined injustices drove them to form alliances against new authority figures. Many of the new officers singled out old adversaries and settled perceived injustices which had occurred during the conflict. These retributions led to outbreaks of violence in pockets of Missouri. In the spring of 1893, small farmers and ranchers in Oklahoma took it upon themselves to revolt against U.S. Deputy Marshals after many of their neighbors were arrested for refusing to pay extortion fees to keep their property. It was perceived by the locals that marshals sent down to ensure land was allocated fairly, used their position to acquire the best parcels in the region for themselves. Locals were also forced to pay under-the-table bribes to acquire land of any value. During the same period, small-time Texas ranchers with herds of around twenty cattle or less continually joined with their neighbors to cut down fencing which farmers and large cattle outfits had installed across the prairies. The "cowboys" detested anyone who put up a fence, as they enjoyed the free range and were bound to keep it just that. Men were shot. Only after the Texas Rangers infiltrated their organizations and arrested their ringleaders did the destruction stop. In all regions of the country, support for such resistance was usually strongest where the majority of people living there did not believe local government was capable of, or chose not to provide, honest and competent representation for all.[47]

The Las Vegas chapter of the Knights of Labor wrote a letter to their national leader, Terence Vincent Powderly. They wanted to give Powderly a sense of what men in Las Vegas associated with the Santa Fe Ring were up to. Such men, they wrote, were "entrenching themselves behind technical forms of law in the possession of vast tracts of community grant land. . . ." Just as it was no secret to many cattlemen that local *nuevo-mexicanos* were involved with *Las Gorras Blancas*, rural farmers and ranchers on the grant were keenly aware that many of the lawyers, surveyor generals and land speculators in San Miguel County were working in such combinations to wrest their land away from them.[48]

As troubles on the grant mounted, deep in the mountains, the Penitente religious chapters thrived. Years earlier, when the Mexican bishop tried to reassert the Church's authority in the region, the Penitentes were instrumental in organizing resistance to such efforts. Since first visiting New Mexico in the early part of the 1830s, Mexican Bishop Zubiría had implemented what he thought were several innovative ways to make isolated churches viable, including requiring fees for certain priestly practices, such as overseeing burial and marriage ceremonies. At the same time, the Mexican government began to enforce the Departmental Plan, which was their way of trying to funnel more money into empty national coffers. They did this by instituting direct taxes upon New Mexico citizens, something which had never been attempted in the northern province.[49]

A decade before annexation, *nuevo-mexicanos* felt trapped between new government policies and Zubiría's edicts. The Chimayó Rebellion began after a centralist official authorized the removal of the Santa de la Cañada *alcalde* from office. This *alcalde* fired Juan José Esquibel after accusing him of nepotism. This created an outcry which erupted into full-blown violence. Factions of *mestizos*, creoles and Pueblo Indians joined together, each angered by the Mexicans for different reasons. Hispano parishioners put a gun to the head of a local priest and demanded he allow burials within the church. The Durango diocese's new restrictions to ancient, religious rituals created a flashpoint in the region. Bishop Zubiría actions were partly fashioned as a response to the growing influence of the Penitentes in Northern New Mexico. He wanted to eliminate them as a force in the mountain villages of the Rio Arriba highlands. He started by trying to reassert priests' authority where the Brotherhood had moved into the breach that was created when so many Spanish padres left after Mexican Independence.[50]

It is important to note why *nuevo-mexicanos*, both traditional Catholics and Penitentes, were so angry about the burial restrictions. Although they were implemented because Zubiría was concerned with the health of the parishioners, the bishop failed to anticipate or understand what the ramifications of such a policy might be. Many rural Hispanos believed salvation of a loved one's soul was contingent upon how close their burial site was to the altar. To be near this holy place, where the faithful communed with God, was of the highest priority. It was the responsibility of those left behind to nurture the souls of the departed. To have this sacred ritual denied them was, to many, a sacrilegious event.[51]

Manuel Martinez recalled that the Penitente chapter of Tecolote de Rincon, which became Rociada, was called the "Society of Father Jesus." Louis Bustos, whose ancestors first settled the same valley, recalled it was a secret brotherhood. If you wanted to join, you had to go and see the *hermano mayor* (major brother). "The faith we all have being Catholics and helping each other out in time of need is a part of our tradition . . . " In the 1890s, the Penitentes still reaffirmed the villages' cultural values and anchored mountain communities with grit, resolve, and a faith independent, yet closely tied to, the Roman Catholics. Like most people of faith, troubled times did not always fracture them, indeed, crisis brought many Hispanos on the grant together. As Juan José Herrera's union activities came to life, so did the local *moradas*.[52]

Such gathering places were scattered throughout the grant. In the company of outsiders, *nuevo-mexicanos* might appear as stoic, seen as respectful, or perhaps docile. Yet if such people were docile, how had they withstood Apache raids, Comanche depredations, and Spanish indifference for over a century? It was not true. Forty years after rebelling against Bishop Zubiría, they chafed at Protestant missionaries' negative assumptions about their faith, they chafed at the French bishop who tried to reassert power over local churches, and they chafed at the surveyors who stretched chains across their valleys. Juan Gomez-Quiñones argues the secret Penitente brotherhood was key to the success of *Las Gorras Blancas*. Both groups were strongest in the mountain villages, where they moved effortlessly between communities, relaying information, and keeping watch over each other's property. As farmers and ranchers, they met after nightfall, usually within the *moradas*, and discussed the changing events on the grant. Prominent in this period's discussions would have been the plight of José Padilla and his brothers. Their struggle was every rural Hispano's struggle. For two years, *Milhiser* v. *Padilla* simmered, brewing a precarious blend of anxiety and anger between most everyone in Las Vegas. Concurrently, authority figures in Las Vegas and Santa Fe played a shell-game with the Court of Private Land Claims over common lands and the public domain. The federal government seemed to approve Surveyor General Julian's goal of carving the *ejido* into thousands of real estate allotments. All the while, Hispanos continued to practice the faith of their fathers, yet now, although they may have entered the chapter houses as agrarians and shepherds, they sometimes left as something else. Issues on the grant were far from settled.[53]

On 3 April 1889, a few months before *Milhiser* vs. *Padilla* was finally resolved, an article ran in the *Las Vegas Optic* that reported what had happened to a group of Tuscola, Illinois officials who were trying to push through the construction of a drainage canal across some of their constituents' property. In the middle of the night, a legislator's barn was burned to the ground. The article called the perpetrators "white caps." About three weeks later, something similar happened on the Las Vegas grant. By early fall, twenty-one locals had been indicted for fence cutting. On 19 November

1889, the first defendant was found not guilty by a jury of his peers. Based on this, Judge James O'Brien, in charge of this proceeding, dismissed the charges on the remaining twenty.[54]

While Judge Elisha V. Long reviewed Colonel Johnson's report, fences continued to go up on the *ejido*. One morning in late April, four miles of Englishmen William Rawlins' and Frank Quarrel's new barbed-wire fence was found cut to pieces. On a different trip to the same property, one of the Englishmen's workers was shot in the leg. His horse was also killed. On another trip to the same property, farm machinery was destroyed. Not long after that, authorities indicted twenty-six men for the destruction of private property on the Las Vegas Land Grant. That summer, in the middle of the night, José Ygancia Lujan was visited three times by the *Las Gorras Blancas*. His farm equipment was destroyed and his fences were cut to pieces. Another time, Lujan's barn was burned to the ground. These were not vague warnings or threats. The last had precipitated his visit to *Ojito Frios*. Many times *Las Gorras Blancas* would first issue a letter to the landowner explaining what would happen if he did not comply with their demands. Such warnings included the simple order that they remove barbed-wire from the *ejido*. If ignored, bad things happened. Barns became smoking heaps of rubble. Expensive farm equipment was destroyed. Although it was rare that someone got hurt, everyone carried guns. Rawlins and Quarrel's employee could attest that they occasionally went off.[55]

Based on previous decisions handed down by the American court system, many *nuevo-mexicanos* anticipated that Judge Long would favor Philip Milhiser and the Las Vegas Land and Cattle Company. They were fed up. On November 1, sixty-three armed *nuevo-mexicanos* rode their horses into Las Vegas and surrounded the courthouse. Their faces covered, the *Gorras Blancas* made it a point to visit Miguel Salazar, the prosecuting attorney, and then paraded around the Plaza, deliberately passing the jail. Judge Long was infuriated by the display, but refused to let it affect his decision regarding Milhiser's suit. He had personal opinions about those masquerading through town but could not control what happened in the streets. District attorney Salazar and others branded the riders "communists" and "anarchists." Yet locals' premonitions about the trial's outcome were wrong. Milhiser lost his case. Hispanos celebrated the decision as a victory over usurpation, yet the owner of the Las Vegas Land and Cattle and Company was not ready to relinquish his quest. The day after the horsemen paraded through town, the last session of the year for the district court, Salazar filed twenty-six new indictments, implicating forty-six men "from 20 to 65," for the destruction of property on the grant.[56]

As it turned out, Judge Elisha V. Long had based his ruling on more than his interpretation of the facts, or Mexican law. The judge's abhorrence of *Las Gorras Blancas* colored his reasoning. He found it repugnant to rule in favor of anyone who wanted fences removed from the grant. Long's desire to wag a finger in the face of the night-rider's defiance impacted his decision. What Milhiser demanded of the Padillas was exactly what rural Hispanos demanded of cattleman Wilson Waddingham and Anglo-American newcomers who believed the grant was private property subject to fencing. Ultimately, as events played out, the ruling hurt Hispano efforts to hold on to the grant.

As mentioned above, when Judge Long named the "town of Las Vegas" as the controlling authority of the commons, he did not define what "town" meant. This opened a path for future arguments. As a result of the Industrial Age, Las Vegas contained an Old Town, and a New Town. The original settlement which grew up around the Plaza was not incorporated, therefore was never legally considered a "town." In defense of Judge Long, the court only required that he determine if Milhiser had the right to force Padilla to remove his fences so he could graze cattle there. This is what the judge ruled on, nothing more. Prior to the official ruling, Philip Milhiser got wind of what Long's decision was going to be and tried to have the suit dropped. Stephen B. Elkins and Thomas B. Catron were also livid with judge. They feared lands won in other partition suits might be jeopardized, setting a precedent. It was too late for that. The results of *Milhiser* v. *Padilla* would contribute to a decrease in illegal fencing of the grant, regardless of Judge Long's intentions, but as 1889 came to a close, anyone with barbed-wire strung across the commons still had reason to be concerned.[57]

In the late fall of 89, while both sides waited for the judge's decision, many of the leaders within the Knights of Labor were beginning to transition some of their organizational skills into the new political party that was forming in San Miguel County. After Long's ruling became public, lingering animosities continued to stoke Old Town Hispano and East Las Vegas

Anglo-American emotions. Rancor and suspicion colored the atmosphere throughout both communities as the new-year approached.

Juan José Herrera denied any complicity in the destructive acts being played out around Las Vegas. Many Anglo-Americans, including the editor of the *Las Vegas Optic*, believed otherwise. Referred to in an editorial as "Captain Herrera," the first paragraph of one article named him as, "the reputed leader of the white caps [lower case]." While admitting Herrera denied the title, *The Optic* continued: "This paper has no desire to persecute or unjustly charge Herrera with crimes that have lately been committed . . . but there is no denying the fact that he is generally charged with being the instigator and the leader and the state of outlawry is charged to him." The same article reminded its readership that it was illegal for anyone to wear firearms in public unless they felt threatened and described what constituted an unlawful assembly.[58]

Although what was considered lawful for some and unlawful for others might seem foggy to many on the grant, it was clear that Herrera was a talented organizer, and had put those skills to use in San Miguel County. He was trilingual. His knowledge of the American legal system made him indispensable to groups looking for advice on how to confront and stop the partition suit in New Mexico. Although most Hispano Las Vegans believed the destruction of fences was warranted, Herrera swore he was not part of violence that involved innocents. The *Las Vegas Optic* challenged him to prove it. To this newspaper and many businessmen in Las Vegas, it seemed obvious that various members of the Knights of Labor, Penitente clans, and *Las Gorras Blancas* were inter-mixed. That Herrera led one of the movements, yet had nothing to do with their less visible counter-parts was hard for some to believe. [59]

In the last decade of the nineteenth century, citizens were faced with more than land grant problems. In 1890, both the benefits and the by-products of the Industrial Age were present on the grant. As with most territorial boomtowns, Las Vegas had its share of murderers, thieves and rustlers to deal with. Criminal elements lurked in the saloons and around the depot, awaiting opportunities to divest honest patrons of their cash, and sometimes, their lives. The *Las Vegas Optic* occasionally opined that law enforcement had been tainted by graft, and was just as likely to look the other way during a crime as jail the perpetrators. Hyman G. Neill, a.k.a. Hoodoo Brown, was a proprietor of a gambling joint in East Las Vegas before becoming its first Justice of the Peace. During the first rash of fence cuttings, Sheriff Lorenzo Lopez of Old Town worked to stop such destruction, but later affiliated himself with leaders of the new political movement. After a falling out with brother-in-law Eugenio Romero, he was cast by fellow Republicans as corrupt; a straw man for Herrera and Vicente Silva.[60]

Vincente Silva also ran a saloon in town. It was purported to operate as a front for illegal activities. Silva led a gang of cattle rustlers and felons who congregated in his establishment while awaiting orders, contributing to the atmosphere of lawlessness which pervaded much of Las Vegas after the arrival of the railroad. Miguel A. Otero Jr. claimed Silva's gang, known as the *Sociedad de Bandidos*, was involved with both *Las Gorras Blancas* and the liberal political party that had formed in San Miguel County. Once Sheriff Lopez abandoned the Republicans, Otero cast him and Herrera in the same light as Silva's thieves. It should not come as much of a surprise that the former territorial governor did this, as he was a rising star in the statewide Republican Party machine, attending its national convention as a delegate in 1888. His father had been one of the most powerful *patrónes* in the Southwest, and Otero Jr. had inherited the mantle. Owner of the San Miguel State Bank and the largest wholesale operation in New Mexico, he stood to lose much from any movement that derided and cast aspersions on Republican ideals.[61]

Events on the grant let to a political atmosphere conducive to backstabbing, yellow journalism, and grandstanding politicians. That some of Silva's henchman rode with *Las Gorras Blancas* does not damn the majority of the local farmers and ranchers who participated in the uprising. Commonfolk were driven to join because of an honest desire to protect their own property. No matter the revolution, whether in Concord or Mexico City, criminals participated. It should come as no shock that all did not serve a higher cause. A percentage of thieves have always participated in battles, sometimes because they happened to be in the vicinity or simply because there was an opportunity to capitalize on events as they unfolded. Even so, adversaries of such movements are prone to use such ne'er do wells as prime examples of the types of citizens involved in revolts to dissuade the majority from joining such a low crowd. Yet regardless of what the *Las Vegas Optic* printed, or Eugenio Romero or Jefferson Raynolds claimed, most rural *nuevo-mexicanos* knew better. Bad guys were drawn to boomtowns. Silva was a criminal. Juan José Herrera was a hero. They knew the difference, and said so with their actions.

Herrera linked the various villages together by using his communication and leadership skills, emphasizing what he knew to be true; that mountain communities were not isolated enclaves, if properly organized could speak as one voice, and that the people living on the grant were not easily intimidated. As the labor union grew, other *nuevo-mexicanos* found ways to step forward, joining in the growing protests against land encroachment. The independent *El Partido del Pueblo Unido* political party was created out of the growth of this movement. It was in response to Republican goals and designs that it became so popular. One man involved in its success was Felix Martinez.[62]

Martinez, who had vouched for José Padilla and sold him land, was from Mora, about twenty-five miles to the north. He began his education there, studying at St. Mary's Christian Brotherhood School for five years. By the time he was fourteen, Martinez was working in Colorado as a grocery clerk. While there, he took a private commercial business course that he used to great advantage, working for a variety of merchants in Colorado. When the Atchison, Topeka, and Santa Fe began to lay tracks to the south, the young businessman followed them over the Raton Pass, through Wagon Mound, and on to various other stops before arriving in Las Vegas in 1879. Within a year, he met and married a young lady from Virginia, named co-incidentally enough, Virginia Buster. He partnered with Simon E. Clements in the retail trade business for several years, establishing himself as an engaging, enterprising young man who seemed to be going places. In 1886, Felix Martinez entered local politics. Although Republicans dominated most positions of local power, as a Democrat, he was elected County Assessor. Not one to let dust collect under his boots, he also started a real estate operation that year, one that would eventually prove to be quite successful. Two years after his first political victory, Felix Martinez was elected to the Territorial Legislative Assembly, a post he would hold with some distinction until 1890. As impressive as these accomplishments were, the thirty-three-year-old Martinez was just getting started.[63]

Felix Martinez. Las Vegas newspaper pub-
lisher and one of the founders of El Partido del
Pueblo. From the Collection of the Las Vegas
Citizen's Committee for Historic Preservation.

Like a lot of politicians, Felix Martinez knew words could be weapons, and if you participated in New Mexico politics, it was best to come armed. In 1890, he purchased a share of the Santa Fe newspaper, *La Voz del Pueblo* (The Voice of the People) from Nestor Montoya and E. H. Salazar, and then moved it to Las Vegas. In 1894, Salazar would begin another paper in Las Vegas, *El Independiete*. There was much to write about.[64]

By 1890, the two towns of Las Vegas were not strangers to the printed word. Forty-four newspapers attempted to garner this town's attention be-tween 1879 and 1900. Shortly after Judge Long decided *Milhiser v. Padilla*, the combined population of Las Vegas was 5,697. By 1890, a large, diverse community was in place. Events on the grant and such a population provided an opportunity to capture subscriptions. Anyone with political aspirations or strong opinions tried to influence the local newspapers. If that proved unsuc-cessful many funded or started papers of their own. Jefferson Raynolds was chief stockholder in the short-lived Republican driven, *Daily Gazette* and the *Gazette Publishing Company*. Fellow Republican J. A. Carruth published the

Free Press, ran a weekly called the *Examiner*, and published the *New Mexico Livestock Journal*. As an indication of the lengths those in power would go to influence such people in the 1890s, several publishers received supplemental income from being appointed to choice local positions as reward for the favorable comments they placed in their newspapers about specific candidates or issues. Such was J. A. Carruth's good fortune. He was hired as the local postmaster by county administrators.[65]

In the latter part of the nineteenth century, putting out a newspaper on a regular basis was hard work and time consuming. As an example, it took two men at least eight hours to create a four-page publication with 1,000 subscribers. Felix Martinez launched his Spanish language *La Voz del Pueblo* on the northeast corner of Douglas Avenue and Eighth Street. He began with two assistants. One, Ezequiel C. de Baca, would later become Governor of New Mexico. The second, Antonio Lucero, became its first Secretary of State. These talented men wrote in defense of the Las Vegas Land Grant, against the likes of the Santa Fe Ring, Republican cronyism, Thomas B. Catron, and men people called "land grabbers." The combined talents of these three *nuevo-mexicanos*, working together in common cause, may be unmatched in New Mexico history.[66]

Vitriolic headlines and damning editorials in defense of party positions were nothing new in Las Vegas, or within any other nineteenth century American newspaper. On the approach of the railroad, the *Revista Católica*, as far back as 2 February 1878, urged Hispano politicians to join together: "What is there about Democrats and Republicans? BE MEXICANS." This cry, originally printed in Spanish, was translated a week later by the *Santa Fe Weekly*. It was well known that a group of Jesuits ran the *Revista Católica*. Led by Father Gasparri, these men were referred to by the *Santa Fe Weekly* as, "Italian refugees . . ." On 20 November 1879, the *Las Vegas Optic* wrote: "East Las Vegas is an American town and will be governed by Americans only!" Certain strains of American nativism began to emerge deep within the heart a country that only a few short decades earlier had been a part of the Republic of Mexico. As 1889 came to a close, Spanish and English newspaper editors reveled in the use of exhortations and exclamation points.[67]

Reverend Donato M. Gasparri. From
Twitchell, *The Leading Facts of New Mexican
History*, vol. 2.

As stated above, after learning which way Judge Long was leaning,
and fearing the impact of such a decision on the region, Philip Milhiser
attempted to withdraw his suit, but it was too late. To corroborate his ruling,
in 1890 Judge Long presented fifty-eight pages of his notes along with his
findings to J. A. Carruth, who published the complete record of the trial,
along with a history of the grant, in pamphlet form. Milhiser, along with
many of his East Las Vegas cohorts, failed in their attempt to prevent future
settlement on the commons. Long's decision had refused to acknowledge
that a select few held exclusive rights to the entire grant, nor could Milhiser
or anyone else claim a portion of the *ejido* as their own. Even so, this did not
stop him from continuing to file suits and pester the U.S. government to act
in his favor. In light of the judge's decision, Philip Milhiser and his backers
took a new tact in the coming year. After a review of Long's reasoning, they
next petitioned the U.S. Secretary of the Interior to issue a patent for the Las
Vegas Land Grant, basing their claims on Judge Long's ruling against the
Las Vegas Land and Cattle Company. I will review these strategies and their
results in the final chapter.[68]

Las Gorras Blancas were pleased yet wary with the trial's outcome. Although fence cutting slowed for a time, newcomers remained confident American courts would eventually acknowledge that the *ejido* was a part of public domain. Such beliefs encouraged settlers to purchase carved out portions of the commons from land speculators, which irritated local *nuevo-mexicanos* enough to spur a new round of destruction. The nightriders once again dropped leaflets of warning. They demanded the removal of all barbed-wire on the commons. Circulars broadcast around town and the surrounding villages called for *nuevo-mexicanos* to stand up for their rights. Max Nordhaus, who earlier testified for Philip Milhiser and was now merchant Charles Ilfeld's general manager, writing to Ilfeld's sheep ranch foreman Max Goldberg, illustrated the concerns citizens held in regard to *Las Gorras Blancas*: "White Caps are cutting all fences in the neighborhood . . . Pastures . . . unsafe." *Las Gorras Blancas* agitated Hispano railway workers. They urged them to fight for wages equal to their Anglo-American counterparts and strike if they were denied. After winter's cold winds gave way to the spring of 1890, highly coordinated attacks once again spread across the grant. The night raiders wore white masks and carried wooden whistles to signal each other. The Penitentes also carried small wooden flutes, called *pitos*.[69]

Nuevo-mexicano railway workers on the Las Vegas grant. From the Collection of the Las Vegas Citizens' Committee for Historic Preservation.

One night, on his way home from town, wealthy Republican stalwart and *jéfe politico* Eugenio Romero found himself surrounded by three-hundred masked riders. He claimed they were "armed to the teeth." They demanded he take down his fences or suffer the consequences. He had been confronted by such men before. Hispano Francisco Manzanares also felt their wrath. Manzanares owned a wholesale operation that had had made good with the coming of the railroad. He distributed local produce and goods to St. Louis and the East Coast. Two miles east of town, *Las Gorras Blancas* cut down his fences. That same spring, three witnesses did not show up to testify against the forty-seven men District Attorney Alverez had charged with fence destruction in 1889. Presiding Judge James O'Brien dropped the charges.[70]

On the day the trial was to begin, everyone that had been indicted, including the Herrera brothers, showed up to face their accusers. After the judge dropped the charges, while onlookers emptied out of the courtroom, District Attorney Salazar stared in disbelief as an impromptu celebration broke out. He claimed his witnesses had been murdered. A victory parade that included much of the general population marched to the Plaza. A few shot off guns and passed around whiskey. It was clear where most Hispanos on the grant stood regarding *Las Gorras Blancas*.[71]

Two months later, as grass-roots resentment against land encroachment continued to bubble to the surface, the same Judge O'Brien that dropped this case wrote a letter to Governor Prince, expressing his views on why fences continued to be torn down. The governor continued to keep an ear turned toward Las Vegas because officials in Washington D.C. were asking questions. The Secretary of the Interior was also cognizant of the problems there, having heard the grumblings of speculators. "To a casual and impartial observer," O'Brien wrote, "ignorant of antecedent causes, the so-called outrages are the protests of a simple, pastoral people against the establishment of large landed estates, or baronial feudalism in their native territory. The term 'White Cap' when used in any other sense, is in my opinion, a misnomer."[72]

On the opposite side of the spectrum, one man wrote to his newspaper, calling the fence cutters "a lawless mob of Mexicans." Coincidentally or not, on 5 April, the *Optic* inserted a supposed educational treatise on local Penitentes calling them, "superstitious fanatics . . ." and writing, "this very class is usually the rabble element of the community." On 14 April 1890, the same paper expressed the opinions of both sides. "Land grabbers," an editorial noted, "who have fenced miles and miles . . . need not look to the *Optic* for sympathy and help in your grabbing schemes." Yet in the same edition it denounced the violence attributed to the "White Caps." Another paper, run by a disgruntled E. H. Salazar of the *Sol de Mayo*, later printed, "that in the end, the White Caps would be found to be the enemy of the people."[73]

Politics, the old cliché goes, oftentimes makes strange bedfellows. Although they followed different paths to leadership, Juan José Herrera and Felix Martinez formed the heart and soul of the new party. Although they were not always on the same page, their similar goals allowed them to work together. According to Miguel Otero Jr., Juan's brother Pablo once served time for murder, but he was still later elected to the territorial legislature's House of Representatives. In 1891, while in the Imperial Saloon, the Herrera brothers got into a bar fight. Two of their adversaries in this brawl were father and son. The son was killed during this melee. A warrant was later issued for Pablo's arrest. On Christmas Eve, a posse of locals caught up with ex-representative. He was shot to death while attempting to escape.[74]

As the new political movement gained its legs in the first quarter of 1890, anyone upset with the way things were being run in Las Vegas were invited to join in, including Anglo laborers and ex-Republicans. F. A. Blake, H. M. Loeb, and T. B. Mills were some of the most prominent Anglo-Americans to join *El Partido del Pueblo*. Regardless of who joined, its base remained *nuevo-mexicano* villagers intent on protecting their common lands. One of the most prominent town leaders to join *El Partido del Pueblo* was the county sheriff and ex-brother-in-law of Eugenio Romero, Lorenzo Lopez. His defection indicated a serious breach had occurred within the San Miguel County Republican power-structure.[75]

The Voice of the People

My wife's father, he tells me when this man Pendaries put up a fence at the edge of the ditch. He came to collect signatures so he could fence a section that was public domain and the people did not give him any signatures. We used to pasture cattle there and Pendaries and other gringos came and they fenced it all in. So that land is ours. But they have the fence.[1]

When Eugenio married Ascension Lopez in 1856, their families' combined power equaled or surpassed any in New Mexico. Trinidad Romero's proposal to Valeria Lopez and their marriage added more weight to this unspoken fact. Lorenzo Lopez's roots, like Eugenio's, ran deep on the Las Vegas Land Grant. While Ascension and Valeria's brother admired the Romeros, he did not necessarily believe his sisters were marrying up. A landowner of some reknown, Lorenzo considered himself equal in stature to any of the Romeros, and was not awed by their successes. Both Lorenzo and Eugenio served as county sheriffs. During the height of the grant's troubles, Lorenzo Lopez held the title. In 1888, after thirty-two years of marriage, Ascension died, leaving Eugenio Romero a widower. It is unknown what effect, if any, Ascension's death had on either man's future actions, yet their relationship, never rock-solid, soon took a turn for the worse. In May of the following year, Sheriff Lopez began to serve the first arrest warrants on *nuevo-mexicanos* charged with the barn-burnings and fence-cuttings in San Miguel County.[2]

As clouds full of snow enveloped the nearby mountains, two seemingly unrelated events occurred that affected many people on the grant. In December, eighty tons of Sheriff Lopez's hay was set on fire. Additionally, eleven miles of his fence was destroyed. Eugenio Romero remarried, taking Deluvina R. de Romero as his new bride. By 1890, a rumor had spread across the county charging Sheriff Lopez with joining the *Gorras Blancas*. Within this same loop of gossip was the information that Lopez was a practicing Penitente. Amid arrest warrants, deaths, remarriage, and fiery infernos of hay, the simmering rift that had been developing between Eugenio Romero and Lorenzo Lopez broke into the open. The county sheriff bolted the Republican Party, throwing in his lot with the leaders of *El Partido del Pueblo*.[3]

While Felix Martinez and Juan José Herrera worked to galvanize their various constituencies in San Miguel County, statewide internal bickering among other *nuevo-mexicano* politicians poisoned efforts to find enough consensus to get a state constitution approved. One of the main bones of contention remained consenting to a non-parochial school system. As recently as the fall of 1889, a new state constitution was presented in Santa Fe for ratification. As David J. Weber points out, Hispanos always out-registered and out-voted Anglo newcomers, so the fact that so many territorial legislatures had failed to reach an agreement in the past revealed the fractious nature of the New Mexican political community. That year, another resolution to form a state constitution failed.[4]

San Miguel County was involved in these political difficulties, yet *El Partido del Pueblo* found a way to get its constituents to act as one. Felix Martinez was a strong advocate of the people and fierce defender of the common lands. While Lorenzo Lopez contemplated the loss of his sister and ruminated over the thousands of acres that it had taken to produce eighty tons of hay, Martinez continued to use *La Voz del Pueblo* and the power of language to claim the moral high ground, branding speculators and cattlemen as "land grabbers," a phrase which became the pejorative catchword throughout the region in the 1890s. Yet Martinez's ideas about the future of New Mexico were not so deep-rooted in past traditions that he could not contemplate an occasional compromise. He had always been a proponent of the American political system, yet only as long as it lived up to its constitutional ideals. He was adamant that *nuevo-mexicanos* receive fair representation. He believed in a strong education system that included non-secular instruction. He advocated introducing American technologies into

New Mexico, but only as a way to introduce opportunity for all. Martinez was willing to compromise with Anglo-Americans as long as they offered to meet him halfway, and believed such a path was the only one that would ever lead to statehood. His name was not associated with *Las Gorras Blancas*. In fact, on one occasion, his fences were torn down.[5]

La Voz del Pueblo in the early part of the twentieth century. This newspaper was located on the corner of Douglas and 8th Street. From the Collection of the Las Vegas Citizens' Committee for Historic Preservation.

Juan José Herrera saw the advantages of joining forces with men such as Martinez, but disagreed with them on key points. Herrera did not trust Anglo-Americans. At fifty-four, he had seen much abuse and corruption in Territorial New Mexico. He warned Martinez and other progressive young Hispanos that it was a mistake to assume Americans would hold to any compromise. Herrera was always on the move, a doer, someone who thought if you stayed in the same place too long, trusted anyone too much, or waited on others too long before taking action, your chance of being put at a disadvantage increased. Juan José was suspect of any promise power brokers made. He knew from experience gained in Colorado that trust was a valuable resource that should only rarely be expended. Herrera was leery of promises. The Las Vegas Land Grant, Herrera argued, was a community grant, and belonged to everyone who lived there. The common lands were not private property that could be sold or fenced. Everyone had a right to graze sheep in the valley or take wood from the forest. He argued the commons was the peoples' land, not the incorporated town of East Las Vegas'. He asked if the city of Denver owned its surrounding land, or any other town for that matter.[6]

The main bone of contention between Herrera and Martinez was how the Las Vegas Land Grant should be governed. Martinez was agreeable to an appointed board that looked after the needs of the people. He did not have a problem with such a group allotting future parcels for new homes or determining how the grant's resources could best be used to benefit *nuevomexicanos* living there. Herrera disagreed with this concept. No board, he argued, should ever be allowed to tell someone living on the grant what he or she could, or could not do with the natural resources God had allocated to that region of New Mexico.[7]

By late spring, not long after the winter snows began to recede into the higher elevations of the Sangre de Cristo Range, emotional wounds and angers aroused in the fall of 1889 began fester and rise up again. Throughout the spring of 1890, acts of destruction, threats and counter-threats, accusations of conspiracy and underhandedness continued. In March, several hundred masked men rode their horses through town, dropping more leaflets around the Plaza and throughout the area, again communicating their concerns and positions on land grant issues. North of Las Vegas and east of Mora, cattleman Wilson Waddingham received a letter of warning to take down his fences or face the consequences. As mentioned above, the *Las Vegas Optic* challenged "Captain Herrera," to prove he was not the leader of *Las Gorras Blancas*. Within a few days, he did, sending a typewritten response to the paper. The editor doubted Herrera was capable of putting together such a reply, even claiming in the headline, "Herrera at Last has a Letter Written for Him. . . . " yet in the interest of "fairness," published it on 7 April 1890. "I have noticed an article," Juan José wrote, "branding me as a dangerous man. I am satisfied [the accusation] . . . is but an outgrowth

[of] designing politicians . . . who through their corruption and mis-doings are the sole cause of the present discontent." Herrera denied he had ever harmed anyone who was innocent of wrong-doing. He also claimed: "While I was born in New Mexico, I rejoice in feeling that I am an American."[8]

Such was the atmosphere in Las Vegas when Governor Prince decided to attend the July 4 festivities on the Plaza. The night before, vespers, Jesús María Alarid led his string band through the streets of Las Vegas as the lead element of a procession that included 1,000 men, riding two-by-two through the town. On Independence Day, what *nuevo-mexicanos* came to call Festival, Nestor Montoya of *La Voz del Pueblo* championed the rights of the working man, accenting why so many had been a part of the previous night's parade. The *Caballeros del Trabajo*, or Knights of Labor, were well-represented on both 3 and 4 July. On the Fourth, Governor Prince surely shifted in his seat as each Herrera took the podium and hailed the valiant efforts of the Hispano laborer. He watched and listened to the crowd cheer Juan José Herrera's words and wondered if the best action might be none at all. He returned to Santa Fe knowing who the leaders of the movement were, and asked for help from the federal government. That proved to be a fruitless exercise. After the Fourth of July, fences continued to come down on the grant.[9]

On 4 August 1890, an article in the *Las Vegas Optic* reported on the negative impact of the nighttime raids upon the local economy. People were losing jobs and money. The Knights of Labor continued to agitate, arguing that log-cutters in the mountains deserved better wages and safer working conditions. The union convinced many of the laborers to strike. *El Partido del Pueblo* demanded timber companies stop deforesting the mountains. The Romero brothers owned some of these logging ventures. *Las Gorras Blancas* torched telephone poles slated for the Las Vegas Power and Light Company. Six-thousand railroad ties Eugenio Romero was to sell to the Atchison, Topeka, and Santa Fe were destroyed. As a result of these actions, the railroad company cancelled further contracts to procure ties in San Miguel County. Disruptions of railroad track construction due to such destruction got the attention of East Coast papers and investors on Wall Street. Local contractors estimated their losses to be at least 100,000 dollars.

An Albuquerque paper claimed the night raids and stoppages were the main reason New Mexico statehood kept getting denied. Business opportunities in Las Vegas began to dry up. Investors looked elsewhere.[10]

Jean Pendaries, his ranch surrounded by mountain villages, was surely aware and concerned with events on the grant, but his opinions were apparently not documented, or at least have not come to light. This may, in large part, be due to an obituary that appeared in the *Optic* on August 5. It announced that his fifty-seven year old wife Mathilde had unexpectedly passed away. As a possible explanation, the paper bluntly noted she was, "being quite fleshy and taking but little exercise." A Catholic service was held in town. Within days, while Pendaries and his family mourned, the cultures and ideologies that made up East Las Vegas and Old Town once again collided over control of the grant.[11]

In mid-August of 1890, an act that symbolized years of frustration and pressure due to the incremental land loss played out on the streets of Las Vegas. After emboldened masked men once again paraded their horses through town, leaving flyers that declared their intentions to protect the people and run encroachers off the grant, banker Jefferson Raynolds decided it was in his best interest to get both sides together and calm things down. The banker was no supporter of Herrera or Martinez but realized his own prosperity depended on Las Vegas' business vitality, which of late was poor. *Las Gorras Blancas* were instrumental in this economic decline. Outside business interests, including land speculators, had stopped putting their money in his bank. On 16 August 1890 he called a town meeting, inviting all interested parties to attend. The object was to find a way to put a stop to the bickering and ill will. L. Bradford Prince made a return appearance to Las Vegas for this meeting, which was probably not a good idea. Prince, pressured by Washington to get a handle on the situation, begged people in the room to come forward and help him put a stop to those who were terrorizing the countryside. Who were the men behind *Las Gorras Blancas*? He wanted names. He wanted arrests. He got neither. Much of what transpired seemed eerily similar to an earlier meeting held a few months earlier.[12]

Territorial Governor L. Bradford Prince. From Ralph Emerson Twitchell, *The Leading Facts of New Mexican History, vol. 2.*

One Saturday evening the previous March, men also came together to discuss the barn-burnings and other acts of destruction. Interpreters were recruited to translate what was being said during this meeting. Back in March, Jefferson Raynolds declared he wanted to create a Committee of Safety. He explained: "There is no doubt now that there exists among us a very dangerous element which has damaged every interest in the Territory, as well as San Miguel County and Las Vegas. It behooves every good citizen to have this fence-cutting and these commissions of other depredations stopped immediately."[13]

Both Felix Martinez and Juan José Herrera attended the March affair. Each spoke. Nestor Montoya translated what Martinez said into English: "The people are to rise in their might and squelch the land grabber as well as the fence-cutter, the fence-cutting was begun with the plea of giving people their rights. . . . The good decisions of a just judge was that the Vegas grant belonged to the town." The words that cut the deepest were reserved for the owner of the Las Vegas Land and Cattle Company. "The man Milhiser, is more than the community, because he is guarded by dogs . . . . Milhiser, under the protection of his bloodhounds, holds the community at bay. He, and other land grabbers are not greater than the mighty will of the people and should be ordered by the courts to vacate. Then there would be no fence cutting, but peace." Later, Herrera spoke in a similar vein, both men receiving a great deal of applause. Certain Anglo-American leaders were unable to get past the anger expressed by so many *nuevo-mexicanos*. By August, tensions had grown worse, leading to the territorial governor's demand for names.[14]

As the August meeting broke up, Felix Martinez and Philip Milhiser found themselves facing one another. Surely Milhiser was still irritated. His attempt to acquire *La Monilla* had been stopped by two of the men attending that meeting. They had received standing ovations for their efforts to disrupt his business plans. In August, Martinez once again spoke, referring to the "just judge," who must have been E. V. Long, and noted that Milhiser was "guarded by dogs." After the 16 August meeting broke up, Martinez and Milhiser got into an argument. Once again, Martinez called Philip Milhiser a "land grabber." Governor Prince was so appalled at his lack of response for names that he later requested U.S. troops be stationed in Las Vegas and requested that government agents infiltrate *Las Gorras Blancas*. Neither request was ever approved. Surprisingly, only words were flung the night of meeting, yet the next day the cattleman approached Felix Martinez on the streets of Las Vegas and threatened him. The publisher of the *La Voz del Pueblo*, normally known to be a reasonable man, took out his pistol and hit Philip Milhiser over the head with it.[15]

If there was one moment which defined this volatile period in San Miguel County, this was it. Most of the personalities that are a part of the fight for the Las Vegas Land Grant eventually fade from history, however prominent they might have been; Felix Martinez does not. In spite of this event, he will later be elected to the Territorial Council. He was instrumental in founding what would become New Mexico Highlands University. He served four years as the District Court Clerk for the Fourth Judicial District, became the point man in Las Vegas' acquisition of the state mental hospital, later owned and published the *El Paso Daily News* and the *Albuquerque Tribune*, and continued to run the *La Voz del Pueblo*. After moving to El Paso, he founded the El Paso and Southwestern Railroad Company, created and became Vice-President of the Southwestern Portland Cement Company, and served on the board of the First National Bank of El Paso. His greatest achievement, at least in the minds of many citizens of El Paso, was overseeing the creation of the Elephant Butte Dam in 1903. Felix Martinez was also utilized as a mediator in the Mexican Civil War and was serving on the Federal Reserve Board in Dallas, Texas, when he died in 1916. The accomplishments of this man are stunning and require a monograph of their own. Suffice to say his moment in the sun did not come when he hit Philip Milhiser on the head with the butt of his pistol. It is unknown, but doubtful that the cattleman was seriously injured. Since history indicates Milhiser threatened Martinez, it is unlikely he was arrested. Martinez promoted American ideals and believed *nuevo-mexicanos* must be allowed to take their rightful place as equal citizens in the United States. Even after leaving for El Paso, his Las Vegas paper would continue to have an impact on the area. Such violence might seem unusual for a man of Martinez's standing, yet that might be the key point to understanding how events unfolded the way they did. Rural common-folk were not violent by nature either, but the defiance most displayed when faced with losing their lands was not any more unusual than the reactions any community might exhibit under similar circumstances. Perhaps Martinez saw the future of San Miguel County in the cattleman's face and reacted.[16]

In October of that year, the newly submitted state constitution was voted down because most village *nuevo-mexicanos* were unwilling to accept the provision that provided for non-secular schools. The *Revista Católica* bragged that the common man had once again outsmarted the Protestant missionaries, old guard *ricos*, and Republicans.[17]

Yet the same spirit which killed ratification of the state constitution was just as instrumental in destroying Republican dominance in San Miguel County. In preparations for the upcoming county elections, Marcus Brunswick, treasurer of the Republican Party, looking for political contributions, wrote to Amsterdam cattleman Wilson Waddington, "if the People's Party is successful, I think they will tax everything high and take down more fences." In another letter, as the election approached, he noted of the raiding masked men, "It is all politics...This will stop when the election is over." When the election was over, *El Partido del Pueblo* had captured 60 percent of the vote, sweeping all the offices in the county. Thomas B. Catron, Eugenio and Trinidad Romero, and other Republicans were astonished that the *nuevo-mexicano* platform rooted in protecting Hispano property rights soundly defeated their candidates. What Martinez and Herrera had pulled off countered everything the Santa Fe Ring represented. In the San Miguel County elections of 1890, the men who had so adroitly manipulated land grant titles in New Mexico for decades were finally defeated.[18]

What would that mean for the future of Las Vegas and its people? Judge Elisha V. Long, in his decision, *Milhiser v. Padilla*, denied the cattleman's claim that his purchase of Sulzbacher's land included a representative percentage of the commons. Philip Milhiser and Thomas B. Catron believed it was illegal for anyone not owning an original portion of the grant to homestead on the commons. They sought "absolute ownership to undivided units of land to which no other party possessed any rights or privileges." Both believed the grant was already divided up and no future settlers should be allowed in. For perhaps the wrong reasons, Long disagreed. In a later court case, *Milhiser et al v. Jose Albino Baca et al.*, the persistent cattleman continued his assault on the grant. In his decision on this case, Judge James O'Brien ruled that any resident on the grant could gain title after living on the land for ten years. With Felix Martinez and fellow party members now in control of government offices, this was amended to five years. That meant a person who had lived on the grant for at least five years could gain title to his portion of it, regardless of whether he had previously secured legal ownership. The maximum amount of property a person could claim was 160 acres, the same as each of the Padilla brothers owned at *La Monilla*. From this case came the final declaration that no property owner could acquire a representative portion of the *ejido*. After the 1890 election, a political structure seemed to be in place that would represent everyday people. The need for *Las Gorras Blancas* diminished. Night raids trailed off. It is true some villagers were dissuaded from continuing such efforts because of the fear of being arrested, yet, as often happens, the success of the movement also contributed to its decline. During the decline, many transitioned from night riding to electioneering.[19]

Not surprisingly, although the People's Party claimed all the offices in the San Miguel County in both 1890 and 1892, the Republicans did not remain idle. Newspapers that fronted each constituency's position continued to lambaste the other. Another Spanish-language press, this one in direct opposition to the views of the *La Voz del Pueblo*, edited by Manuel C. de Baca and financed by Eugenio Romero, called *El Sol De Mayo*, continued to try to convince the locals that Felix Martinez, the Herrera brothers, and traitor Lorenzo Lopez were false prophets. To counter Romero's acquisition, Juan José Herrera purchased the Albuquerque *El Defensor del Pueblo* and, like Martinez, espoused the cause through the printed word. The competing newspapers ridiculed each's political stances, finding little common ground. Such printed diatribes by both parties fractionalized and diminished the community as a whole. Las Vegas continued to wane as a viable place to do business even after the violence stopped. The two town's splintered governments could not focus on the common good, and therefore were unable to come up with a strategic plan to combat the loss of revenue. A new rail distribution center operating through Texas, Tucumcari, and points west eliminated Las Vegas as a main rail-hub. Even so, later events did not cloud earlier accomplishments.[20]

In the late 1880s and early 90s, Juan José Herrera and his brothers combined several factions and communities into a coordinated, efficient organization which meshed with the beliefs of forward thinking men like Felix Martinez, whose paper, *The Voice of the People*, damned bossism and hailed the land rights of *nuevo-mexicanos*. People who thirsted for the partitioning of the Las Vegas grant, men like Philip Milhiser and Thomas B. Catron, would remain dry-mouthed a few more years. For a moment in time, the people were one, and their voices were heard.

Conclusion: Emotional History

A Fissured Memory

In 1905, Florencio Aragon, herding sheep along the Gallinas River, met several men carrying a host of chains and other equipment. They were surveyors working for the government. One of them told Florencio he would have to move his animals over the Ortiz Grant because he was on private property. The herder later met the cook for this party. The cook told Aragon the land now belonged to Las Vegas. Florencio said: "It was all a straight line . . . Each mile they got up a high stone marker." All the boundaries, he continued to repeat, were, "straight lines."[1]

Even today, straight lines are a foreign concept in New Mexico. The state is known for its geographic majesty, a land of curves and jagged edges, high peaks, and swirling waters. In such country, the horizon is fluid, one moment full of mountains, the next obliterated by fog and clouds, serenity and danger, all tied within the same knot. The landscapes' palate constantly adjusts to the motion of the earth. The sky becomes a deeper blue as the day slides by. Varying shades of violet, orange, and red paint the horizon as the sun falls behind the mountains. Hellish wind storms transform forests of serene ponderosa pines into dancing, rubbery stalks of mayhem. In such a region, one's imagination becomes a powerful force, opening itself to mystical concepts, one conducive to strong faith, loyalty, and love. *Nuevo-mexicanos* retain a relationship with their land that connects them to their God and their ancestors. William deBuys wrote: "In an unforgiving environment, small errors yield large consequences." I would add that such an environment stokes the souls of *nuevo-mexicanos* with a vibrancy and emotion that forges their character and guides their lives, even if not in ways they always desire.[2]

It is the avoidance of the straight line that still fractures the town of Las Vegas. Usurpation continues to cast a shadow over the community. Eighty years would pass before East and West Las Vegas came together. In 1970, New Town and Old Town merged into one town. In a municipality of only 15,000 people, there are still two independent school districts. The town's rich heritage remains a big part of its present, evident in its buildings, the surrounding landscape, and its people, yet just as it did in 1879, 1890, and 1903, opinions differ on what the future of Las Vegas should look like.

Much of old Las Vegas stokes the imagination, recalling American boomers' notions of what the Wild West must have looked like. The old Plaza remains remarkably intact. Elegant, turn of the century buildings stare down on an historic square. West of this square a variety of adobe homes stand; while to the east many examples of the territorial style that followed the railroads remain. At present, a commercial rejuvenation project has spurred the exterior refurbishing of many of the old buildings. A few art shops and jewelry stores are established on Bridge Street and around the Plaza. City officials and new business enterprises are making an earnest effort to draw tourist dollars to Las Vegas by playing off the childhood memories of an older generation that fondly recalls Roy Rogers, John Wayne, and Indian culture. Art merchants strive to capture the same market drawn to the venues located in Santa Fe and Taos.

The portion of town which grew up along the railroad tracks, long ago christened East Las Vegas, a once bustling, Anglo-American business center on the edge of the frontier, has not stood up as well as Old Town. A remnant of itself, New Town, comprised of a few three-story, vacant brick buildings that occasionally cave in on one another, barely hints at the boom that drove this part of the Southwest in the 1880s. Yet even here, there are recent signs of life. The historic train depot has been renovated. A bustling antique store claims a corner where saloons and gambling halls once roared with life. Although many of the buildings are gone, enough of East Las Vegas' architecture remains to give an idea of what happened in the first years after the railroad came, and how disheartening it must have been for many to watch such growth develop away from the heart of Old Town.

As the Citizens' Committee for Historic Preservation will proudly tell you, the city has over 900 buildings on its historic register. There are at least three identifiable town footprints in Las Vegas, the old Plaza area, East Las Vegas, and an amalgamation of twentieth century storefronts that arose in the 1960's. Many of the buildings on the register are nineteenth-century Victorian homes and stucco-style, single-story dwellings. All hark back to the heady days of the Santa Fe Trail, cattle barons, and the railroad boom. New Mexico Highlands University sits just east of the Gallinas River on a rise where Colonel Kearney's Army of the West first camped. San Miguel County is ripe with the history of New Mexico, its Old West footprint still visible, yet much of what happened here remains dormant, unknown, and forgotten.[3]

Nuevo-mexicanos never thought of themselves as inhabitants of the "Old West." What became the American Southwest used to be Spain and Mexico's northern frontier. Las Vegas was an engaged, active center of trade, as well as a self-sufficient farming community long before the Americans got there. A barter economy connected it to Chihuahua and Mexico City, the Pacific Coast, the Arkansas River Basin, and the *Llano Estacado*. To name only a few, this cultural crossroads included Puebloans, Jicarilla Apaches, Navajos, Spaniards, *Nuevo-Mexicanos*, and Comanches. At the forefront of this trade were the Hispano comancheros, adept middle-men that took advantage of their location in the heart of the cultural shatter-zone that was and still is New Mexico. Las Vegas did not realize it was not a part of civilization until after the Americans got there.

Strong divisions still exist between Anglos and Hispanos on the Las Vegas grant. Many of the fissures that remain can be traced back to how land grant issues were resolved in 1902. The future health of the community requires that any revitalization incorporate a history more reflective of the majority population. What happened in the last part of the nineteenth century remains important. Events which occurred shortly after the turn of the century still eat at the soul of this community. Like Jean Pendaries, many Anglos living in Las Vegas today may be quite earnest in their attempts to make San Miguel County a better place to live, yet without a true understanding of the emotional toll the grant's history has played upon Hispanos, it is hard for such people, however earnest they are, to relate to its true consequences. To the many *nuevo-mexicanos* on the grant who feel disfranchised, any attempt at revitalization, without this recognition, will ring hollow.[4]

The Creation of the Land Grant Board

Political victories in 1890 and 1892 enabled San Miguel County residents' fairer representation at the territorial level, but the grass-roots movement which catapulted *nuevo-mexicanos* to victory carried little weight on the national scene. In 1891, the federal government created the Court of Private Land Claims to sort out the conflicting petitions and lawsuits regarding personal property on land grants. *El Partido del Pueblo* supported such acts as long as the Court provided fair judgments for everyone concerned. Yet as the wheels of national government began to turn, Hispanos in charge of the local movement began to realize legal and political momentum was beginning to roll away from them, and became apprehensive.[5]

As stated above, in 1860, after the de Baca dispute was settled, Congress declared the 1835 Las Vegas Land Grant awarded by Mexican authorities to a community of settlers was the legal entity that owned the Gallinas River settlement. Surveyor General William Pelham's review of both petitions found fault with neither. Pelham wrote, "it is firmly believed that the land embraced in either of the two grants [the de Baca claim and the 1835 community claim] is lawfully separated from the public domain and entirely beyond the disposal of the general government. . . ." Congress, unwilling to contest Pelham's findings or open a legal hornet's nest, approved both and gave the de Baca clan a corresponding amount of land elsewhere [6]

Usurpation of common land occurred differently throughout the territory, yet specific patterns of *nuevo-mexicano* land loss that developed in 1880s New Mexico disproportionally favored Anglo-Americans. Such patterns were often shaped by judges and federal appointees' decisions. Thirty years after Texan Pelham's report reached Washington, D. C., Congress created the Court of Private Land Claims to weed through unresolved issues, forgotten petitions, and deficiencies in the original format to settle all outstanding claims and counter-claims in New Mexico. This court found no problem revising the rules originally set up to confirm or deny grant petitions. They noted that the surveyor generals had admitted they could not adequately fulfill their responsibilities.

After creation of this body, a new wave of Anglo-American

interpretations concerning Spanish and Mexican land laws began to impact New Mexicans. For grants not already confirmed, decisions of authenticity could no longer be made based on pre-existing evidence of settlement. Just because an Hispano ancestors had lived on the same plot of land for over a hundred years no longer guaranteed him ownership. In Santa Fe, the Court of Private Land Claims, consisting of five judges, after reviewing 282 New Mexico petitions, decided that if the original Spanish or Mexican grant had not been approved by the contemporary governor of the province, the claim was not legal. Wherever an *alcalde*, or any authority *other* than the Spanish or Mexican governor had approved the award, the grant, the judges reasoned, was not valid. The court also re-interpreted the legality of the *ejido*, ruling it fell within the definition of public domain. This was essentially the same argument Surveyor General G. W. Julian had touted in prior years.[7]

Both Julian and the Court of Private Land Claims believed the Spanish and Mexican governments owned the common lands, not the people that settled the grant, therefore, they declared the U.S. government had inherited the *ejido* after annexation. Historian Malcolm Ebright argues that neither the Supreme Court nor the Court of Private Land Claims dug deep enough into Spanish law when assembling their cases and argues their conclusions were flawed. Harking back to Castilian precepts, he writes there were two definitions within Spanish land law regarding public domain. One was noted as *tierra conegiles*, which referred to protection of a community or pueblo rights, including the commons. More appropriately defined as a *private* domain by its originators, this law was provided to prevent public officials and individuals from acquiring the *ejido* for their personal use. The U.S. courts and G. W. Julian completely misconstrued, ignored, or more likely, did not understand this portion of Spanish law, which should have protected the commons after annexation, not opened it up to settlement.[8]

Ironically, in Las Vegas, Jefferson Raynolds, Philip Milhiser, and others disagreed with the court's decision, but not due to any proficiency in Castilian law. Most East Las Vegans, as well as the newest surveyor general, Edward Hobart, preferred the grant remain intact, barring outsiders. They did not want the commons to become public domain. Hobart, like Milhiser, owned property on the grant. He was keenly aware of the impact of *Las*

Gorras Blancas in San Miguel County. He too, ignored demands to remove his fences from common lands. As a result, at one point Hobart's house mysteriously burned to the ground. Anglo-American cattlemen, businessmen, and their Hispano counterparts knew that if the Court of Private Land Claim's decision regarding the public domain held, the representative portion of the *ejido* they claimed as their own would evaporate. New settlers would stake homestead claims on lands they desired. In 1893, Raynolds filed suit against the Department of the Interior to halt such a change in Las Vegas. In 1897, a Washington, D.C. district court agreed, stating "the Town of Las Vegas . . ." had an "indefeasible title." The same judge noted the grant should be resurveyed and a patent issued. It is interesting to note that as far back as Pelham, all officials described the "town of Las Vegas," as the legal term for the grant, yet similar to Long's finding in 1888, in 1897, the D.C. judge did not explain who or what that controlling authority was. Raynolds, attempting to save the common lands for himself and his friends, had at least put the brakes on the complete dismantling of the grant, even though that was not his intention.[9]

Under this decision, the commons in Las Vegas remained the property of the grant, yet who would actually control this property remained an unanswered question. Only one thing was for certain in 1897, the federal government had declared the Las Vegas Land Grant one entity. Two factions vied for the patent. Ezequiel C. de Baca represented a group from Old Town, west of the river. This contingent finally decided to incorporate as the "town of Las Vegas." Surprisingly, the original community that developed around the Plaza had never been incorporated as a legal entity. In 1879, when East Las Vegas came out of the ground, there had been a move to combine the two centers of commerce, but a popular vote to create only one town failed. The two separate communities continued to operate independently of one another. In 1882, another vote to create one Las Vegas passed, but the territorial legislature disallowed it. Later, in the midst of the grant troubles and during the *Milhiser* v. *Padilla*, court case, the New Towners, decided to move forward on their own, incorporating themselves in 1888. East Las Vegas was still the only legally incorporated "town" in Las Vegas in 1897.[10]

Only after the district judge in D.C. ruled a patent should be issued for the grant did the citizens of Old Town finally move to incorporate. The de Baca group planned to let local officials nominate a commission or board to oversee the business of the grant. Jefferson Raynolds and Territorial Senator Charles Spiess, both East Las Vegas Republicans, argued against this, lobbying that a local district judge, not a commission of town leaders, should appoint a Board of Trustees to manage the Las Vegas Land Grant.[11]

It was not the first time a local group had tried to create a board to manage the grant. In 1873, a citizens' group put together a commission to apportion property to new settlers. Miguel Garcia, Juan Romero, and May Hays were elected and charged with designating forty and eighty acre tracts to newcomers. The grant's original families fought this commission and their authority to carve out parcels within the *ejido*. The intent of Raynolds' suit against the Department of the Interior twenty years later was very similar to earlier efforts that resulted in the acquisition of an 1873 restraining order that halted unrestricted settlement on the commons.[12]

In 1888, incoming Anglo-Americans, like the original settlers, argued the Las Vegas grant was a closed property system which legally prevented future settlement to anyone without a chain of title which originated from 1835. Such was Philip Milhiser's argument when he bought property from Louis Sulzbacher. Lawyer Sulzbacher dabbled in real estate and liked to flip land for profit. He did this when he sold land he had purchased from grant heirs Pablo Ulibarri to Milhiser. The arrival of the railroad had changed the land's dynamics. No one knew this better than banker Jefferson Raynolds, merchant Eugenio Romero, and host of other town leaders interested in making money on the grant. The locomotive created an urgency, a sense among some, that it was important to gain control of the grant as soon possible or lose any future opportunity to develop the commons as they saw fit. San Miguel County kept the law profession busy as the nineteenth century came to a close.[13]

The D.C. district judge that called for a grant patent prompted East Las Vegas Republicans to file suit in the district court to force the issue. They did not want control of the grant's untapped resources to be decided by a local commission. Senator Charles Spiess and the Veeder law firm pushed their agenda before District Judge William J. Mills. Mills happened to be Wilson Waddingham's father-in-law. Like most cattlemen and land speculators, Waddingham had received his share of threatening notices from *Las Gorras Blancas* about his fences. Previous to Spiess' suit, in New Mexico, the commonly accepted practice for creating a body that would oversee a grant was for a county commission or the territorial governor to approve and direct a popular election to choose a grant board, one representative of the people who lived there. This is similar to the plan the Old Town committee was pursuing. East Las Vegans wanted to head-off such a design. That is why Senator Spies and his lawyers' put their suit before Judge Mills. They preferred that a judge appoint a land grant board, not the people. Mills concurred with the senator and his East Las Vegas supporters. For the first and only time in New Mexico history, a judge appointed a land grant board to oversee all activity on that entity, including the right to borrow money in its name or sell off common lands as needed. The territorial legislature was in session at the time. After the ruling, Spiess quickly returned to Santa Fe and obtained a waiver legalizing Mill's actions. Over the next five years, several counter-suits were brought forth in an effort to have the Mill's decision thrown out. All failed. Mills Avenue now immortalizes the judge on the streets of Las Vegas.[14]

The first meeting of the Board of Trustees of the Las Vegas Land Grant occurred on 22 December 1902. It was held in Judge William J. Mills chamber. The minutes recount that seven trustees were appointed. They were prominent banker Jefferson Raynolds, successful mercantilist Charles Ilfeld, retired Judge E. V. Long (presiding judge in *Milhiser* v. *Padilla*), manager of the El Agua Para Water Company, F. H. Pierce, prominent rancher Felix Esquibel, timber contractor and land speculator Isidoro Gallegos, and businessman Eugenio Romero. The minutes also reveal that these men met on 7 December and elected officers. Jefferson Raynolds became the Las Vegas Land Grant Board's first president. As its first secretary, E. V. Long would record the minutes of subsequent meetings.[15]

President Raynolds was gracious enough to offer a "suitable room in the First National Bank . . . and to furnish the same with proper conveniences for the use of the Board. . . ." Over the next several months the trustees would meet to discuss land grant business at the bank, newly located in

East Las Vegas. During these sessions they set pricing for commons' timber and directed the secretary to advertise lots for sale. The Board made it clear that no resources were to be removed from the grant for business purposes unless proper protocols and transactions were followed. They hired men to watch over these resources and report back when someone illegally grazed on pasturelands or cut down trees.[16]

As it turned out, the survey conducted in 1900 as a prerequisite to the new patent found a 65,000 acre discrepancy. Instead of the 496,000 acres surveyed by William Pelham in 1860, the Las Vegas grant only totaled 431,653. This was due to Pelham not accounting for the Tecolote land grant, which, as stated above, was awarded at about the same time as the 1835 Las Vegas grant. The Board immediately ordered another survey to recover this land, but ultimately relented to the new boundary.[17]

Many locals hoped that with an end to the court battles, land on the grant could be properly administrated. Both sides had promised this would happen once they were in control. *Nuevo-mexicano* farmers sought approval of petitions for land they already worked, and more clarification on access to unused portions of the grant. Submissions to the board did not always get a quick response. Only after Felix Martinez's paper, *La Voz del Pueblo*, wrote about the delays, did Raynolds and the others finally move forward on the numerous applications involving 160 acres or less.[18]

The Board exercised its right to utilize the commons as they saw fit. At the top of their list was to convert "wasted" land into profitable ventures. Raynolds and other board members promoted several risky ventures which failed, leading to loss of much of the commons and money put forth in the grant's name. One such enterprise involved damming the Gallinas River to create irrigation canals to funnel water to arid bottomlands east of town. Elisha V. Long recorded for the trustees a summary of his meeting with land surveyor B. F. Johnson. The surveyor convinced Long a dam along the Gallinas would provide all the water needed to create a fertile oasis downstream, enough to irrigate 150,000 acres. "Mr. Johnson," Long wrote to his colleagues, "is an examiner of surveys and an engineer of large experience and travel in this and foreign Countries [*sic*] and he assured me that this is the best irrigation proposition he has ever seen." Although funds were set aside for construction and future downstream lots were sold, the dam never materialized, at least not in the time period the Board planned for. The enterprise was a complete failure. Johnson might have been a good surveyor but he was less than clairvoyant. Two decades later a dam was built there, creating Storrie Lake. It was named after the engineer who built it. Yet the idea that a dam could turn the bottomlands into fertile cropland never panned out. Property values never went up. Large amounts of cash extracted out of the common's resources went down a rathole.[19]

The Board chalked up their mistakes to experience but never seemed to learn much, continuing to fail at various projects using other people's money. As a result, the grant lost sections of the *ejido* or its resources funding failed business ventures. In 1906, 50,000 acres was purchased by A. W. Thompson, who believed he could sell thousands of homesteads to Easterners. Such sales and other schemes contributed to the loss of over 300,000 acres of the *ejido* by 1931. The Easterners never came, at least not in the numbers speculators envisioned. For at least a century, Anglo-Americans had been developing a talent for converting land into money. For decades, Jefferson Raynolds and men like him had thirsted for a similar opportunity on the grant. Everyone appointed to the Board by Judge Mills was familiar with success. American history is full of stories of such men. Confident and poised, Ilfeld and Gallegos, Esquibel, Romero and Raynolds, even Judge Long, never considered failure a possibility. They were certain of the prosperity that would fall their way once placed in charge of making decisions on the Las Vegas Land Grant. It did not happen. The arid New Mexico environment was not conducive to the same type of agrarian success stories that, time after time, were replicated east of the Mississippi. Men like Jefferson Raynolds were deaf to, or incapable of grasping the wisdom inherent within so many of the *nuevo-mexicanos* that lived on the grant. Adapt to the flow of the river. If one listened instead of talked, anticipated the weather instead of ignored it, remained respectful and a little fearful of one's surroundings, and remained faithful to God, life could be sustained on the grant. The Hispano farmer did not control the natural rhythm of the surrounding environment, nor force his will upon it.[20]

In the District Court of the Fourth Judicial District of the Territory of New Mexico, sitting in and for the County of San Miguel.

In the matter of the application for the appointment of Trustees to take charge of and administer the Las Vegas Grant:- No.5545.

To the Honorable Court aforesaid
and the Honorable William J. Mills,
Judge of said Court.

WHEREAS on the 13th day of May, A.D.1902, there was filed in the above named District Court, and afterwards presented to the Judge thereof, a certain petition by residents of the Town of Las Vegas, as defined in the papers confirming the Las Vegas Grant, interested therein, and in the administration of said Grant, and afterwards after full consideration by an order of said Court bearing date December 9, 1902, the undersigned were individually and collectively appointed by said Court as Trustees, to meet, organize, and as such Trustees to administer the trust set up, described and referred to in said petition and as such Trustees, subject to the orders and directions of the court from time to time, to do all and singular, the acts and things mentioned and intended by said trust and apply the said grant to the use and benefit of the said Town of Las Vegas, meaning thereby, as the undersigned Trustees understand, the inhabitants within the boundaries of said grant, and the villages, towns, settlements and cities therein situated, and all of them; and afterward by the order of said court published in the

The minutes of the first Las Vegas Land Grant Board meeting, page 1. From NMSRCA, "Record Group Las Vegas Land Grant," Box A-Roll 1. Copy located on 2nd floor of Donnelly Library, New Mexico Highlands University.

Daily Optic and Daily Record in the City of Las Vegas, on the 10th day of December, 1902, the public, the residents within said grant and the undersigned, were notified of the action of said court and the appointment of the undersigned Trustees to administer said trust;

NOW, we being willing, under the direction of the court, to undertake the duties contemplated by said order and having taken the oath to fairly and impartially discharge our said duties, a copy of which oath is attached hereto, we hereby inform the said court and the Judge thereof that we, severally and collectively, accept said appointment. We also report herewith proof of the publication of said notice that the same may be made a matter of record.

[signatures]

Territory of New Mexico)o(
)o(ss
County of San Miguel.   )o(

We, the undersigned, whose names are hereunto attached, do solemnly swear that we will fairly and impartially, to the best of our ability, discharge the duties of our appointment as Trustees, appointed by the above named District Court, to administer the trust named by the Court in its said order of appointment.

[signatures]

The minutes of the first Las Vegas Land Grant Board meeting, page 2. From NMSRCA, "Record Group Las Vegas Land Grant," Box A-Roll 1. Copy located on 2nd floor of Donnelly Library, New Mexico Highlands University.

Upon reviewing the minutes of the Board of Trustees first meetings, a couple of interesting bits of information are worth noting. E. V. Long recorded receiving a letter dated 24 February 1903, from Philip Milhiser. Milhiser's letter anticipated another communication, this one from Alfonso Hart, of Washington, D.C, which was to reach the Board on March 3. Milhiser's letter informed the Trustees that he agreed with what Hart was asking for, which was compensation for services rendered in connection with the patent for the Las Vegas Land Grant. Two years later, the Board discussed another request from Mr. Hart, dated 27 June 1905, that was presented by Hart personally, the next day, for compensation regarding work done to acquire control of the grant. The Board agreed to pay Alfonso Hart either $15,000 or 15,000 acres out of the Las Vegas Land Grant *ejido*. Another lawyer, this one local, Lewis C. Fort, received 2,560 acres as payment for providing the Board members legal advice. All the trustees received both salaries and thousands of acres of the grant's commons as payment for their diligence. By 1942, only 29,000 acres of the *ejido* remained. In 2004, the Las Vegas grant's commons consisted of 10,340 acres.[21]

Honor and Defiance

The fight for the Las Vegas Land Grant was nothing new for *nuevo-mexicanos*. Standing up for their homes, for honor and faith, was habit in New Mexico. Alongside neighbors and ancestral kin, they fought for the right to worship and raise a family as they saw fit. When the Bishop of Durango attempted to gain control of the northern provinces and implemented a series of fees and new rules, the Chimayó Rebellion occurred. Attacks from Apache, Comanche, and Navajo were woven into the history of their culture, as was the adaptive and innovative trade networks the *pobladores* developed with these same nations. The southeastward trekking Comanchero was every bit as intrepid, brave, entrepreneurial, and successful as the westward trekking French-Canadian fur trappers. In 1841, *nuevo-mexicanos* humiliated and turned back the Texas Santa Fe Expedition. A few years later, they were willing and prepared to meet the Army of the West at Apache Pass. It was only after their leadership failed them that they turned away. Ten years after the Chimayó Rebellion of 1836, another revolt, this time against the United

States, led to the death Governor Bent and many other Americans, including soldiers. *Nuevo-mexicanos* traveled as far as fifty-seven miles to volunteer for Union duty during the Civil War. They fought and died at the Battles of Valverde and Glorieta Pass. It would have been more surprising if a group such as *Las Gorras Blancas* had never materialized on the Las Vegas Land Grant. Coming together as a people to defend their way of life had always been a part of *nuevo-mexicano* culture.[22]

Fecundo Valdez, in describing village culture wrote: "*un hombre con mucha vergüenza*," a man is a person who depends on no one to make a living. Such a man owns his own property. If he were to lose it, a lack of honor, a sense of shame, would pervade his life. Without land, there was shame. Without honor, life was hardly worth living. Technological superiority certainly placed the Hispano on an unequal footing with the Americans after annexation, but that was not their undoing, nor why they lost their lands. It was the means of economic transaction which destroyed their subsistent lifestyle. The insertion of the cash economy into a land devoid of cash, and its inaccessibility to *nuevo-mexicanos* destroyed their ability to hold on to their property. They could not pay the lawyers who represented them, or the surveyors who measured off their lots, nor come up with the money for the taxes, with beans and oats.

Historian Andrés Reséndez uses the term "market persuasion" to illustrate that the American economy benefited and enticed the Mexican entrepreneur away from Mexico and toward the United States. I agree that the border was a fluid place and there were certainly plenty of Hispanos who looked forward to annexation, helped make it happen, and quickly adapted to their new country's ways. But they were not the majority. It was the landed elite who truly benefited. The *patrón*. The Hispano mercantilist.[23]

The rural *nuevo-mexicanos* did not reap the same rewards upon annexation. Many lost their lands and had to resort to wage-work to get by. It was the Hispano elite that were appointed to the land grant board, not the common folk. True, the insertion of manufactured goods into Hispano villages improved their lifestyles, yet such barter did nothing to protect their property. Land loss bred a sense of shame which could only be met with honor. Honor was tied up in the *nuevo-mexicano's* perception of self. Loss of honor; shame, required a reply. That such a reply led to positive results on the Las Vegas Land Grant is directly attributable to the religious beliefs the mountain communities practiced.[24]

Without a strong religious community in place, there still may have been barn-burnings on the grant in the late 1880s, but it is doubtful *Las Gorras Blancas* would have had the same impact. When Juan José Herrera came back from Colorado in 1887, secret societies were already in place throughout the mountains. The Penitente Brotherhood was made up of rural farmers and ranchers who practiced an ancient faith that required stern discipline and abeyance to its beliefs. Its members met at night and kept their practices secret unless a holy occasion warranted their participation with the rest of the village.

The Hispanos who visited the *moradas* were family men steeped in cultural traditions, unafraid to defend their way of life or do what was right for the village. Herrera had grown up on the grant, so knew the character of the people and from where to solicit help. As it turned out, so did Lorenzo Lopez. With Herrera's talent for organization and first-hand knowledge of similar encroachments in Colorado, he was able to take advantage of the secret organization already in place to help create a grass-roots movement that thwarted westward expansion. Lopez added credibility to the movement. He was influential in helping to unwind the Republican stranglehold on the county. His name lent credence to upstart candidates running against the establishment.

In November 1892, Eugenio Romero ran against Lorenzo Lopez for San Miguel County Sheriff. Lopez won. On 17 December 1892, Romero filed a motion in court contesting the victory. This suit eventually made its way to the New Mexico Supreme Court. Romero testified that several men voting for Lopez had not paid their poll tax, and argued their vote should not count. If their vote did not count, Romero contended, he was the true winner of the election. Andrieus A. Jones, Lopez's lawyer and also a prominent Democrat at the time, proved that his client had won the contest fair and square. Mr. Jones then countersued Romero for court costs. Lorenzo Lopez was awarded $753.25.[25]

That *Las Gorras Blancas* were instrumental in slowing grant encroachment is indisputable. Consider Judge Long's decision on *Milhiser* v. *Padilla*. Recall that Jose Padilla and his brothers put up fences on land Philip Milhiser declared his. This included the additional 25, 860 acres of common lands Milhiser deduced he owned because he had purchased private plots from Sulzbacher. This was the typical expansionist mentality *nuevo-mexicanos* faced on the Las Vegas Land Grant. Anglo-American ideas about land and property lines were inconsistent with Hispano laws and customs. Both Felix Martinez and Juan José Herrera testified that the cattleman was wrong. When Judge Long made his ruling, he was cognizant of the fencing issues surrounding the entirety of the grant. Masked men had set fire to thousands of acres of hay to make their point. Such acts are comparable to someone blowing up an oil tanker today. Hay was the energy resource of the era, a hot commodity in Territorial New Mexico. It fueled the cavalry's mobile operations, supplied sustenance for working livestock and fed the growing cattle herds throughout the Southwest. In a land that averaged twenty inches of annual rainfall, one acre could produce 3,000 pounds of hay. Charles Ilfeld, Jean Pendaries, and José Padilla all sought markets for this valuable product. In an ironic twist, *Las Gorras Blancas* paraded through Las Vegas to protest the very actions the Padillas had taken to protect their property. Judge Long believed he would have been playing right into the hands of men he despised if he ruled that José Padilla's fence had to be removed.[26]

Pretend for a moment there were no masked-riders destroying property in San Miguel County. What would Judge Long have ruled in *Milhiser v. Padilla*? Would he have been as concerned about Mexican law and future colonization? Was he more concerned about a ruling that could be construed as favorable by a group he considered antagonizers and law-breakers? Perhaps if there had been no night-riders, it is at least conceivable that he would have ordered the Padillas to remove their fences without disturbing the status-quo. Cattleman Milhiser could then have more easily established ownership of a portion of the commons, just as land speculators did at Las Trampas. A successful court verdict for the cattleman may have provided the opening East Las Vegas businessmen were looking for to carve up the land grant, moving them closer to a partitioning of the *ejido*. It did not happen. At least not the way Milhiser and other Anglo-Americans hoped. At the time, local Hispanos saw the verdict as a victory. Ultimately, Milhiser and Raynolds did use the judge's term, "the town of Las Vegas," to push forward a new way to gain control of the grant, the creation of a patent that required the appointment of men to run the land almost as if it were their own.

Yet, the Las Vegas Land Grant was never partitioned and did not meet the same fate as many other New Mexico grants. When Judge James O'Brien released forty-six men from indictments concerning fence destruction and other mayhem, it was obvious from the subsequent celebrations that the majority of the town backed *Las Gorras Blancas* and what they stood for. Only after District Court Judge Mills and Senator Spiess worked around the democratic process did control of the grant fall into the hands of men who believed more in the market-economy than the majority population's sense of what was best for the land they lived on.

Perhaps if the differing factions throughout the state had put aside their fractious loyalties earlier and formed a coalition that supported statehood, some of the legislative and legalistic maneuverings that took place on the Las Vegas grant would not have happened. If authorities had been more concerned with the overall welfare of their territory earlier, perhaps a different kind of board would have been elected, not appointed, to run the grant. This point alone indicates the fractious, inter-territorial political strife that haunted the territory in the nineteenth century impacted *nuevo-mexicanos'* ability to hold on to their usufructuary rights. New Mexico did not become a state until 1912. That year, its Supreme Court required any person living on grant land to personally be notified regarding any partition suit involving their property. After statehood, in the 1920s, the New Mexico legislature created laws and regulations to ensure that Boards of Trustees better represented the grants, ensuring heirs would be more involved and have more control appointing their own board members. This does not mean all land grant problems were eliminated after statehood. Indeed the *ejido* continued to be frittered away. Yet it is clear that after the Civil War, a window of opportunity was open to New Mexico to become a state that was allowed to close. Under the cover of territorial ambivalence, the inability or recalcitrance on the part of territorial legislatures to create a united front contributed to land loss throughout New Mexico.[27]

The *nuevo-mexicanos'* ability to wrest control from Republicans in San Miguel County during the 1890 and 1892 elections was a culmination of various factions that came together under the leadership of Felix Martinez and Juan José Herrera. These men rose on the crest of the wave of indignation that swept the Santa Fe Ring out of Las Vegas politics. Yet the victory belonged to the Hispanos and Hispanas of the Las Vegas Land Grant. A people of faith, honor, and defiance.

Welcome to Las Vegas

Today, as the business district moves forward with plans to invigorate the town by highlighting its great history, I propose that no plan will succeed that does not include a fair representation of that heritage. Las Vegas has a rich legacy, one which began along the bison trails that skirted the southern rim of the Sangre de Cristo Mountain Range. Many paths crossed here. They are what make this place so dynamic. All that followed the ancient trails through Las Vegas should be represented in this history; the Comanche, the Jicarilla Apache, Navajo, Pueblo, Kiowa, and comanchero. Fort Union soldiers, the merchants, innovators, the railroad and the Wild West, all played a role in defining the rich heritage of this town, but none more so than the Las Vegas *pobladores* and *nuevo-mexicanos*. Where are they in the renovation plans? Where is the statue of Felix Martinez, leaning over the *La Voz del Pueblo*, the ink still wet, his co-workers Antonio Lucero and Ezequiel C. de Baca looking on?

Can there be no monument to the men who stood up for the rights of the people? Imagine for a moment, driving north out of town, past Storrie Lake and beyond the slow rise of hills, the Rocky Mountains to the left, the high plains to the right, the worn ruts of the Santa Fe Trail still dimpling the prairie-grass; just off the road, a group of bronze horsemen, masked, in full regalia, as Eugenio Romero once said, "armed to the teeth," their leader just a few feet in front, the wind blowing his hat back, arm extended, finger pointing toward the Las Vegas Plaza. *Las Gorras Blancas* on the march. Welcome to the *Las Vegas Grandes*, where the history of the land still beats in the hearts of all who live there.[28]

Exhibit I

The documentary evidence submitted by Philip Milhiser to substantiate his claim of title is summarized below.

On 17 March 1879 Pablo Ulibarri and wife Maria, original heirs to the Las Vegas grant, sold one undivided half interest from same to Louis Sulzbacher and Benigno Jaramilla.

On 4 June 1881 Pablo Ulibarri sold an additional share of the grant to Henry L. Waldo and wife Lucy.

On 30 November 1886 Luis Sulzbacher purchased a portion of the land Henry L. Waldo and wife Lucy's bought from Ulibarri.

Recorded in the county deed books on 13 July 1883 Eulojo Segura and wife Maria sold their share in the Las Vegas grant to the partnership of William H. Meyer, Henry L. Waldo and Luis Sulzbacher.

On 6 December 1886 Sulzbacher purchased Benigno Jaramilla's and wife Petra's share in the undivided half interest in the grant Jaramilla had originally obtained with Sulzbacher in 1879.

On 15 June 1887 Henry L. Waldo and Lucy sold another part of their grant holdings to Sulzbacher.

Philip Milhiser and the Las Vegas Land and Cattle Company purchased grant land from Sulzbacher and his partners on two different occasions in the last month of 1887. A major purchase of 3,100 dollars was made on 2 December and one of 600 dollars on 30 December.

(All above information taken from E.V. Long Papers "The History of the Las Vegas Grant," 1890.)

Exhibit II

The documentary evidence submitted by José Padilla to substantiate his claim of title is summarized below.

On 10 February of 1879 Padilla filed his plot for 160 acres in the deed records.

A declaratory statement dated 6 July 1885 was recorded in the county deed records and on 10 August 1885 another noted Padilla's claim of land per the Homestead Laws.

On 7 September 1887, Jose L. Padilla and brothers Pablo, Francisco, Faustin, and Clemente purchased on "undivided interest" in the Las Vegas grant from Felix Martinez and his wife Virginia for 300 dollars.

José testified: "I have 160 acres according to my papers, and have been in possession since 1877, in the month of February." He also swore, "I fenced a part of my land before I filed my declaratory statement, the other part I did afterwards. In 1877 I built a house and corral, and the stone wall . . . I have an interest in the Las Vegas Grant which I hold by deeds of conveyance made to me and others." Pg 48

Referee Johnson asked Felix Martinez to explain why he believed the land the Milhiser's had purchased from Sulzbacher was not the property Padillas resided on. Martinez argued the land Sulzbacher purchased from original heir Ulibarri was " situated below the town of Las Vegas, and adjoining the Gallinas River . . ." The land Martinez sold to Padilla came from original heir Tomas Baca, completely separate from Ulibarri property, therefore Martinez testified that ". . . the lands occupied and claimed by the claimants and the land occupied and claimed by the defendants, is no part of the land allotted to the grantors." Pg 48

[All above information taken from E. V. Long's publication of transcript, entitled, "The History of the Las Vegas Grant," 1890.]

Exhibit III

Las Vegas Daily Optic Volume XI, No. 110, Tuesday Evening, 11 March 1890.
Report of what was on the leaflets *Las Gorras Blancas* were distributing.

OUR PLATFORM

Not wishing to be misunderstood, we hereby make this our declaration:

Our purpose is to protect the rights and interests of the people in general, and especially those of the helpless classes.

We want the Las Vegas grant settled to the interest of all concerned, and this we hold is the entire community on the grant.

We want no "land grabbers" or obstructionists of any sort to interfere. We will watch them. We are not down on lawyers as a class, but the usual knavery and unfair treatment of the people must be stopped.

Our judiciary hereafter must understand that we will sustain it only when "Justice" is the watchword.

The practice of "double dealing" must cease.

There is a wide difference between New Mexico's "law" and "justice." And justice is God's law, and that we must have at all hazards.

We are down on race issues, and will watch race agitators. We are all human brethren under the same glorious flag.

We favor irrigation enterprises, but will fight any scheme that leads to monopolize the supply of water courses to the detriment of residents living on lands watered by the same streams.

We favor all enterprises, but object to corrupt methods to further the same.

We do not care how rich you get so long as you do it fairly and honestly.

The people are suffering from the effects of partisan "bossism" and these bosses had better quietly hold their peace. The people have been persecuted and backed about in every which way to satisfy their caprice. If they persist in their usual methods, retributions will be their reward.

We are watching "political reformers."

We have no grudge against any person in particular, but we are the enemies of bulldozers and tyrants.

We must have a free ballot and fair county and the will of the majority shall be respected.

Intimidation and the "indictment" plan have no further fear for us. If the old system should continue, death would be a relief to our sufferings. And for our rights our lives are the least we can pledge.

If the fact that we are law abiding citizens is questioned, come out to our houses and see the hunger and desolation we are suffering, and "this" is the result of the deceitful and corrupt methods of "bossism."

Be fair and just and we are with you, do otherwise and take the consequences.

THE WHITE CAPS

1,500 Strong and Gaining Daily

Exhibit IV

Excerpt of Surveyor General William Pelham' Report to Congress on the Las Vegas
  Land Grant
18 December 1858

By the Surveyor General for the said Territory of New Mexico report on the
  eighteenth day of December, one thousand eight hundred and fifty-eight, which
  my report is in the words and figures following to wit:
The Heirs of Louis M[a] Baca
  and
The Town of Las Vegas
The first of the above mentioned cases was filed in this office on the 19th June 1855
  and the second on 11th September of the same year.
These cases were set for trial at different periods but owing to the absence of
  counsel and witnesses were not brought a final close until the 11th December.
The claim of the heirs of Luis Maria de Baca is based on the following facts as set
  forth in the original papers files in the office of claimants.
On the 16th, January 18 1821 Luis Maria de Baca in his own name and that of
  seventeen male children petitioned the Provincial Deputation of the State of
  Durango under whose jurisdiction he avers the province of New Mexico was a
  tract of public land able for cultivation and pasture, called the Vegas Grandes on
  the Gallinas River, in the jurisdiction of El Bado. IN this petition he states that
  a like petition had been made to the authorities of the province of New Mexico
  and that by the decree of the 18th February 1820 the land was granted to him
  and eight other person but as these persons already possessed land elsewhere
  they took no interest in its cultivation and prays that the grant be made to himself
  and his aforementioned children, with the following boundaries to wit. On the
  north the Chapellotte River, on the south the border of El Bado, on the west the
  summit of the mountain and on the East, the Aguaje de la Llegua and the boundary of Don Antonio Ortiz. On the 29th May Diego Garcia Conde and Miguel de
  Zubiria President and Secretary of Provincial Deputation of Durango informed
  Facundo Melgares the Governor of New Mexico that, on the supposition the
  companions of Don Luis Maria Cabeza de Baca had other lands whereon to
  pasture their cattle, that Deputation had determined to confer upon the said
  Baca the land commonly called Vegas Grandes, provided the other parties had

erected no buildings on the land or made any other improvements, unless it was voluntarily agreed between the parties that Baca should reimburse them or any improvements they might have made, and that an equal quantity land should be assigned to them wherever they would select in place of those donated to Baca and the Governor of New Mexico was requested to inform the parties of what had been done.

On the 17th day of October 1823 Bartolomé Baca, Political Chief of New Mexico directed the Alcalde of El Bado to place Luis Maria Cabeza de Baca in possession of the land called for in his possession of the land called for in his petition as the eight individuals who accompanied him in the first petition had place no improvements on the land, and the Alcalde was required to certify at the foot of the order the proceedings had by him in the premises.

On the 27th day of February 1825, Juan Bautista Vigil, the Secretary of the Most Excellent Deputation of New Mexico certified that at the session of the 16th of the same month a petition of Don Juan Antonio Cabeza de Baca, son of Luis Maria C. de Baca and one of the grantees, was read in which he refers to the grant made in the year 1821, by the Provincial Deputation of Durango to which corporation New Mexico at that time belonged [underline is Pelham's], and it was resolved, that a record of the proceedings in the case be made and a true copy thereof given to the petitioner, and ratifying the grant made by the corporation of Durango on the date aforementioned. The petitioner was required to present himself before the territorial Justice of El Bado with the copy above referred to, who having then the grant made to Salvador Montoya was required to place the aforesaid Luis Maria de Baca and male children in possession of the aforesaid land in accordance with the proceedings had in the premises and without injuring to any third party.

On the 26th December 1825 Tomas Sena the Constitutional Justice of El Bado assigned as a reason for not placing the parties in possession of the land that he had been ordered to do, that a proclamation had been issued for the election of his successor, at which he was compelled to attend; and that on the second day after the election had commenced he was taken violently ill and was compelled to postpone the elections as was well known to the messengers of Don Luis Maria Cabeza de Baca.

On the 13th of January 1826, Governor Narbona again ordered the Constitutional Justice to place the parties in possession of the land granted.

The testimony of Manuel Antonio Baca, shows that the parties were placed in possession of the land, although there is no documentary evidence of the fact.

The claim of Las Vegas is based on the following proceedings. On the 20th day of March 1835, Juan de Dios Maese, Miguel Archuleta, Manuel Duran and Jose Antonio Casaos [Casados], for themselves and in the name of twenty five others petitioned the corporation of El Bado for a tract of land for cultivation and pasture, situated in the county of El Bado and bounded as follows: On the north by the Sapello River on the south by the boundary of the grant of Don Antonio Ortiz; on the east by the boundary of the Town of El Bado.

On the same day the corporation of El Bado transmitted the petition to the Territorial Deputation with the recommendation that the petition be granted.

On the 23rd of March of the same year the grant was made by the Territorial Deputation with the boundaries asked for, with the further provision that persons who owned no lands were to be allowed the same privileges of settling upon the grant as those who petitioned for it.

On the 24th of the same month and year Francisco Sarracino the acting Governor or Political Chief directed the Constitutional Justice of El Bado to place the parties in possession which was done on the 6th day of April of the same year.

It is not supposed that Congress intended upon the establishment of the office of the Surveyor General of New Mexico that he should be required to determine questions of right between parties but simply to ascertain whether the claims presented to him were of such a nature as to separate the land embraced within the boundaries set forth on them, from the public domain, and that conflicting claims between parties should be adjudicated before the proper tribunals of the country having jurisdiction in the premises.

Under this view of the case it will not be necessary to refer to any other points made by counsel than those touching the sufficiency of the titles given and under which the representative parties claim.

It is contended by the last [underline is Pelham's] grantees that the concession made to Baca by the Provincial Deputation of Durango was void for want of power in the tribunal that assumed to make it.

At the time the grant was made to Baca the Country was in a state of confusion arising from the severance of Mexico from the parent country, many of the States had not yet given their adhesion to the new order of things and in some places as remote in the interior as New Mexico were not even aware that a new order of things had been established, therefore the several authorities of the country exercised the power entrusted to them by the King of Spain or his lawful authorities and as it is not disavowed that the state of Durango held jurisdiction over the Province of New Mexico it is supposed even in the absence of any positive proof that the Deputation of that state acted within the scope of its authority when it made the grant by the Territorial Deputation of New Mexico in 1825 it conceded that the province of New Mexico was under the jurisdiction of that state, and that any grant made by its legally constituted authorities was a good and valid one. In the case under consideration no condition was attached, the grant was an absolute one and it has been held by our Courts that when no conditions were attached they could not be raised by implication. So satisfied was Governor Melgares that the Deputation of Durango had . . . [indecipherable] right to make the concession that he ordered the grantees to be placed in immediate possession, which he would not have done had he doubted in the least that the authorities of that state had exceeded their powers in granting lands in the province over which he presided as Governor.

But supposing the grant made to Baca by the Deputation of Durango to have been null and void its confirmation by the Territorial Deputation of New Mexico in 1825, at which period it is not denied it had the power to grant lands, would be equivalent to a new grant, and as it is complete in itself so far as the severance of the land granted is concerned to separate it from the public's domain, it is a matter of very little importance whether the former grant by the Deputation of Durango was valid or not. This grant is therefore deemed to be a good and valid one.

The grant made to Juan de Dios Maese and others is not contested on the ground of any want of formality in the proceedings, but as far as the documentary evidence shows is made in strict conformity with the laws and usages of the country at the time.

Testimony is introduced to show that the heirs of Baca protested in 1837 against the occupancy of the land by the claimants under the latter grant, and that they went upon the land knowing the existence of a prior grant, but as these matters are not deemed to be pertinent to the case so far as this office is concerned it is not necessary to comment upon them.

It is firmly believed that the land embraced in either of the two grants is lawfully separated from the public domain and entirely beyond the disposal of the general government, and that in the absence of the one, the other would be as good and valid grant but as this office has no power to decide between conflicting parties they are referred to the proper tribunals of the country for the adjudication of their respective claims and the case is hereby respectfully referred to Congress through the proper channel, for its actions in the premises.

Wm. Pelham

Surveyor General

Surveyor General's Office

Santa Fe, New Mexico,

December 18th, 1858.

Marginal: Ter. Of New Mex. Sur. Gen'ls Office, This Document is duly recorded in Vol. 2 on pages 25, 26, 27, 28, 29, & 30 of the records of this office.

Notes

Introduction

1. Maurilio E. Vigil, *Los Patrones: Profiles of Hispanic Political Leaders in New Mexico History* (Washington, DC: University Press of America, 1980), p. 72; Malcolm Ebright, *Land Grants and Lawsuits in Northern New Mexico* (Albuquerque: University of New Mexico Press, 1994), fn 51, p. 342. On nomenclature I use scholars Richard L. Norstrand's use of Hispano and Hispana found in Richard L. Norstrand, "The Hispano Homeland in 1900," *Annals of the Association of American Geographers* 70, no.3 (Sept., 1980): p. 382-396; and the lower case, *nuevo-mexicano* in Andrés Reséndez, *Changing National Identities At The Frontier: Texas and New Mexico, 1800–1850* (Cambridge, UK: Cambridge University Press, 2005).
2. Clark S. Knowlton, "The Town of Las Vegas Community Land Grant: An Anglo-American Coup D'Etat," *Journal of the West* 19, no. 3 (1980): p. 13. Also see Antonio Ortiz comments concerning common land after fifth condition noted in the "Original Decree for the San Miguel Del Bado Land Grant," in David J. Weber, ed., *Foreigners in their Native Land: Historical Roots of the Mexican Americans* (Albuquerque: University of New Mexico Press, 1973), pp. 30-32.
3. Lynn I. Perrigo, *Gateway to Glorieta: A History of Las Vegas* (Santa Fe: Sunstone Press, 2010), p. 111; Robert J. Rosenbaum, *Mexicano Resistance in the Southwest: "The Sacred Right of Self-Preservation"* (Austin: University of Texas Press, 1981), p. 109; Weber, *Foreigners in Their Native Land*, pp. 236-238.
4. Joseph Schumpeter, *Capitalism, Socialism and Democracy* (1942, revised, New York, 1947) in Bradley J. Birzer, "Expanding Creative Destruction: Entrepreneurship in the American Wests," *Western History Quarterly* 30, no. 1 (Spring 1999): p. 47.
5. Some of these ideas come from William deBuys, *Enchantment and Exploitation: The Life and Hard Times of a New Mexico Mountain Range* (Albuquerque: University of New Mexico, 1985).
6. Malcolm Ebright, *Land Grants and Lawsuits in Northern New Mexico* (Albuquerque: University of New Mexico Press, 1994), p. 218.
7. Anselmo F. Arellano, "The People's Movement: Las Gorras Blancas," in *The Contested Homeland: A Chicano History of New Mexico*, eds. Erlinda Gonzales-Berry and David R. Maciel (Albuquerque: University of New Mexico Press, 1994), p. 69.

Chapter 1 / Going Home

1. Arellano, in *Contested Homeland*, p. 69.

2. Ralph Emerson Twitchell, *The Leading Facts of New Mexican History*, vol. 2. New Edition (Santa Fe: Sunstone Press, 2007), p. 400.

3. Arellano, in *Contested Homeland*, p. 68.

4. Rosenbaum, *Mexicano Resistance*, p. 109; Lynn I. Perrigo, "The Original Las Vegas" vol. 2, unpublished manuscript, n.d. (Carnegie Library, Las Vegas, New Mexico), p. 497.

5. On Herrera's age at the time see, Anselmo F. Arellano and Julian Josue Vigil. *Las Vegas Grandes on the Gallinas: 1835–1985* (Las Vegas, N.M.: Editorial Teleraña, 1985), p. 58. This work states Herrera was 62 in 1898, thus I worked backward to 1890. As for his father, see Arellano in *Contested Homelands*, p. 63. *Las Vegas Daily Optic*, 7 April 1890.

6. Arellano, in *Contested Homelands*, p. 69. Interviews compiled by Cathryn A. Gallacher, conducted in 1975–1976, *Southwest Oral History Association*, Los Angeles, California, (Oct., 1986), in Carnegie Library, Las Vegas: New Mexico, 68-1. Hereinafter these interviews will be cited with interviewee's name, *SOHA*, and designated interview number and page, such as 68-1. Rosenbaum, *Mexicano Resistance*, p. 104.

7. Arellano in *Contested Homelands*, p. 69.

8. John L. Kessell, *Spain in the Southwest: A Native History of Colonial New Mexico, Arizona, Texas, and California* (Norman: University of Oklahoma Press, 2002), p. 38.

9. Kessell, *Spain in the Southwest*, p. 96; José A. Rivera, *Acequia Culture: Water, Land and Culture in the Southwest* (Albuquerque: University of New Mexico Press, 1998), p. 3.

10. Kessell, *Spain in the Southwest*, pp. 95, 120-123.

11. Ibid., p. 93 and 95; Reséndez, *Changing National Identities*, p. 55.

12. Fray Angelico Chavez, "Pohé-Yemo's Representative," quoted in Richard N. Ellis, ed., *New Mexico Past and Present: A Historical Reader*, p. 56; Kessel, *Spain in the Southwest*, p. 172.

13. Kessell, *Spain in the Southwest*, pp. 171-173; Oakah L. Jones, Jr., "Pueblo Warriors and the Spanish Conquest," in Ellis, *New Mexico Past and Present*, pp. 73-74.

14. One of the few monographs to address the common Hispanic settler is Oakah L. Jones, *Los Paisanos: The Spanish Settler on the Northern Frontier of New Spain* (Norman: University of Oklahoma Press, 1979). Juan Gomez-Quiñones, *The Roots of Chicano Politics 1600–1940* (Albuquerque: University of New Mexico Press, 1994), p. 15.

15. Kessell, *Spain in the Southwest*, pp. 160-165.

16. This settlement was located twenty miles downriver from the Pecos Pueblo, Malcolm Ebright, *Land Grants and Lawsuits*, p. 173. Also see, Kessell, *Spain in the Southwest*, p. 333; David J. Weber, ed., *Foreigners in their Native Land: Historical Roots of the Mexican Americans* (Albuquerque: University of New Mexico Press, 1973), pp. 143-145.

17. Ebright, *Land Grants and Lawsuits*, p. 149 and 146.

18. Ibid., p. 147.

19. Kessell, *Spain in the Southwest* p. 38 and 333.

20. Ibid., p. 333.

21. William Pelham's Report to Congress, December 18, 1858. New Mexico State Records and Archives (hereafter noted as NMSRA), Box A-Roll 1, (Copy located on 2cnd floor of Donnelly Library, New Mexico Highlands University); Ebright, pp. 176, 181-183, 296, 297; Knowlton, "The Town of Las Vegas," p. 13. The 1835 boundaries were

different than the original de Baca grant. The north and east lines were the same, but the southern border of the first de Baca grant was the San Miguel del Bado grant, and the western border was the Pecos Mountains. The de Baca grant was larger. For the best examination of the Las Vegas boundaries see Malcolm Ebright, *Land Grants and Lawsuits*, p. 177.

22. Ebright, *Land Grants and Lawsuits*, pp. 177-178; Knowlton, "The Town of Las Vegas," p. 14.

23. Perrigo, *Gateway to Glorieta* (Santa Fe: Sunstone Press, 2010), pp. 101-102. On the specific names of first settlers, see Ebright, *Land Grants and Lawsuits*, p. 181.

24. Ebright, *Land Grants and Lawsuits*, p. 179; Arellano, in *Contested Homeland*, p. 63.

25. Ebright, *Land Grants and Lawsuits*, pp. 182-183.

26. Ibid., p. 182; Pelham report to Congress, December 18, 1858.

27. Perrigo, *Gateway to Glorieta*, pp. 101-102; Ebright, *Land Grants and Lawsuits*, p. 181; Knowlton, "The Town of Las Vegas," p. 14.

28. For the discrepancies regarding the number of original settlers, see Pelham report to Congress, December 18, 1858, and Ebright, *Land Grants and Lawsuits*, p. 181, fn 62, p. 331.

29. José A. Rivera. *Acequia Culture: Water, Land and Culture in the Southwest*, pp. 3-4.

30. William deBuys, *Enchantment and Exploitation*, p. 196.

31. Manuel Martinez, *SOHA*, 6-4. On the *ejido* also see Phillip B. Gonzales, "Struggle for Survival: The Hispanic Land Grants of New Mexico, 1848–2001," *Agricultural History* 77, no. 2 (2003): pp. 296-297; Victor Westphall, *Mercedes Reales: Hispanic Land Grants of the Upper Rio Grande Region* (Albuquerque: University of New Mexico Press, 1983), p 10.

32. Skip Miller, "La Hacienda De Los Martinez," in David J. Weber, *On the Edge of Empire: The Taos Hacienda of los Martinez* (Santa Fe: Museum of New Mexico Press, 1996), p. 19; plus Weber, *On the Edge of Empire*, p. 28.

33. On women plastering the homes, see Sarah Deutsch, *No Separate Refuge: Culture, Class, and Gender on an Anglo-Hispanic Frontier in the American Southwest, 1880–1940* (New York: Oxford University Press, 1987), p. 52 and 54; also de Buys, *Enchantment and Exploitation*, p. 194; and Maurilio Vigil, "The Political Development of New Mexico Hispanas," in *Contested Homeland*, pp. 192-193.

34. For a good review of the animosities and power struggles between the Franciscan friars and Spanish authorities in seventeenth century New Mexico, see Kessell, *Spain in the Southwest*, pp. 107-110; France V. Scholes, "Church and State in New Mexico," in Ellis, *New Mexico Past and Present*, pp. 40-45.

35. Scholes, in Ellis, *New Mexico Past and Present*, p. 33; Kessell, *Spain in the Southwest*, p. 113; Douglas Monroy, *Thrown Among Strangers: The Making of Mexican Culture in Frontier California* (Berkeley: University of California Press, 1990), pp. 30-34.

36. Kessell, *Spain in the Southwest*, p. 106.

37. On the origination of Hispanic faith in New Mexico, the Penitentes, and John Mackey's quote, see Warren A. Beck, "The Cultural Contributions of the Penitentes," (Paper presented at the 1968 October Western History Association Conference) in Ellis, *New Mexico Past and Present*, pp. 172-177; Kessell, *Spain in the Southwest*, p. 34.

38. Reséndez, *Changing National Identities*, p. 133. On women and religion, see Deutsch, *No Separate Refuge*, p. 50.

39. Beck, "The Cultural Contributions of the Penitentes," in Ellis, *New Mexico Past and Present*, pp. 181-182.

40. Ibid., pp. 177-183; Juan B. Rael, *The New Mexican Alabado* (Stanford, CA: Stanford University Press, 1951), pp. 12-15; Robert Darnton, *The Great Cat Massacre: And Other Episodes in French Cultural History* (New York: Random House, 1984), p. 262.

41. Beck quoted in Ellis, *New Mexico Past and Present New Mexico Past and Present*, p. 179; Rosenbaum, *Mexicano Resistance*, p. 10.

42. Beck quoted in Ellis, *New Mexico Past and Present*, pp. 178-183; Rosenbaum, *Mexicano Resistance*, p. 27.

43. Beck quoted in Ellis, *New Mexico Past and Present*, pp. 178-183. On women participating during Holy Week, see Deutsch, *No Separate Refuge*, p. 50; Rael, *The New Mexican Alabado*, p. 12.

44. Deutsch, *No Separate Refuge*, pp. 9-10.

45. Ibid., p. 10; Rosenbaum, p. 146.

46. Brian Delay, *War of a Thousand Deserts: Indian Raids and the U. S.–Mexican War* (New Haven & London: Yale University Press, 2008), pp. 58-59.

47. See, Frederick Jackson Turner, "The Significance of the Frontier in American History," in Richard W. Etulain, ed., *Does the Frontier Experience Make America Exceptional?* (Boston & New York: St. Martin's Press, 1999), pp. 27-28.

48. Deutsch, *No Separate Refuge*, pp. 37-38; Ebright, *Land Grants and Lawsuits*, pp. 182-183.

49. David Dary, *The Santa Fe Trail: Its History, Legends and Lore* (New York: Penguin Books, 2000), p. 146.

50. Ibid., p. 69.

51. Reséndez, *Changing National Identities*, p. 104

52. Dary, *Santa Fe Trail*, p. 194.

53. Reséndez, *Changing National Identities*, pp. 34-35; Westphall, *Mercedes Reales*, p. 52 and 57; Montoya, *Translating Property*, pp. 32-33.

54. Reséndez, *Changing National Identities*, pp. 68-69; Howard R. Lamar, *The Far Southwest: 1846–1912, A Territorial History*, rev. ed. (Albuquerque: University of New Mexico Press, 2000), pp. 42-43.

55. Stephen Watts Kearny, 15 August 1846, Las Vegas, New Mexico, available at webct. nmhu.edu/2006301334_HIST453/Kearney.htm: (accessed 7/6/2006). On the Treaty, see Reséndez, pp. 99-101; Knowlton, "The Town of Las Vegas," 15; Phillip B. Gonzales, "Struggle for Survival: The Hispanic Land Grants of New Mexico, 1848–2001," *Agricultural History* 77, no. 2 (Spring 2003): p. 300.

56. Congress justified eliminating Article 10 by claiming they wanted to do away with feudalism and peonage, yet felt different about similar inequalities in the South. See Montoya, *Translating Property*, pp. 47-48; deBuys, *Enchantment and Exploitation*, p. 105; Gonzales, "Hispanic Land Grants," pp. 298-300; Ebright, *Land Grants and Lawsuits*, pp. 29-30. "The Treaty of Guadalupe Hidalgo," February 2, 1848, available at: www.yale.edu/lawweb/avalon/diplomacy/mexico/guadhida.htm: (accessed 5 July 2006).

57. Montoya, *Translating Property*, p. 35 and 212; Reséndez, *Changing National Identities*, p. 96 and 254; Perrigo, *Gateway to Glorieta*, pp. 12-13; Ebright, *Land Grants and Lawsuits*, p. 220.

58. On possible bribe, see deBuys, *Enchantment and Exploitation*, p. 105. Carlos R. Herrera, "New Mexico Resistance to U.S. Occupation," in *Contested Homeland*, pp. 28-29.

59. For New Mexico demographics during the period, see Richard R. Greer, "Origin of the Foreign-Born Population of New Mexico During the Territorial Period," *New Mexico Historical Review* 17, no. 4 (Oct., 1941): pp. 281-283. Reséndez, *Changing National Identities*, p. 237; Knowlton, "The Town of Las Vegas," p. 14.

60. Lynn I. Perrigo, *Hispanos: Historic Leaders in New Mexico* (Santa Fe: Sunstone Press, 1985), p. 59; M. C. Gottschalk, "Pioneer Merchants of the Las Vegas Plaza," (Unpublished manuscript), First Edition, 2nd printing (Carnegie Library, Las Vegas, New Mexico, 2000), pp. 5-6.

61. debuys, p. 106; Gottschalk, "Pioneer Merchants of the Las Vegas Plaza," pp. 5-6.

62. Reséndez, *Changing National Identities*, p. 239 and 97; Dary, *Santa Fe Trail*, p. 147 and 150; debuys, *Enchantment and Exploitation*, p. 106.

63. Reséndez, *Changing National Identities*, p. 257-258; Montoya, *Translating Property*, pp. 20, 32-35.

64. Charles Bent to Manuel Alvarez, Dec 25, 1842, #60, Charles Bent Collection, Denver Public Library, 5'th floor, WH28 Box 1; Reséndez, *Changing National Identities*, p. 257; Charles Bent to Manuel Alvarez, 1846, #84, Charles Bent Collection, Denver Public Library.

65. I have retained the exact spelling found in this letter, Charles Bent to Manuel Alvarez, Taos, April 8, 1846; Montoya, *Translating Property*, p. 35; Lamar, *The Far Southwest*, p. 60; Herrera, in *Contested Homeland*, p. 31.

66. Herrera, in *Contested Homeland*, p. 33.

67. Montoya, *Changing National Identities*, p. 212; Reséndez, *Changing National Identities*, p. 116 and 97. A good account of the battle between U.S. forces and insurgents is found in Paul I. Wellman, *Glory God and Gold*, ed. Lewis Gannett (Garden City, New York: Doubleday, 1954), pp. 290-291.

68. James A. Crutchfield, *Tragedy at Taos: The Revolt of 1847* (Plano: The Republic of Texas Press, 1995), p. 123 and 126.

69. James A. Crutchfield, *Tragedy at Taos: The Revolt of 1847* (Plano, Texas: The Republic of Texas Press, 1995), p. 123 and 126; Eugene H. Hanosh, "A History of Mora, 1835–1837." (Master's thesis, New Mexico Highlands University, 1967), pp. 35-36; Herrera, in *Contested Homeland*, pp. 34-35.

70. Lewis H. Garrard, *Wah-to-yah: And the Taos Trail, or Prairie Travel and Scalp Dances, with a look at Los Rancheros from Muleback and the Rocky Mountain Campfire* (Norman: University of Oklahoma Press,1974, 2nd printing), pp. xiv, 172, 173, 177, 197.

71. Dary, *Santa Fe Trail*, pp. 216-217; Knowlton, "The Town of Las Vegas," p. 14.

72. Gottschalk, "Pioneer Merchants of the Las Vegas Plaza," p. 15.

73. Ibid., p. 15. There is little information on what property was selling for on the Plaza. There is a note on page 15 of *Pioneer Merchants* that states in 1877 William H. Shupp

paid Trinidad and Andrés Sena $300 for their lot. For details on Romero's businesses also see Gottschalk, p. 16. On Upper Town, see Perrigo, *Gateway to Glorieta*, p. 160.

74. Perrigo, *Gateway to Glorieta*, p. 9; Rosenbaum, *Mexicano Resistance*, pp. 26-27; Maurilio E. Vigil, "*The Political Development of Hispanic New Mexicans: the Struggle for Political Equality.*" (Paper presented at the 1985 Spring Conference of the Western Social Science Association, Ft. Worth, Texas, 24-27 April 1985), p. 8; Richard White, "*It's Your Misfortune and None of My Own*" (Norman: Oklahoma University Press, 1991), p. 237; Perrigo, *Hispanos: Historic Leaders in New Mexico*, p. 28.

75. Westphall, *Mercedes Reales*, p. 10; Montoya, *Translating Property*, p. 11.

76. Westphall, *Mercedes Reales*, p. 10.

77. Ibid., p. 11.

78. Chris Emmett, *Fort Union and the Winning of the Southwest* (Norman: University of Oklahoma Press, 1965), p. 33.

79. Westphall, *Mercedes Reales*, p. 10 and 80; Montoya, *Translating Property*, p. 10; Gonzales, "Hispanic Land Grants," pp. 298-299.

80. Westphall, *Mercedes Reales*, p. 12.

Chapter 2 / The Barter Economy, Capitalism, and the Arrival of Civilization

1. Reséndez, p. 77; Erlinda Gonzalez-Berry and David R. Maciel, "The Nineteenth Century: An Overview," in *Contested Homeland*, p. 12.

2. Floyd S. Fierman, *Roots and Boots: From Crypto Jew inn New Spain to Community Leader in the Southwest* (Hoboken, N.J.: KTAV Publishing House, 1987), pp. 20-21, 188; Henry Tobias and Charles E. Wodehouse, "New York Investment Bankers and New Mexico Merchants: Group Formation and Elite Status among German Jewish Businessmen," *New Mexico Historical Review* 65 (January 1990): p. 24.

3. Fierman, *Roots and Boots*, p. 21; Tobias and Wodehouse, "New York Investment Bankers and New Mexico Merchants," p. 35; John M. Neito-Phillips, *The Language of the Blood* (Albuquerque: University of New Mexico Press, 2004), p. 115.

4. William Parish, *The Charles Ilfeld Company, A Study in the Rise and Decline of Mercantile Capitalism in New Mexico* (Cambridge: Harvard University Press, 1961), p. 13.

5. Parish, *The Charles Ilfeld Company*, p. 15 and 8; Henry J. Tobias, *A History of the Jews in New Mexico* (Albuquerque: University of New Mexico Press, 1990), p. 76.

6. Richard White, "*It's Your Misfortune and None of My Own*," p. 172.

7. Lamar, *The Far Southwest*, p. 24; Tobias, *A History of the Jews in New Mexico*, p. 72; Neito-Phillips, *The Language of the Blood*, p. 60; Deutsch, *No Separate Refuge*, p. 28; Maurilo E. Vigil, "The Political Development of Hispanic New Mexicans," p. 8.

8. Fierman, *Roots and Boots*, fn 1, p. 199.

9. Thomas W. Kavanagh, *The Comanches: A History, 1706–1875* (Lincoln: University of Nebraska Press, 1999), pp. 143, 205-206; Patricia Limerick, *Legacy of Conquest: The Unbroken Past of the American West* (New York: W.W. Norton, 1987), p. 82.

10. On the Navajo, see James F. Brooks, *Captives and Cousins: Slavery, Kinship and Community in the Southwest Borderlands*, (Chapel Hill: University of North Carolina Press,

2002), p. 293. On the Ute, see Ned Blackhawk, *Violence Over the Land: Indians and Empires in the Early American West* (London: Harvard University Press, 2006), p. 140; Elliot West, *Contested Plain: Indians, Goldseekers and the Rush to Colorado* (Lawrence: University of Kansas, 1998), p. 65.

11. Kavanagh, *The Comanches*, pp. 208-209.

12. Limerick, *Legacy of Conquest*, p. 82; deBuys, *Enchantment and Exploitation*, p.15. On Goodnight, see James F. Brooks, *Captives and Cousins*, pp. 337-344.

13. On the Mora mill see deBuys, *Enchantment and Exploitation*, p. 111. For information on Pendaries, see Parish, *Charles Ilfeld*, p. 59. Henry J. Tobias, *A History of the Jews of New Mexico*, p. 76; Perrigo, *Gateway to Glorieta*, p. 34.

14. deBuys, *Enchantment and Exploitation*, p. 15 and 111.

15. Maurilo E. Vigil, *Los Patrones*, pp. 65-70.

16. Parish, *Charles Ilfeld*, p. 59.

17. deBuys, *Enchantment and Exploitation*, p. 111.

18. Parish, *Charles Ilfeld*, p. 15.

19. Vigil, "The Political Development of Hispanic New Mexicans," p. 46.

20. Deutsch, *No Separate Refuge*, p. 39.

21. deBuys, *Enchantment and Exploitation*, p. 172; Westphall, *Mercedes Reales*, pp. 98-99; Ebright, *Land Grants and Lawsuits*, p. 38; Phillip B. Gonzales, "Struggle for Survival: The Hispanic Land Grants of New Mexico, 1848–2001," *Agricultural History* 77, no. 2 (2003): p. 301, Lamar, *The Far Southwest*, pp. 103, 123-124.

22. William Pelham Report to Congress, December 18, 1858. Perrigo, *Gateway to Glorieta*, pp. 104-105.

23. Lamar, *The Far Southwest*, pp. 63-64; Parish, *Charles Ilfeld*, p. 61.

24. Martin Hall, "Sibley's New Mexico Campaign," in Ellis, pp. 122-125; Lamar, *The Far Southwest*, pp. 103-106; David J. Mullen, "Ceran St. Vrain: Leading Citizen of New Mexico," (New Mexico Highlands University, Master's thesis 2002), pp. 88-93.

25. Chris Emmett, *Fort Union and the Winning of the Southwest* (Norman: University of Oklahoma Press, 1965), p. 186 and 190.

26. Dary, *Santa Fe Trail*, p. 256-258.

27. See Donald S. Frazier, *Blood and Treasure: Confederate Empire in the Southwest* (College Station: Texas A&M Press, 1995). For a different perspective on the performance of New Mexican volunteers at the battle of Valverde see Jacqueline D. Meketa, *Legacy of Honor: The Life of Rafael Chacon, a Nineteenth-Century New Mexican* (1986).

28. Lee Myers, "New Mexico Volunteers, 1862–1866," *The Smoke Signal* no. 37 (Spring 1979): p. 143; NMSRCA Box 22, 10822 0102, Muster Rolls, Santa Fe, New Mexico.

29. White, *"It's Your Misfortune and None of My Own,"* pp. 142-146.

30. Lynn I. Perrigo and Vera A. Perrigo, "Centennial Pageant," A Paper Presented at the Las Vegas, New Mexico United Methodist Church, 1979, p. 2, Carnegie Library.

31. Perrigo, *Gateway to Glorieta*, p. 160 and 11.

32. Fierman, *Roots and Boots*, p. 199; Parish, *Charles Ilfeld*, p. 21.

33. Porter Stratton, *Territorial Press of New Mexico: 1834–1912* (Albuquerque: University of New Mexico Press, 1969), p. 147; Victoria E. Dye, *All Aboard the Santa Fe: Railroad*

Promotion of the Southwest, 1890 to 1930s (Albuquerque: University of New Mexico Press, 2005), p. 12.

34. Parish, *Charles Ilfeld*, fn 58, p. 376; Stratton, *Territorial Press*, p. 150.

35. Stratton, *Territorial Press*, p. 150.

36. Gottschalk, "Pioneer Merchants of the Las Vegas Plaza," p. 40.

37. John Hoyt Williams, *A Great and Shining Road: The Epic Story of the Transcontinental Railroad* (New York: Random House, 1988), p. 126.

38. Perrigo, *Gateway to Glorieta*, pp. 168-169; Paxton Price, "The Railroad, Rincon and the River," *New Mexico Historical Review* 65, no. 4 (October 1990): p. 440.

39. Miguel Otero Jr., *Otero-Events of the Days of 1879–1882*, (original unpublished manuscript, n.d., Carnegie Public Library, Las Vegas, New Mexico, 87701), p. 2.

40. Perrigo, *Gateway to Glorieta*, p. 36.

41. Otero, *Otero-Events of the Days of 1879–1882*, p. 2. On the influence of railroad on Las Vegas see, Marian Mosley, "Las Vegas Before the University," (unpublished manuscript, Carnegie Library, Las Vegas, New Mexico, 1948), pp. 2 and 4.

42. Donald Meinig, "American Wests: Preface to a Geographical Interpretation," *Annals of Association of American Geography* 62 (June 1972), pp. 160, 170, 173-75, 179, 181, quoted in William G. Robbins, "Western History: A Dialectic on a Modern Condition," *The Western Historical Quarterly* 20, no. 4 (November 1989): p. 437; Mosley, "Las Vegas Before the University," p. 5.

43. Stratton, *Territorial Press*, p. 60.

44. Citizens Committee for Historic Preservation, (One-page Pamphlet), *Historic Las Vegas, New Mexico: Along the Santa Fe Trail*; Mosley, "Las Vegas Before the University," p. 15.

45. Gottschalk, "Pioneer Merchants of the Las Vegas Plaza," p. 46; Mosley, "Las Vegas Before the University," p. 5.

46. Louis Harris Ivers, "The Montezuma Hotel at Las Vegas Hot Springs, New Mexico" *The Journal of the Society of Architectural Historians* 33, no. 3 (Oct. 1974): p. 206.

47. Otero, *Otero-Events of the Days of 1879–1882*, p. 4; James Marshal, *Santa Fe: The Railroad that Built an Empire* (New York: Random House, 1943), pp. 162-163; Gottschalk, "Pioneer Merchants of the Las Vegas Plaza," p. 5.

48. Price, "The Railroad, Rincon and the River," p. 444 and 449; Perrigo, *Gateway to Glorieta*, p. 168.

49. White, *"It's Your Misfortune and None of My Own,"* p. 282; Parrish, *Charles Ilfeld*, p. 87.

50. White, *"It's Your Misfortune and None of My Own,"* p. 304; Stratton, *Territorial Press*, p. 175; Perrigo, "The Original Las Vegas, vol. 2," Carnegie Library, Las Vegas, New Mexico, (unpublished manuscript, n.d.), p. 373.

51. Howard Bryan, *Wildest of the Wild West: True Tales of a Frontier Town on the Santa Fe Trail* (Santa Fe: Clearlight Publishers, 1988), pp. 104-106.

52. Parish, *Charles Ilfeld*, p. 28.

53. Ibid., p. 49.

54. Ibid., p. 49.

55. On Jefferson Raynolds, see Ben E. Adams, "Pioneer Bankers of the West: Boom to Bust, Civil War to Great Depression," *undecipherable* (Nov./Dec., n.d.): pp. 317-322, Rare

Book Room, Special Collections, New Mexico Highland University Library; Gottschalk, "Pioneer Merchants of the Las Vegas Plaza," p. 44; Parish, *Charles Ilfeld*, pp. 48-56. On Raynolds' election as treasurer, see *Livestock Feed and Farming*, 1 December 1888, on reel 2 *The Stock Grower* September 15, 1888–March 9, 1888, Donnelly Library, 2nd floor, New Mexico Highlands University.

Chapter 3 / A Tangled Web

1. White, *"It's Your Misfortune and None of My Own,"* p. 309; Duetsch, *No Separate Refuge*, p. 28; Cheryl J. Foote, *Women in the New Mexico Frontier, 1846–1912* (Albuquerque: University of New Mexico Press, 2005 (originally published by Niwot: Colorado: University Press of Colorado, 1990), p. 10 and 102.
2. Foote, *Women in the New Mexico Frontier*, p. 102.
3. On Pendaries see Parish, *Charles Ilfeld*, fn 10, p. 377; Gottschalk, "Merchants," p. 11; Oliver LaFarge, *Behind the Mountain* (Santa Fe: Sunstone Press, 2008), p. 51.
4. Gerald McKevitt, "Italian Jesuits in New Mexico: A Report by Donato M. Gasparri, 1867–1869," *New Mexico Historical Review* 67, no. 4 (October, 1992): p. 358. For complete details on Father Martinez's problems with the new French Bishop and his ex-communication, see Angélico Chávez, *But Time and Chance: The Story of Padre Martinez of Taos, 1793–1867* (Santa Fe: Sunstone Press, 1981).
5. McKevitt, "Italian Jesuits in New Mexico," p. 389; Stratton, *Territorial Press*, p. 137 and 139.
6. Surveyor General William Pelham's 18 December 1858 report to Congress was incorrect, overstating the total by 60,000, acres. For actual acres see U.S. General Accounting Office, Report to the Congressional Requestors, "Treaty of Guadalupe Hidalgo: Findings and Possible Options Regarding Longstanding Community Grant Claims in New Mexico,"(June 2004), p. 128, www.gao.gov. (accessed 7/27/2008).
7. Juan Gomez-Quinones, *The Roots of Chicano Politics*, p. 279; Westphall, *Mercedes Reales*, p. 10 and 36; Gonzales, "Hispanic Land Grants," p. 496.
8. White, *"It's Your Misfortune and None of My Own,"* p. 261.
9. Howard R. Lamar, "The Santa Fe Ring," from *The Far Southwest, 1846–1912*, pp. 136-155, in Ellis, *New Mexico Past and Present*, p. 158; Victor Westphall, *Thomas Benton Catron and His Era*, (Phoenix: University of Arizona Press, 1973), pp. 22, 28-29; Westphall, *Mercedes Reales*, pp. 98-99; Neito-Phillips, *The Language of the Blood*, pp. 60-61, 283.
10. Westphall, *Catron and His Era*, p. 72 and 160.
11. Westphall, *Mercedes Reales*, p. 40; Howard R. Lamar, *The Far Southwest*, p. 131-132; Arellano in *Contested Homeland*, p. 62.
12. Westphall, *Mercedes Reales*, p. 13.
13. Gonzalez, "Hispanic Land Grants," p. 300; Westphall, *Mercedes Reales*, pp. 12-13; Ebright, *Land Grants and Lawsuits*, pp. 214-215; de Buys, *Enchantment and Exploitation*, p. 182.
14. deBuys, *Enchantment and Exploitation*, pp. 179-183; Gonzales, "Hispanic Land Grants," p. 302.

15. Westphall; *Mercedes Reales*, p. 47; Knowlton, "The Town of Las Vegas," p. 17.

16. Ebright, *Land Grants and Lawsuits*, pp. 151-154, deBuys, *Enchantment and Exploitation*, p. 181.

17. Ebright, *Land Grants and Lawsuits*, pp. 152-155; de Buys, *Enchantment and Exploitation*, pp. 180-181.

18. Reséndez, *Changing National Identities*, pp. 62-64.

19. Westphall, *Mercedes Reales*, pp. 101-103; White, *"It's Your Misfortune and None of My Own,"* p. 177; Montoya, *Translating Property*, p. 115.

20. Montoya, *Translating Property*, pp. 28, 29, 73-75; Gonzales, "Hispanic Land Grants," p. 304.

21. On Spencer's shenanigans see Montoya, *Translating Property*, p. 90. On Chafee and House Bill 740, see Montoya, *Translating Property*, pp. 88-92. Neito-Phillips, in *Contested Homeland*, p. 107. For the remaining acres, U.S. General Accounting Office, Report to the Congressional Requestors, "Treaty of Guadalupe Hidalgo: Findings and Possible Options Regarding Longstanding Community Grant Claims in New Mexico,"(June 2004), p. 128, www.gao.gov. (accessed 7/27/2008).

22. Westphall, *Mercedes Reales*, pp. 101-103; White, *"It's Your Misfortune and None of My Own,"* p. 177.

23. Montoya, *Translating Property*, p. 79

24. Gonzales, "Hispanic Land Grants," p. 302; Montoya, *Translating Property*, pp. 79, 94-95.

25. Montoya, *Translating Property*; William Kelleher, *The Maxwell Land Grant: A New Mexico Item.* New Edition (Santa Fe: Sunstone Press, 2008).

26. Montoya, *Translating Property*, pp. 114-117; Lamar, *The Far Southwest*, p. 128.

27. Montoya, *Translating Property*, p. 218; Ebright, *Land Grants and Lawsuits*, pp. 39-40; Lamar, *The Far Southwest*, pp. 128-129.

28. Montoya, *Translating Property*, p. 218

29. Ebright, *Land Grants and Lawsuits*, p. 270

30. deBuys, *Enchantment and Exploitation*, pp. 174-175; Rosenbaum, *Mexicano Resistance*, p. 10 and 146; Gomez-Quiñones, *Roots of Chicano Politics*, p. 284.

Chapter 4 / Incremental Ambitions

1. David Remley (on Watts), *The Bell Ranch: Cattle Ranching in the Southwest, 1824–1947* (Albuquerque: University of New Mexico, 1993), p. 48; Westphall, *Catron and His Era*, p. 308.

2. Parish, *Charles Ilfeld*, p. 153; Vigil, *Los Patrones*, p. 37; Perrigo, *Gateway to Glorieta*, p. 34; White, *"It's Your Misfortune and None of My Own,"* pp. 222-225.

3. Tobias Duran, "Francisco Chavéz, Thomas B. Catron, and Organized Political Violence in Santa Fe in the 1890s," *New Mexico Historical Review* 59, fn 3 (July 1984), pp. 291-292.

4. Donald J. Pisani, *To Reclaim a Divided West: Water, Law and Policy, 1948–1902* (Albuquerque: University of New Mexico Press, 1992), p. 10.

5. White, *"It's Your Misfortune and None of My Own,"* pp. 176-177; Lamar, *The Far Southwest*, pp. 63-70.

6. Westphall, *Catron and His Era*, p. 308 and 322.

7. Ibid., p. 308.

8. Ibid., p. 318 and 332.

9. Ellis, *New Mexico Past and Present*, p. 190.

10. White, *"It's Your Misfortune and None of My Own,"* p. 177.

11. Manuel Martinez, Interview no. 6, *SOHA*, 1-25, p. 6-4.On the relevancy of oral histories, see Charles L. Briggs and John R. Van Ness, *Land, Water and Culture: New Perspectives on Hispanic Land Grants* (Albuquerque: University of New Mexico Press, 1987), p. 25.

12. On my ideas about *vergüenza* see Brooks, *Captives and Cousins*, p. 8; and deBuys, *Enchantment and Exploitation*, p. 195.

13. Arellano, in *Contested Homelands*, p. 76.

14. Hilario Rubio, Jr. *La Gente Del Otro Lado: A Historical Economic and Geneologic Survey of Rociada, New Mexico* (Santa Fe: Yucca Speedway Printers, 1980), p. 27.

15. Rubio, Jr. *La Gente Del Otro Lado*, p. 27; Knowlton, "The Town of Las Vegas," fn 19, p. 21; *1870 Census San Miguel County, New Mexico Territory*, file 21 of 29, available from www.rootsweb.com/~census/ (accessed 2 October 2007).

16. Rubio, Jr. *La Gente Del Otro Lado*, p. 27 and 3. The Pendaries Ranch included the valley and portions of the mountains that surrounded it. This land straddled the Mora and Las Vegas grants. All land north of the Sapello River was originally part of the Mora grant. When San Miguel County came into being, it incorporated the valley where Pendaries built his home and grist-mill, from "Rociada, Quadrangle," (Denver, Co.: U. S. Geological Survey, 1965).

17. Oliver La Farge, *Behind the Mountain*. New Edition (Santa Fe: Sunstone Press, 2008), p. 51.

18. Gottschalk, "Pioneer Merchants of the Las Vegas Plaza," p. 11. On daughters' original names see Rubio, Jr., *La Gente Del Otro Lado*, p. 31. On Rudolph as manager of Plaza Hotel, see advertisement in *Las Vegas Optic*, 3 January 1890; Westphall, *Catron*, p. 105.

19. Agnesa Lufkin Reeve, *From Hacienda to Bungalow: Northern New Mexico Houses, 1850-1912* (Albuquerque: University of New Mexico Press, 1988), p. 118; Parish, *Charles Ilfeld*, p. 59.

20. Diane Fulton-Rudolph, *RUDOLPH-L Archives, Re: Zebulon, Edward, Julia Rudolph of Maryland and Kansas*. From Boards.ancestry.com/mbexec/msg/rw/YIEBAEB/235.1.1.1.2.1: (accessed 29 June 2007); Rubio, Jr., *La Gente Del Otro Lado*, p. 27.

21. In various accounts, the name Milhiser is also spelled Milhizer, Millhizer and Milhieser. I retain one L and the S, not the Z, and leave out the interior E. Perrigo, *Gateway to Glorieta*, p. 109.

22. Ebright, *Land Grants and Lawsuits*, p. 210; Rosenbaum, *Mexicano Resistance*, p. 102, Perrigo, *Gateway to Glorieta*, p. 109. On Sulzbacher, see Fierman, *Roots and Boots*, p. 94. Westphall, *Catron*, pp. 22, 28-29; Elisha V. Long, "The History of the Las Vegas Land Grant" (East Las Vegas: J. A. Carruth, 1890), copy in the Rare Book Room, Donnelly Library, New Mexico Highlands University, p. 39.The Judge did not publish the transcripts to make money, but to explain why he did what he did. Philip Milhiser was thirty years old in 1888. He died in 1906 when he was 48. See "Las Vegas and Vicinity

Johnson Mortuary Death Certificate Index 1905–1987," in "Locked Room," Carnegie Library, Las Vegas, New Mexico.

23. Ebright, *Land Grants and Lawsuits*, p. 210; Rosenbaum, *Mexicano Resistance*, p. 102; Perrigo, *Gateway to Glorieta*, p. 109; Elisha V. Long, "The History of the Las Vegas Land Grant," p. 17-20. Using Milhiser's argument, I divided 431,000 acres (roughly the final total acreage of the 1900 survey), and then divided it by one-sixth, or .06, which was the share of the commons he was claiming. This calculates to 25,860 acres.

24. Ebright, *Land Grants and Lawsuits*, p. 210; Rosenbaum, *Mexicano Resistance*, p. 102; Perrigo, *Gateway to Glorieta*, p. 109; Elisha V. Long, "The History of the Las Vegas Grant" p. 17. On Sulzbacher, see Fierman, *Roots and Boots*, p. 94.

25. See calculation in note 23. Long, "The History of the Las Vegas Grant," p. 18.

26. Ibid., p. 42.

27. Ibid., p. 45.

28. Ibid., p. 45.

29. Ibid., p. 46.

30. Ebright, *Land Grants and Lawsuits*, p. 210; Long, "History of the Las Vegas Grant," p. 17 and 44.

31. Ibid., pp. 40-41.

32. Ibid., pp. 46-49. The Herrera homestead was at *El Salitre*. See Arellano, in *Contested Homeland*, p. 63.

33. Long, "History of the Las Vegas Grant," p. 50.

34. Ebright, *Land Grants and Lawsuits*, p. 155; Rosenbaum, *Mexicano Resistance*, p. 103.

35. Ebright, pp. 211-213; Perrigo, *Gateway to Glorieta*, p. 109.

36. Ebright, *Land Grants and Lawsuits*, p. 207.

37. Ibid., p. 213.

38. Robert Larson, "The White Caps of New Mexico: A Study in Ethnic Militancy in the Southwest." *Pacific Historical Quarterly* 44 (May 1975): p. 178; Ebright, *Land Grants and Lawsuits*, pp. 206-208. On Ilfeld's indictment, also see Ebright, p. 214. On Sulzbacher in Kansas City and Puerto Rico, see Tobias, *A History of the Jews in New Mexico*, p. 231 and 117.

39. Perrigo, *Gateway to Glorieta*, pp. 106-107; Elwin Eugene Bearrow "The History of Las Vegas Land Grant," (M. A. thesis, New Mexico Highlands University, 2001), p. 23.Not to be confused with E. V. Long's 1890 document of the same title. I will use Bearrow's last name only when referring to his thesis. When referring to the 1890 document, printed by J. A. Carruth, I will use author's name, Long.

40. Larson, "White Caps," p. 184; Robert W. Larson, "Populism in the Mountain West: A Mainstream Movement," *Western Historical Quarterly* 13 no. 2 (April 1982): pp. 160-161.

41. Arellano, in *Contested Homeland* p. 63; Ebright, p. 193.

42. Arellano, in *Contested Homeland*, p. 79-80.

43. Larson, "White Caps," p. 184.

44. Arellano, in *Contested Homeland*, pp. 64, 78-79.

45. Robert W. Larson, "The Knights of Labor and Native Protests in New Mexico," in Robert Kern, ed. *Labor in New Mexico: Unions, Strikes and Social History Since 1881*

(Albuquerque: University of New Mexico Press, 1983): p. 37; Larson, "White Caps," p. 179; Bryan, *Wildest of the Wild West*, p. 210.

46. Rosenbaum, *Mexicano Resistance*, pp. 167-168.

47. Richard White, "Outlaw Gangs of the Middle Border: American Social Bandits," *Western Historical Quarterly* 4, no. 12 (Oct., 1981): pp. 397-398; Walter Prescott Webb, *The Texas Rangers: A Century of Frontier Defense* (Austin: University of Texas Press, 1965), pp. 432-433.

48. Tobias Duran, ""Francisco Chavez, Thomas B. Catron and Organized Political Violence in Santa Fe in the 1890s," *New Mexico Historical Review* 59, no. 3 (July 1984): p. 293; Leon Fink, ed., *Major Problems in the Gilded Age and the Progressive Era* (New York: Houghton Mifflin Company, 2001), pp. 35-36.

49. Reséndez, *Changing National Identities*, p. 176.

50. Ibid., p. 178.

51. Reséndez, *Changing National Identities*, p. 178; Ellis, *New Mexico Past and Present*, p. 177.

52. Reséndez, *Changing National Identities*, pp. 179-181; Manuel Martinez, Interview no. 6, *SOHA* 1-25, p. 6-2; Louis Bustos, Interview no. 6, *SOHA* 1-25, p. 6-3; Quinones, *Roots*, p. 280 and 284; Rubio, Jr. *La Gente Del Otro Lado*, p. 11.

53. Quiñones, *Roots*, p. 280 and 284.

54. Arellano, quoted in *Contest Homelands*, pp. 64-65; *Las Vegas Optic*, 3 April 1889; *Las Vegas Optic*, 25 November 1889.

55. I have changed the spelling from the source's Luhan, found in Rosenbaum, pp. 104-105.

56. Ibid., pp. 104-105.

57. Parish, *Charles Ilfeld*, p. 176. On Long's decision, see Ebright, *Land Grants and Lawsuits*, pp. 212-213. On the destruction of Rawlins & Quarrell's fences and the shooting, see Rosenbaum, *Mexicano Resistance*, p. 99 and 103.

58. For the newspapers perspective on the town's general embarrassment regarding *Las Gorras Blancas* activities and paper's reference to Herrera as its leader, see the *Las Vegas Optic*, 5 April 1890, "The White Caps", pp. 1-2 (Donnelly Library, New Mexico Highlands University), microfilm, box titled "Las Vegas, N M: *Las Vegas Daily Optic* 1/3/1890–12/9/1890"; also, Robert Larson, "The White Caps of New Mexico: A Study in Ethnic Militancy in the Southwest," *Pacific Historical Quarterly* 44 (May 1975): pp. 180-181.

59. Rosenbaum, *Mexicano Resistance*, p. 126. On the paper's challenge to Herrera, see *Las Vegas Optic*, 5 April 1890.

60. Doris Meyer, *Speaking For Themselves: Neomexicano Cultural Identity and the Spanish-Language Press, 1880–1920* (Albuquerque: University of New Mexico Press, 1996), p. 50; Bryan, *Wildest of the Wild West*, p. 219.

61. Vigil, *Los Patrones*, p. 102; Meyer, "New Mexico Volunteers," p. 219.

62. Rosenbaum, *Mexicano Resistance*, p. 126.

63. Vigil, *Los Patrones*, pp. 87-88.

64. Stratton, *Territorial Press*, p. 26 and 37.

65. Ibid., pp. 25, 35, 273-274.

66. Ibid., p. 17 and 26; Vigil, *Los Patrones*, p. 88.

67. Stratton, *Territorial Press*, p. 138 and 129.

68. Rosenbaum, p. 103; *Las Vegas Optic*, 10 March 1890.

69. Westphall, *Catron*, p. 177; Stratton, *Territorial Press*, p. 130; Rosenbaum, *Mexicano Resistance*, p. 120; Ellis, *New Mexico Past and Present*, pp. 178-183.

70. Rosenbaum, *Mexicano Resistance*, p. 120 and 108; Vigil, *Los Patrones*, p. 81.

71. Rosenbaum, *Mexicano Resistance*, p. 103.

72. Ibid., pp. 119-118.

73. *Las Vegas Optic*, 5 April 1890, p.1 (Donnelly Library, New Mexico Highlands University), microfilm, box titled "Las Vegas, NM: *Las Vegas Daily Optic* 1/3/1890– 12/9/1890"; Stratton, *Territorial Press*, p. 130; Rosenbaum, *Mexicano Resistance*, p. 118.

74. Miguel Antonia Otero, *My Life on the Frontier, 1864–1882* (New York: Press of the Pioneers, 1935): pp. 248-251, quoted in Fink, *Major Problems in the Gilded Age*, p. 52; Bryan, *Wildest of the Wild West*, p. 216.

75. Rosenbaum, *Mexicano Resistance*, p. 127; Arellano, in *Contested Homeland*, p. 72.

Chapter 5 / The Voice of the People

1. Manuel Martinez, Interview no. 6, *SOHA* 1-25, p. 5-3.

2. Rosenbaum, *Mexicano Resistance*, p. 127; Vigil, *Los Patrones*, pp. 70-71.

3. Rosenbaum, *Mexicano Resistance*, p. 132; Bryan, *Wildest of the Wild West*, p. 228; Perrigo, *The Original Las Vegas*, p. 495; Arellano, in *Contested Homeland*, pp. 70-72, 80.

4. David J. Weber, *Myths and the History of the Hispanic Southwest* (Albuquerque: University of New Mexico Press, 1988), p. 24; Quiñones, *Roots*, pp. 60-61; Arellano, in *Contested Homeland*, p. 65.

5. Rosenbaum, *Mexicano Resistance*, pp. 127, 167-168. To calculate the amount of acreage it would take to grow 80 tons of wheat, I turned to the *Production of Field Crops*, using an average yield of 150 lbs. per acre for western hay at high altitudes, first coming up with 2,000 lbs. (per acre) and then dividing by 150 lbs., from which I determined that it would take 1,066 acres to create 80 tons of hay. As a side note, I also noted that 11 miles of Lorenzo Lopez's fence had been destroyed, which could have encompassed the amount of hay that was torched pretty easily, M.S. Kipps and T.K. Wolfe, *Production of Field Crops* (New York: McGraw-Hill, 1959), p. 554.

6. Rosenbaum, p. 127. As mentioned above, on Herrera's age, I utilized information in Arellano, *Las Vegas Grandes*. It notes that in 1898, Juan was 62 years old.

7. Rosenbaum, *Mexicano Resistance*, p. 132.

8. Arellano, in *Contested Homeland*, p. 66; *Las Vegas Optic*, 7 April 1890, p. 2.

9. Arellano, in *Contested Homeland*, pp. 69-70.

10. Parish, *Charles Ilfeld*, p. 176; *Las Vegas Optic*, 4 August 1890, p. 2; Rosenbaum, *Mexicano Resistance*, pp. 108-109. On Romero's loss of railroad ties see Arellano, in *Contested Homeland*, p. 67.

11. *Las Vegas Optic*, 5 August 1890, p. 4. One of Pendaries' son-in-laws, Charles R. Rudolph, did become treasurer of the *Partido del Pueblo*, but nothing has surfaced regarding the patriarch's politics.

12. Perrigo, *Gateway to Glorieta*, p. 111; Rosenbaum, *Mexicano Resistance*, p. 109.
13. Weber, *Myths, and History*, p. 236; Rosenbaum, *Mexicano Resistance*, p. 110.
14. Weber, p. 237. Perrigo, *Gateway to Glorieta*, p. 111
15. Perrigo, *Gateway to Glorieta*, p. 111; Rosenbaum, *Mexicano Resistance*, p. 109; David J. Weber, ed., *Foreigners in Their Native Land: Historical Roots of Mexican Americans* (Albuquerque: University of New Mexico Press, 1973), pp. 236-238.
16. Vigil, *Los Patrones*, pp. 89-91; Robert Rankin White, "Felix Martinez: A Borderland Success Story," *El Palacio* 87 (Winter 1981): p. 15.
17. Stratton, *Territorial Press*, pp. 141-142; Weber, *Foreigners in the Native Land*, p. 214.
18. Parish, *Ilfeld*, p. 177; Rosenbaum *Mexicano Resistance*, pp. 127-128; Weber, *Foreigners*, p. 214.
19. Rosenbaum, *Mexicano Resistance*, p. 126; Meyer, *Speaking for Themselves*, p. 49.
20. Quinõnes, *Roots*, p. 281 and 283.

Conclusion: Emotional History

1. Florencio Aragon, Interview no. 39, *SOHA* 1-25, p. 39-3.
2. deBuys, *Enchantment and Exploitation*, p. xix.
3. Emmett, *Fort Union and the Winning of the Southwest*, p. 33.
4. Jean Pendaries lived to the ripe old age of 83. He died in Rociada on 17 March 1909. See "Las Vegas and Vicinity Johnson Mortuary Death Certificate Master Index 1905–1987," found in Carnegie Library, "Locked Room," Las Vegas, New Mexico.
5. Rosenbaum, *Mexicano Resistance*, p. 129.
6. Pelham Report to Congress, December 18, 1858.
7. Rosenbaum, *Mexicano Resistance*, p. 129; Ebright, *Land Grants and Lawsuits*, pp. 136-140; Gonzales, p. 306.
8. Ebright, *Land Grants and Lawsuits*, p. 113.
9. Perrigo, *Gateway to Glorieta*, p. 113; Rosenbaum, *Mexicano Resistance*, p. 104, Ebright, *Land Grants and Lawsuits*, pp. 212-213; Pelham, Report to Congress, December 18, 1858.
10. Ebright, *Land Grants and Lawsuits*, p. 217; Calvin R. Wilson, "The Political Consolidation of Las Vegas," (M.A. thesis, New Mexico Highlands University, 1971), p. 19.
11. Ebright, *Land Grants and Lawsuits*, p. 217.
12. Perrigo, *Gateway to Glorieta*, pp. 106-107.
13. Long, "The History of Las Vegas," p. 38.
14. Ebright, *Land Grants and Lawsuits*, p. 217; Gonzales, "Hispanic Land Grants," p. 306; Knowlton, "The Town of Las Vegas," p. 20.
15. Ebright, *Land Grants and Lawsuits*, p. 217, E. V. Long, Minutes of 22 December 1902 Board of Trustee Meeting, NMSRCA "Record Group Las Vegas Land Grant," Box A-Roll 1. Copy located on 2nd floor of Donnelly Library, New Mexico Highland University.
16. E. V. Long, Minutes of 31 January 1903, Board of Trustee Meeting; E.V. Long, Minutes of 11 April 1903, Board of Trustees Meeting. All records originate from same roll cited in note 15.

17. Bearrow, p. 26. Also see Ebright on the creation of Tecolote grant, *Land Grants and Lawsuits*, pp. 182-183.

18. Arellano and Vigil, *Las Vegas Grandes on the Gallinas*, p. 69.

19. E. V. Long, Minutes of 31 January 1903, Board of Trustees Meeting; Perrigo, p. 113.

20. Ebright, *Land Grants and Lawsuits*, p. 180.

21. E. V. Long, Minutes, of 21 August 1905, Board of Trustees Meeting. Hart was Judge Long's law partner. Donald L. Craig, "Land, Water and Education: An Administrative History of the Las Vegas Land Grant," (Master's thesis, New Mexico Highlands University, 1990); Ebright, fn 65, p. 343; on trustee payment, also see Ebright, *Land Grants and Lawsuits*, p. 218. E. V. Long, Minutes, 24 February 1903, there is a reference to approving using Lewis C. Fort and J. D. Veeder as legal advisors. On Fort's payment, see Bearrow, p. 29.On remaining acreage, see Arellano, in *Contested Homelands*, p. 218.

22. Reséndez, *Changing National Identities*, pp. 80, 179, 197, 254.

23. Reséndez, *Changing National Identities*, p. 5.

24. On Valdez, see Brooks, *Captive and Cousins*, p. 100.

25. *Eugenio Romero* v. *Lorenzo Lopez* 1894 , Box 55, folder 594, Territorial Supreme Court Cases, NMSRCA, Santa Fe, New Mexico.

26. For the calculations on hay, see James E. Sherow, *A Sense of the American West* (Albuquerque: University of New Mexico Press, 1998), p. 97.

27. Gonzales, "Hispanic Land Grants," p. 312; Ebright, *Land Grants and Lawsuits*, p. 152.

28. Vigil, *Los Patrones*, p. 88; Rosenbaum, *Mexicano Resistance*, p. 108 and 120.

Glossary

Acalde mayor. Executive officer of district or town.

Ayuntamiento. Municipal Council.

acequia. Irrigation ditch.

cofradía. Catholic lay brotherhood.

compuertas. The headgate off the irrigation ditch or acequia.

ejido. Common land.

fanega. Grain measure, approximately two bushels or 100 pounds.

genízaro. Detribalized nomadic Indians, reduced to slavery, converted, resettled in Spanish homes or villages and deployed as military auxilaries.

hermano mayor. Head of *Cofradía*.

jéfe politico. Political boss.

maderous. Penitente wooden cross, up to fifteen feet in length.

mestizo. Mixed-blood of European and Indian ancestry; loosely, any mixed-blood.

patrón. Landed, leaders of the community with influence over the laborers and citizens who lived there.

partido. Livestock lending and raising system; contract for same.

partidario. Obligee under *partido* sheep lending and leasing.

placita. Small village.

pobladores. Settler.

pueblo. Town or village.

ranchero. Rancher.

rico. Rich or rich person.

sangria. Literal meaning, blood or red. In regards to acequias, sangrias were the lateral lines that ran off the main ditch, supplying water to the farmer's field.

tierra conegiles. Land rights.

vara. Spanish yard, approximately thirty-three inches.

vergüenza. A virtue. Tied to a code or sense of honor whereby a person did not profit off another. A person that owned his own land was considered to have a lot of *vergüenza*. Loss of *vergüenza* contributed to a person's sense of shame.

Bibliography

Primary Sources:

1870 Census San Miguel County.

Charles Bent Collection. 5th floor, WH28 Box 1, Denver Public Library.

Eugenio Romero v. Lorenzo Lopez, 594 New Mexico Supreme Court (1894), New Mexico State Records Center and Archives, Santa Fe.

New Mexico State Records Center and Archives. "Record Group Las Vegas Land Grant," Box A-Roll 1. Copy located on 2nd floor of Donnelly Library, New Mexico Highland University.

Las Vegas Optic. (New Mexico Highland University, Donnelly Library Microfilms) Box titled 'Las Vegas, NM: *Las Vegas Daily Optic* 1/3/1890–12/9/1890.

E. V. Long "The History of the Las Vegas Grant," 1890. East Las Vegas: Printer: J. A. Carruth. Rare Book Room, Donnelly Library, New Mexico Highlands University. This document is also located at NMSRCA in Elisha V. and Boaz W. Long Papers, 1857–1970, Collection 1972 - 003.

Oral History Collection, Southwest Region. Los Angeles: Southwest Oral History Association, 1986 October. Carnegie Library, "Locked Room" Las Vegas, New Mexico.

"Las Vegas and Vicinity Johnson Mortuary Death Certificate Master Index 1905–1987," Carnegie Library, "Locked Room" Las Vegas, New Mexico.

Secondary Sources:

Books

Arellano, Anselmo F. and Julian Josue Vigil. *Las Vegas Grandes on the Gallinas: 1835–1985.* Las Vegas, NM: Editorial Teleraña, 1985.

Blackhawk, Ned. *Violence Over the Land: Indians and Empires in the Early American West.* London: Harvard University Press, 2006.

Briggs, Charles L. and John R. Van Ness, eds. *Land, Water, and Culture: New Perspectives on Hispanic Land Grants.* Albuquerque: University of New Mexico Press, 1987.

Brooks. James F. *Captives and Cousins: Slavery, Kinship and Community in the Southwest Borderlands.* Chapel Hill: University of North Carolina Press, 2002.

Bryan, Howard. *Wildest of the Wild West: True Tales of a Frontier Town on the Santa Fe Trail.* Santa Fe: Clear Light Publishers, 1988.

Burke, John Francis. *Mestizo Democracy: The Politics of Crossing Borders.* College Station: Texas A&M Press, 2002.

Chávez, Angélico. *But Time and Chance: The Story of Padre Martinez of Taos, 1793–1867.* Santa Fe: Sunstone Press, 1981.

Cleaveland, Norman. *The Morleys: Young Upstarts on the Southwest Frontier.* Albuquerque: Calvin Horn, 1971.

Crutchfield, James A. *Tragedy at Taos: The Revolt of 1847.* Plano: The Republic of Texas Press, 1995.

Darnton, Robert. *The Great Cat Massacre: And Other Episodes in French Cultural History.* New York: Random House, 1984.

Dary, David. *The Santa Fe Trail: Its History, Legends and Lore.* New York: Penguin Books, 2000.

deBuys, William. *Enchantment and Exploitation: The Life and Hard Times of a New Mexico Mountain Range.* Albuquerque: University of New Mexico Press, 1985.

Deutsch, Sarah. *No Separate Refuge: Culture, Class, and Gender on an Anglo-Hispanic Frontier in the American Southwest, 1880–1940.* New York: Oxford University Press, 1987.

Dye, Victoria E. *All Aboard the Santa Fe: Railroad Promotion of the Southwest, 1890 to 1930s.* Albuquerque: University of New Mexico Press, 2005.

Ebright, Malcolm. *Land Grants and Lawsuits in Northern New Mexico.* Albuquerque: University of New Mexico Press, 1994.

Ellis, Richard N., ed. *New Mexico Past and Present: A Historical Reader.* Albuquerque: University of New Mexico Press, 1971.

Emmett, Chris. *Fort Union and the Winning of the Southwest.* Norman: University of Oklahoma Press, 1965.

Fierman, Floyd S. *Roots and Boots: From Crypto-Jew in New Spain to Community Leader in the American Southwest.* Hoboken, NJ: KTAV Publishing House, 1987.

Foote, Cheryl J. *Women in the New Mexico Frontier, 1846–1912.* Albuquerque: University of New Mexico Press, 2005.

Garrard, Lewis H. *Wah-to-Ya: And The Taos Trail, or Prairie Travel and Scalp Dances, with a look at Los Rancheros from Muleback and the Rocky Mountain Campfire.* 2nd printing. Norman: University of Oklahoma Press, 1974.

Gonzales-Berry, Erlinda and David R. Maciel, eds. *The Contested Homeland: A Chicano History of New Mexico.* Albuquerque: University of New Mexico Press, 1994.

Gomez-Quiñones, Juan. *The Roots of Chicano Politics 1600–1940.* Albuquerque: University of New Mexico Press, 1994.

González, Deena J. *Refusing the Favor: The Spanish Mexican Women of Santa Fe, 1820–1880.* New York: Oxford University Press, 1999.

Hämäläinen, Pekka. *The Comanche Empire.* New Haven & London: Yale University Press, 2008.

Jones, Oakah, L. *Los Paisanos: The Spanish Settler on the Northern Frontier of New Spain.* Norman: University of Oklahoma Press, 1979.

Kessell, John L. *Spain in the Southwest: A Native History of Colonial New Mexico, Arizona, Texas and California.* Norman: University of Oklahoma Press, 2002.

LaFarge, Oliver. *Behind the Mountains.* New Edition, Santa Fe: Sunstone Press, 2008.

Lamar, Howard R. *The Far Southwest: 1846–1912, A Territorial History.* Albuquerque: University of New Mexico Press, Revised Edition, 2000.

Limerick, Patricia. *Legacy of Conquest: The Unbroken Past of the American West.* New York: W.W. Norton, 1987.

Marshal, James. *Santa Fe: The Railroad that Built an Empire.* New York: Random House, 1945.

Meyer, Doris. *Speaking For Themselves: Neomexicano Cultural Identity and the Spanish-Language Press, 1880–1920.* Albuquerque: University of New Mexico, 1996.

Montoya, Maria E. *Translating Property: The Maxwell Land Grant and the Conflict over Land in the American West, 1840–1900.* Lawrence: University of Kansas Press, 2005.

Monroy, Douglas. *Thrown Among Strangers: The Making of Mexican Culture in Frontier California.* Berkeley: University of California Press, 1990.

Neito-Phillips, John M. *The Language of Blood: The Making of Spanish American Identity in New Mexico, 1880s–1930s.* Albuquerque: University of New Mexico, 2004.

Parish, William. *The Charles Ilfeld Company-A Study in the Rise and Decline of Mercantile Capitalism in New Mexico.* Cambridge: Harvard University Press, 1961.

Perrigo, Lynn I. *Gateway to Glorieta: A History of Las Vegas New Mexico.* New Edition, Santa Fe: Sunstone Press, 2010.

Pisani, Donald J. *To Reclaim a Divided West: Water, Law and Policy, 1848–1902.* Albuquerque: University of New Mexico Press, 1992.

Reeve, Agnesa Lufkin. *From Hacienda to Bungalow: Northern New Mexico Houses, 1850–1912.* Albuquerque: University of New Mexico Press, 1988.

Rael, Juan B. *The New Mexican Alabado.* Stanford: Stanford University Press, 1951.

Remley, David. *The Bell Ranch: Cattle Ranching in the Southwest, 1824–1947.* Albuquerque: University of New Mexico, 1993.

Reséndez, Andrés. *Changing National Identities at the Frontier: Texas and New Mexico, 1800–1850.* New York: Cambridge University Press, 2005.

Rivera, José A. *Acequia Culture: Water, Land and Culture in the Southwest.* Albuquerque: University of New Mexico Press, 1998.

Rosenbaum, Robert J. *Mexicano Resistance in the Southwest: The Sacred Right to Self Preservation.* Austin: University of Texas Press, 1981.

Rubio, Hilario Jr. *La Gente Del Otro Lado: A Historical Economic and Geneologic Survey of Rociada, New Mexico.* Santa Fe: Yucca Speedway Printers, 1980.

Stratton, Porter. *Territorial Press of New Mexico, 1834–1912.* Albuquerque: University of New Mexico Press, 1969.

Tobias, Henry J. *A History of the Jews of New Mexico.* Albuquerque: University of New Mexico Press, 1990.

Twitchell, Ralph Emerson. *The Leading Facts of New Mexican History*, vol. 2. New Edition, Santa Fe: Sunstone Press, 2007

Vigil, Maurilo E. *Los Patrones: Profiles of Hispanic Leaders in New Mexico History*. Washington, DC: University Press of America, 1980.

Webb, Walter Prescott. *The Texas Rangers: A Century of Frontier Defense*. Austin: University of Texas Press, 1965.

Weber, David, J. *Myths and the History of the Hispanic Southwest*. Albuquerque: University of New Mexico Press, 1988.

_____. *On the Edge of Empire: The Taos Hacienda of los Martinez*. Santa Fe: Museum of New Mexico Press, 1996.

_____, ed. *Foreigners in Their Native Land*. Albuquerque: University of New Mexico Press, 1973.

Wellman, Paul I. *Glory, God and Gold*. Edited by Lewis Gannett. Garden City, New York: Doubleday, 1954.

West, Elliot. *Contested Plains: Indians, Goldseekers and the Rush to Colorado*. Lawrence: University of Kansas Press, 1998.

Westphall, Victor. *Mercedes Reales: Hispanic Land Grants of the Upper Rio Grande Region*. Albuquerque: University of New Mexico Press, 1983.

_____. *Thomas Benton Catron and His Era*. Tuscon: University of Arizona Press, 1973.

White, Richard. *"It's Your Misfortune and None of My Own,"* Norman: Oklahoma University Press, 1991.

Williams, John Hoyt. *A Great and Shining Road: The Epic Story of the Transcontinental Railroad*. New York: Random House, 1988.

Journal Articles and Presentations

Birzer, Bradley J. "Expanding Creative Destruction: Entrepreneurship in the American Wests." *Western History Quarterly* 30, no. 1 (Spring, 1999): 45-63.

Beck, Warren, A. "The Cultural Contributions of the Penitentes." Paper presented at the Western History Association, October 1968.

Duran, Tobias. "Francisco Chavéz, Thomas B. Catron, and Organized Political Violence in Santa Fe in the 1890s." *New Mexico Historical Review* 59, no. 3 (July 1984): 291-310.

Greer, Richard R. "Origin of the Foreign-Born Population of New Mexico During the Territorial Period," *New Mexico Historical Review* 17 no. 4 (Oct., 1941): 281-287.

Gonzales, Phillip B. "Struggle for Survival: The Hispanic Land Grants of New Mexico, 1848–2001." *Agricultural History* 77, no. 2 (2003): 293-324.

Ivers, Louis Harris. "The Montezuma Hotel at Las Vegas Hot Springs, New Mexico." *The Journal of the Society of Architectural Historians* 33, no. 3 (October 1974): 206-213.

Knowlton, Clark S. "The Town of Las Vegas Community Land Grant: An Anglo-American Coup D'Etat." *Journal of the West* 19 no. 3 (1980): 12-21.

Larson, Robert W. "The White Caps of New Mexico: A Study in Ethnic Militancy in the Southwest." *Pacific Historical Quarterly* 44 (May 1975): 171-86.

_____. "Populism in the Mountain West: A Mainstream Movement." *Western Historical Quarterly* 13, no. 2 (April 1982): 143-164.

_____. "The Knights of Labor and Native Protests in New Mexico," in Robert Kern, ed. *Labor in New Mexico: Unions, Strikes and Social History Since 1881.* Albuquerque: University of New Mexico Press, 1983.

McKevitt, Gerald. "Italian Jesuits in New Mexico: A Report by Donato M. Gasparri, 1867–1869." *New Mexico Historical Review* 67, no.4 (October, 1992): 357-391.

Meinig, Donald. "American Wests: Preface to a Geographical Interpretation." *Annals of Association of American Geography* 62 (June 1972): 160-181.

Meyers, Lee. "New Mexico Volunteers, 1862–1866." *The Smoke Signal* no. 37 (Spring 1979): 138-151.

Nostrand, Richard L. "The Hispano Homeland in 1900." *Annals of the Association of American Geographers* 70, no. 3 (September 1980): 382-396.

Price, Paxton P. "The Railroad, Rincon and the River," *New Mexico Historical Review* 65, no. 4 (October 1990): 437-454.

Perrigo, Lynn I. and Vera A. Perrigo, "Centennial Pageant." A Paper Presented at the Las Vegas, New Mexico United Methodist Church, 1979, Carnegie Library, Las Vegas, New Mexico.

Robbins, Willliam. "Western History: A Dialectic on the Modern Condition." *Western Historical Quarterly* 20, no. 4 (November, 1989): 429-449.

Tobias, Henry and Charles E. Wodehouse. "New York Investment Bankers and New Mexico Merchants: Group Formation and Elite Status among German Jewish Businessmen." *New Mexico Historical Review* 65 (January 1990): 21-47.

White, Richard. "Outlaw Gangs of the Middle Border: America's Social Bandits." *Western Historical Quarterly* 12, no. 4 (Oct., 1981): 387-408.

White, Robert Rankin. "Felix Martinez: A Borderlands Success Story." *El Palacio* 87, (Winter 1981): 13-17.

Vigil, Maurilo E. "The Political Development of Hispanic New Mexicans: The Struggle for Political Equality." Paper presented at the Spring Conference of the Western Social Science Association, Fort Worth, Texas, 24-27 April 1985.

Unpublished Manuscripts

Blackshear, James Bailey. "The Fight for Land and Honor in Las Vegas, New Mexico." M.S. thesis, Texas A&M University–Commerce, 2008.

Bearrow, Elwin Eugene. "The History of the Las Vegas Land Grant." M.A. thesis, New Mexico Highland University, 2001.

Hanosh, Eugene H. "A History of Mora, 1835–1837." M.A. thesis, New Mexico Highlands University, 1967.

Mosley, Marian. "Las Vegas Before the University." Unpublished manuscript, Carnegie Library, Las Vegas New Mexico, 1948.

Mullen, David J. "Ceran St. Vrain: Leading Citizen of New Mexico." M.A. thesis, New Mexico Highland University, 2002.

Otero, Miguel Jr. "Otero-Events of the Days of 1879–1882." Original manuscript, n.d. Carnegie Library, Las Vegas, New Mexico.

Perrigo, Lynn I. "The Original Las Vegas, vol. 2." Unpublished manuscript, n.d. Carnegie Library, Las Vegas, New Mexico.

Wilson, Calvin R. "The Political Consolidation of Las Vegas." M.A. thesis, New Mexico Highlands University, 1971.

Internet Archives

Fulton, Diane. *RUDOLPH-L Archives, Re: Zebulon, Edward, Julia Rudolph of Maryland and Kansas.* Available from, ancestry.com: accessed 29 June 2007.

Kearny, Stephen Watts. "Proclamation–15 August 1846, Las Vegas, New Mexico," webct.nmhu.edu/2006301334_HIST453/Kearney.htm (accessed 7/06/2006).

The Treaty of Guadalupe Hidalgo. www.yale.edu/lawweb/avalon/diplomacy/mexico/guadhida.htm (accessed 5 July 2006).

U.S. General Accounting Office, *Treaty of Guadalupe Hidalgo: Findings and Possible Options Regarding Longstanding Community Grant Claims in New Mexico,* Report to the Congressional Requestors, (June 2004), 128, www.gao.gov. (accessed 7/27/2008)

Pamphlets

Citizens' Committee for Historic Preservation. *Historic Las Vegas, New Mexico: Along the Santa Fe Trail,* 2006.

Index

Quarrell, Frank G., 188

Raynolds, Jefferson, 83-84, 119-120, 132-133, 144-145, 154-159, 165
Republican Party, 110, 117, 131-134, 137-138, 140, 147-148, 156, 164, 166
Reséndez, Andrés, 163
retalbos, 38
Rice, Russell B., 120
Ricos, 43-44, 47, 54, 59, 91, 96, 107, 147
Rolf, Julian, 82
Romero, Eugenio, 11, 19-20, 45, 53-54, 59, 64, 88, 107, 117, 122, 131-132, 137-140, 143, 149, 156-157, 164, 167
Romero, Juan, 156
Romeroville, New Mexico, 122
Rosenbaum, Robert J., 39
Rosenwald, John, 59, 63, 65, 114
Rudolph, Charles, 116
Rudolph, Milnor, 64, 110

Salazar, Miguel, 128
Saloons, 14, 72, 76-78, 82-83, 88, 130, 151
San Miguel National Bank, 84
Santa Fe Weekly, 123, 134
Sapello, New Mexico, 27, 29, 31, 41, 63-64, 174, 186
Schurz, Carl, 99
Seguro, Elugio, 114, 117
Sena, Tomas, 29, 173
Silva, Vicente, 131-132
Sociedad de Bandidos, 131
Spencer, T. Rush, 96-97, 99
Spiess, Charles, 156-157, 166
St. Vrain, Ceran, 48, 50-52, 63, 65, 69, 71
statehood, 102-106, 141, 144, 166
Sulzbacher, Louis, 113-114, 116, 121, 148, 156, 165, 168-169

Taos Revolt, 48, 51-52, 57, 86, 113
Taylor, John, 116
Tecolote de Rincon, New Mexico, 41, 63, 106, 109, 111, 126
Tecolote grant, 32, 43, 191
Thompson, A. W., 159
Tierra Amarilla, 94-95
Tipton, Will, 120
Trementina, 81

Ulibarri, Pablo, 32, 114, 117, 156, 168
Union Pacific Railway, 75
Usufruct rights, 93

Valdez, Fecundo, 163, 191
Valverde, Hispano involvement in Battle of, 69-70, 163, 183
vara, 33, 192
Vargas, don Jose Diego de, 23-27, 36
Velasco, Luis de, 22
vergüenza, 106-108, 163, 186, 192
Vigil, Cornelio, 48, 49
Villebrumier, France, 108

Waddingham, Wilson, 97, 101, 103, 129, 142, 157
Waldo, Henry L., 114, 168
Waldo, Lawrence W., 51
Watrous, Sam, 63
Watts, John S., 67, 101
Weber, David J., 140
White Caps, 18, 124, 127, 130, 136, 138, 171
White, Richard, 59, 71, 106

Zubiría, Bishop, 125-127, 172

www.ingramcontent.com/pod-product-compliance
Lightning Source LLC
Chambersburg PA
CBHW020533270326
41927CB00006B/561